T4-ATX-075

ZYNE CEURVORSTELYKE DOORLUGTIGHEYD VAN BRUNS-
WIC LUNENBURG VOORTREFFELYKE LUSTPLAATS GENAAMT HERRENHAUSEN.
7. Le Jardin à Fleurs et la Meloneric. 8 L'Amphitheatre. 9 Le Theatre pour les Comedies. 10 La Fontaine derrier du Theatre. 11 Le grand Bassin au Vieux
Jardin. 12 Le grand Bassin au Jardin neuf. 13 Les deux Berceaux Plaisantes au nouveau Jardin. 14 Les deux maisons plaisantes sur le Coin du grand Canal.

SOPHIE
ELECTRESS OF HANOVER

BY THE SAME AUTHOR

LETTERS FROM LISELOTTE

SOPHIE

ELECTRESS OF HANOVER

a personal portrait

by

MARIA KROLL

LONDON
VICTOR GOLLANCZ LTD
1973

© Maria Kroll 1973

SBN 0 575 01585 3

Printed in Great Britain by
The Camelot Press Ltd, London and Southampton

DD
491
·H274
K76

KB

Blackwells 1977

For Alexander, Simon, Nicholas

DISCARDED
WILLIAM D. McINTYRE LIBRARY
UNIVERSITY OF WISCONSIN · EAU CLAIRE

310703

CONTENTS

LIST OF ILLUSTRATIONS

ACKNOWLEDGMENTS

Respectful thanks to TRH the Prince and Princess of Hanover for their kind response to the author's requests; grateful thanks also to Godfrey Scheele of the British Museum, to whom she is deeply obliged for reading this book in typescript and saving her from many a slip; to N. J. Kroll for translating diplomatic reports from the Latin; to Dr Maya Slater for helping to bring Sophie's French up to date; to Claire Hunt for help with the index; to Dr Jill Parker for her professional opinion on the ailments of both Palatines and Hanoverians; to Elizabeth Tonge; to Marsha Evans; to Inge Niemöller, Librarian of the German Cultural Institute, London; to Douglas Matthews of the London Library; to Veronica Mathews of Sotheby's; and to the directors of museums and institutions, who were both kind and helpful.

The author is also indebted to generations of scholars from Leibniz onwards for their annotations of Sophie's letters and Memoirs, and particularly to the work of her most recent biographer, Dr Mathilde Knoop, not least for her helpful bibliography. Finally, profound and special thanks to Sheila Bush in her capacity of helper, editor and friend.

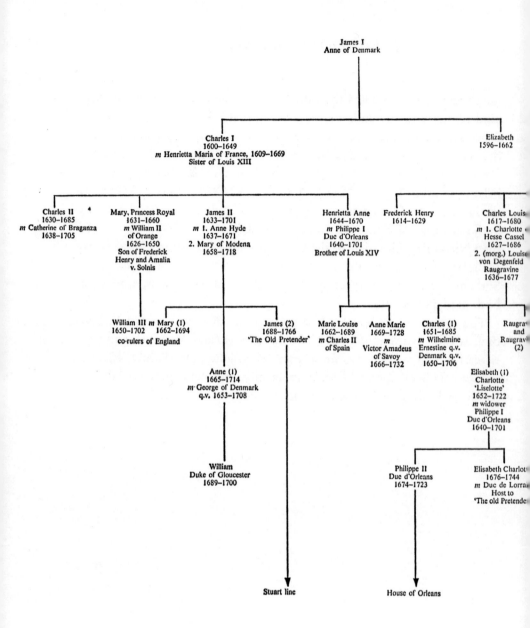

James I
Anne of Denmark

Charles I
1600–1649
m Henrietta Maria of France, 1609–1669
Sister of Louis XIII

Elizabeth
1596–1662

Charles II
1630–1685
m Catherine of Braganza
1638–1705

Mary, Princess Royal
1631–1660
m William II
of Orange
1626–1650
Son of Frederick
Henry and Amalia
v. Solnis

James II
1633–1701
m 1. Anne Hyde
1637–1671
2. Mary of Modena
1658–1718

Henrietta Anne
1644–1670
m Philippe I
Duc d'Orleans
1640–1701
Brother of Louis XIV

Frederick Henry
1614–1629

Charles Louis
1617–1680
m 1. Charlotte
Hesse Cassel
1627–1686
2. (morg.) Louise
von Degenfeld
Raugravine
1636–1677

William III m Mary (1)
1650–1702   1662–1694
co-rulers of England

James (2)
1688–1766
'The Old Pretender'

Marie Louise
1662–1689
m Charles II
of Spain

Anne Marie
1669–1728
m
Victor Amadeus
of Savoy
1666–1732

Charles (1)
1651–1685
m Wilhelmine
Ernestine q.v.
Denmark q.v.
1650–1706

Raugra
and
Raugrav
(2)

Anne (1)
1665–1714
m George of Denmark
q.v. 1653–1708

Elisabeth (1)
Charlotte
'Liselotte'
1652–1722
m widower
Philippe I
Duc d'Orleans
1640–1701

William
Duke of Gloucester
1689–1700

Philippe II
Duc d'Orleans
1674–1723

Elisabeth Charlot
1676–1744
m Duc de Lorra
Host to
'The old Pretende

Stuart line

House of Orleans

Only the people appearing in the text are shown.

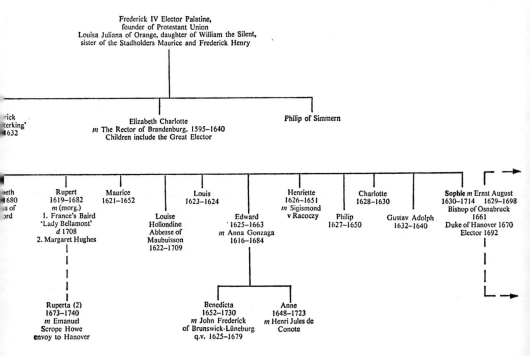

Frederick IV Elector Palatine,
founder of Protestant Union
Louisa Juliana of Orange, daughter of William the Silent,
sister of the Stadholders Maurice and Frederick Henry

'rick
terking'
1632

Elizabeth Charlotte
m The Rector of Brandenburg. 1595–1640
Children include the Great Elector

Philip of Simmern

eth
680
s of
ord

Rupert
1619–1682
m (morg.)
1. France's Baird
'Lady Bellamont'
d 1708
2. Margaret Hughes

Maurice
1621–1652

Louise
Hollondine
Abbesse of
Maubuisson
1622–1709

Louis
1623–1624

Edward
1625–1663
m Anna Gonzaga
1616–1684

Henriette
1626–1651
m Sigismond
v Racoczy

Charlotte
1628–1630

Philip
1627–1650

Gustav Adolph
1632–1640

Sophie m Ernst August
1630–1714 1629–1698
Bishop of Osnabruck
1661
Duke of Hanover 1670
Elector 1692

Ruperta (2)
1673–1740
m Emanuel
Scrope Howe
envoy to Hanover

Benedicta
1652–1730
m John Frederick
of Brunswick-Lüneburg
q.v. 1625–1679

Anne
1648–1723
m Henri Jules de
Conote

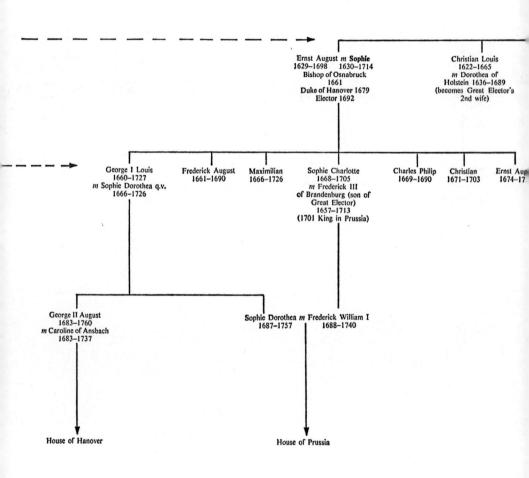

Ernst August *m* **Sophie**
1629–1698   1630–1714
Bishop of Osnabruck
1661
Duke of Hanover 1679
Elector 1692

Christian Louis
1622–1665
m Dorothea of
Holstein 1636–1689
(becomes Great Elector's
2nd wife)

George I Louis
1660–1727
m Sophie Dorothea q.v.
1666–1726

Frederick August
1661–1690

Maximilian
1666–1726

Sophie Charlotte
1668–1705
m Frederick III
of Brandenburg (son of
Great Elector)
1657–1713
(1701 King in Prussia)

Charles Philip
1669–1690

Christian
1671–1703

Ernst Aug
1674–17

George II August
1683–1760
m Caroline of Ansbach
1683–1737

Sophie Dorothea *m* Frederick William I
1687–1757   1688–1740

House of Hanover

House of Prussia

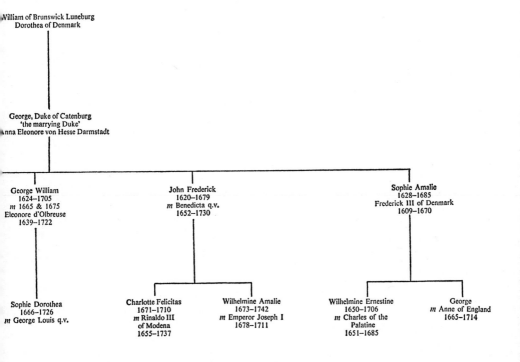

William of Brunswick Luneburg
Dorothea of Denmark

George, Duke of Catenburg
'the marrying Duke'
Anna Eleonore von Hesse Darmstadt

George William
1624–1705
m 1665 & 1675
Eleonore d'Olbreuse
1639–1722

John Frederick
1620–1679
m Benedicta q.v.
1652–1730

Sophie Amalie
1628–1685
Frederick III of Denmark
1609–1670

Sophie Dorothea
1666–1726
m George Louis q.v.

Charlotte Felicitas
1671–1710
m Rinaldo III
of Modena
1655–1737

Wilhelmine Amalie
1673–1742
m Emperor Joseph I
1678–1711

Wilhelmine Ernestine
1650–1706
m Charles of the
Palatine
1651–1685

George
m Anne of England
1665–1714

Only the people appearing in the text are shown.

PREFACE

The material for this book is drawn chiefly from Sophie's own writings, and from the letters exchanged by her friends and relations. Like her mother, the Winter Queen, and her niece Liselotte, the Duchess of Orléans, Sophie was a gifted and indefatigable letter-writer. Her communications tended to be treasured by the recipients, and quantities are preserved in German archives.

Sadly, there are two great gaps. Her entire correspondence with her daughter, who became Queen of Prussia, has gone without a trace; and her letters to Liselotte, whose twice-weekly outpourings over more than forty years elicited as many replies, exist no longer. They were, reluctantly, burned by Liselotte at the request of Sophie's eldest son, who feared the rattle of skeletons in the family cupboard after he had ascended the throne of England as George I. However, thanks to Liselotte's admirable habit of dealing point by point with her aunt's observations, and of repeating whole paragraphs before commenting on them, the content of Sophie's letters may be said to survive in her niece's celebrated correspondence.

Liselotte once told Sophie that her letters were 'so wise and witty that if they ever came to be printed they'd sell out at once'; but even when Sophie wrote her Memoirs she did not write for publication, and was careful to say so in her opening sentences. These Memoirs, like most of her surviving letters, eventually appeared in print, first in the original French, then in German translation; the Memoirs and some of the letters have also appeared in English editions.

Sophie's Memoirs were based on her letters to her brother, the Elector Palatine, which were returned to her after his death. She seems to have resisted the temptation of tailoring them with the benefit of hindsight: Sophie writing at fifty is seen to endorse the record produced by her younger self, and to expand it on subjects on which she had preferred to leave her brother in ignorance.

Sophie's omissions reveal her character just as much as her subject-matter: she good-humouredly deals with numerous episodes that hurt her *amour propre*, but draws heavy veils of silence over matters that might be prejudicial to the honour of her family. Her personal papers do not invariably contain the whole truth, but they seem to contain nothing but the truth as she, and others, saw it. Documentary evidence by hands other than hers show her to have been, on the whole, an accurate reporter, and subjective though all memoirs and letters are by their very nature, Sophie's are more revealing than most, not least between the lines.

Surprisingly, it is her many acts of real kindness that emerge obliquely: her unfailing generosity to her brother's illegitimate daughters, to whom she sent presents accompanied by letters somehow suggesting that acceptance would be a favour to her; or the adoption as her life-pensioner of one of Rupert's discards, who was not only a Catholic but a Jacobite. Sophie was outspoken in her views of people. Her sardonic comments, not always justified, are in striking contrast to her good opinion of herself, which was something of a trial to her present biographer, although it was largely shared by her contemporaries.

It was posterity that was to be sharply divided in its assessment of Sophie. Partisans of her luckless daughter-in-law, of Königsmarck fame, present her as the heartless persecutor of an innocent charmer, driven by overweening pride. Yet such men as Sir Winston Churchill speak of her 'illuminating intelligence' and 'her homely candour and common sense', and in Thackeray's lectures on *The Four Georges* she became 'one of the handsomest, the most cheerful, shrewd, accomplished of women . . .'

Like that distinguished author, who did not set out to write 'about battles, politics, about statesmen and measures of state . . . but to give a peep here and there into that bygone world', this writer's aim is not 'to give grave historical treaties' but to produce a personal portrait of Sophie. Therefore, political events and manœuvres have been sketched in only so far as they touched on the life of this remarkable woman, 'whose eyes,' says Thackeray, 'were so keen that she knew how to shut them on occasion'.

Sophie, Electress of Hanover

PROLOGUE

The huge allegorical picture on the west wall of the Painted Hall in Greenwich contains the figure of an elderly goddess with an intelligent face. She is Sophie of Hanover, who would have become Queen of England had she not died a few weeks before Queen Anne. Thornhill put her into classical draperies, miniver-trimmed for the occasion, and gave her a mural crown—emblem of civic fortune in ancient Greece. Whether this is intended to denote Hanover's good fortune in acquiring the English throne, or England's in acquiring the Hanovers and a secure Protestant succession, is not clear.

From her celestial throne of cloud, Sophie presides over three generations of her heirs: her eldest son, George I, in black armour, ceremonial *Allongé* wig and royal crown; her grandson, who followed him as George II; and her great-grandson, Poor Fred, who died before he had the chance of succeeding, but not before he had become the father of the future George III.

Sophie and her princes owe their position—and indeed their existence—to the fact that on St Valentine's Day, 1613, James I signed the marriage contract between his daughter Elizabeth and Frederick V, Elector Palatine, shortly after entering into a treaty with the Union of Protestant Princes, of which Frederick was the titular head. The marriage sealed the alliance by which James hoped to increase his influence in the Holy Roman Empire of the German Nations: a vast patchwork of more or less autonomous states—some Protestant, some Catholic, according to the religion of their rulers—covering the area, roughly, where German was, and is, spoken. The emperor presiding over this conglomeration was dependent on the support of the Empire's Electors,* whose task and privilege it was to appoint him in the first place, and who alone had the power to convene the Diets at which the business of state was done.

Although a long succession of Catholic Habsburgs of the Austrian line—

---

* In 1613 the Electoral College consisted of the Protestant rulers of the Palatinate, Brandenburg and Saxony and the Catholic Prince Bishops of Mainz, Cologne and Trèves. The seventh member was the elective King of Bohemia, who attended only the Imperial elections and had no further voice in the Empire's affairs.

junior cousins of the Habsburgs in Spain—had contrived to occupy the Imperial throne for generations, the Imperial office remained elective. Naturally Frederick and his colleagues the Electors, enjoying hereditary prerogatives that were royal in all but name, regarded themselves as the equals of any crowned head.

However, James' consort, Anne of Denmark, did not think the groom grand enough for her daughter. For all that he was Germany's premier Protestant Prince, with a lineage as ancient as her own, for all that his domains—the Lower Palatinate, straddling the Rhine, and the Upper, bordering Bohemia—were of strategic importance, for all that his castle in Heidelberg, with its porphyry floors and its famous library of Codices, was the most elegant in all Europe, she considered the Elector to be no more than an obscure prince of an Empire where princes were thirteen to the dozen. She would have preferred her daughter to become an important queen, and began making hurtful jokes about 'Goody Palatine' even before Inigo Jones' wedding decorations had been dismantled.

In the event, King James' high hopes of his son-in-law were to be disappointed. England gained no political advantages from the match; indeed, it soon turned into a political embarrassment. But it was a great success with the young people themselves. They had satisfactorily fallen in love at their first meeting—neither was yet seventeen—and were to remain devoted to each other until Frederick's premature death after an unusually disaster-filled life.

His troubles began in 1618, when insurgent Bohemian Protestants, fearing for their religious freedom, pushed three Habsburg councillors out of the Hradçany window—the incident known as the Defenestration of Prague, which plunged the Empire into the Thirty Years' War. After deposing their Habsburg King, bigoted Ferdinand, cousin and elected successor to the Emperor, the rebels offered Frederick the Bohemian crown.

Urged on by his Dutch uncles, Maurice and Frederick Henry of Orange Nassau, and by his own over-ambitious chancellor, Frederick accepted. His mother begged him not to be so foolish; his father-in-law strongly advised against it; and Ferdinand, the deposed King of Bohemia, who had meanwhile succeeded to the Imperial throne, absolutely forbade it. Frederick defied them all. In 1619, six years after he had installed his wife in his splendid pink sandstone castle at Heidelberg, where she had borne three handsome children and made great improvements to the garden, he carried her and their eldest prince off to Prague. His mother, left behind in charge of the younger children, was heard to murmur as the travellers departed, 'The Palatinate has gone to Bohemia' in the tones of '. . . to the devil'. Then she burst into tears.

Frederick's reign proved to be of short duration, much as Ferdinand's mentors, the Jesuits, had soothingly predicted at its onset. They were sure that the Elector 'would be but a Winter King and gone with the melting snows', and in November 1620, a year after his arrival, Frederick lost his kingdom without so much as attending the battle that cost him his throne. The news that his troops had been defeated by an army of the Catholic League—counterpart to the Protestant Union and headed by Maximilian, Duke of Bavaria—reached him at the palace, where he was paying a call on the Queen from whom he could not bear to be parted for long.

Forced to flee Bohemia, the couple hurriedly gathered attendants, goods, chattels and the Queen's pets. Their crown prince had earlier been sent to safety, but Prince Rupert, born in Prague, nearly came to grief in the commotion. Stowed away in a carriage, he was flung into the boot when the vehicle bumped into motion, but luckily attracted the attention of the occupants by his cries before any real damage was done. One of the Queen's little monkeys was altogether forgotten, to be rescued by a Duke of Saxony, who dined out on this feat for years.

The party aimlessly moved north. There was no returning to Heidelberg, now occupied, like the rest of the Lower Palatinate, by Spanish forces, while the Duke of Bavaria's soldiers held the Upper Palatinate. Frederick had nowhere to go and no one to turn to. The Empire's Protestant princes were unhelpful. Even Frederick's brother-in-law, the Elector of Brandenburg, did not wish to offend the Emperor by harbouring the rebel King. The situation of the 'Bohemian rovers' became desperate, while broadsheets and cartoons mocked their fate.

No invitation arrived from England, for James I was conducting a short-lived flirtation with Spain and did not consider this an auspicious moment to create disharmony between himself and any Habsburg, whether Austrian or Spanish. He pointed out that his treaty with the Protestant Union—united no longer—had been purely defensive, and offered little more than envoys to plead for Frederick at the Imperial Court in Vienna. There, to his daughter's disgust, the matter rested, except that a body of

English volunteers, led by Sir Horace Vere, was sent to the aid of the Palatinate, and Parliament in due course voted Elizabeth a pension.

In the end the Princes of Orange Nassau persuaded the Estates of Holland to offer their nephew and his family asylum in The Hague, but Elizabeth had after all to interrupt her journey in Brandenburg. There, in a horridly inconvenient palace at Küstrin, grudgingly made available by her host on special Imperial permission, she gave birth to her fifth child, whom she called Maurice after his helpful great-uncle. After the shortest possible lying-in, during which the refugees ran out of money even to pay for '*les viandes ordinaires pour la reine*', she moved on. The new baby travelled only as far as Berlin, where it stayed, together with the nursery contingent that had since arrived from Heidelberg with Frederick's mother. Only Rupert accompanied his parents, to be joined by the eldest prince as they crossed into the Low Countries in the spring of 1621.

The Wassenaer Hof in The Hague had been splendidly redecorated for them. In time, Frederick succeeded in extricating from Heidelberg the contents of his wine-cellar and Elizabeth's family portraits. A pension from Messieurs les Etats enabled the exiles to keep their heads above water, and between almost annual babies there was a good deal of hunting, dancing and play-acting. All these pastimes, which Elizabeth greatly enjoyed, only depressed Frederick, described even in his heyday as 'cogitative, or as they call it here, melancholy'.

His depression was well-founded. In 1621 he had been proscribed by the Emperor, and although he had some friends left in the Empire—particularly the Landgrave of Hesse—their exertions on his behalf had all proved ineffective. In 1623 the Emperor unconstitutionally transferred the Palatinate and its Electorship to Maximilian of Bavaria. None of Frederick's visits to friendly Courts, or the letters that he ceaselessly wrote to his royal relations—and few Royals were not related to him—brought assistance. The Oranges were involved in war with Spain. The King of Denmark accused him of being the cause of disaster for the entire Empire. James I continued to offer ambassadors, and promised to insert a clause regarding the Palatine restitution in the marriage contract between his son Charles and Henrietta Maria of France which he was negotiating. When he died in 1625, his son Charles I offered Frederick more ambassadors still, but nothing else.

The King of Denmark, subsidised by England and the Netherlands, entered the war in 1626. He did this not for the love of Frederick, but to protect his own possessions in the Protestant north of the Empire. It was hoped that he would stay the progress of the Catholic forces: both the Emperor's own army and the League's were scoring such victories as would intolerably increase the power of the Austrian Habsburgs. Even the German Catholic Princes, who valued their independence, viewed the situation with apprehension, to say nothing of the Protestants, or of Sweden, involved in war with Poland, or of France, with its long-standing power-struggle with the senior Spanish Habsburg dynasty.

In view of the wider issues now involved, Frederick's rights and wrongs inevitably faded into the background. It did not matter any longer who had sparked off the powder-keg, nor was the Palatine restoration of immediate concern to anyone but the suffering Palatine subjects and their exiled Elector.

The Palatines, ruined by the armies of friends and enemies alike, firmly placed the blame on Elizabeth. They vividly remembered her aloofness. She had never made any visible efforts to fill her post while she was among them, and had never even troubled to learn their language. Rumour said she had declared a preference for Sauerkraut at a king's table over roast meats at an elector's. Clearly, then, this proud daughter of the English King had urged their good Elector to his doom, and brought on their own misery. For a while, Elizabeth was called 'the Helen of Germany' because of her supposed responsibility for launching a thousand armies. But then, as the legend of her colossal charm spread from The Hague—a Brunswick duke, who had never set eyes on her, rode into battle with her glove on his helmet and her colours on his sleeve—she became the Queen of Hearts and no more was heard of Helen.

For the unfortunate Palatines, mediaeval chivalry was a poor substitute for effective assistance. This seemed as distant as ever until Gustav Adolph of Sweden, having dealt with Poland, landed in Germany in July 1630, three months before Elizabeth gave birth to her twelfth child.

CHAPTER ONE

Winter Children
(1630–1650)

ON 14TH OCTOBER 1630 the Princess Sophie was born at the Wassenaer Court, where dry-rot and dilapidation had long set in. Spirits were low. Her parents had been shattered by the accidental death of their eldest son, drowned in the previous year. Their eleventh child, Sophie's immediate predecessor, had followed him to the grave shortly afterwards. In her famous Memoirs, written fifty years later, Sophie says that her own arrival on the gloomy scene caused her parents little joy, 'beyond a feeling of relief at my vacating the place I had until then occupied'.

Even her christening was fraught with problems. Her parents, having run out of ideas for names, and of godmothers who might have provided theirs, resorted to drawing names written on slips of paper out of a hat. 'Chance made me Sophie': bitterness is never wholly absent when Sophie discusses her early years. In fact, the Winter Queen had once had a sister named Sophie who died in infancy: so it was a perfectly respectable family name, and the Queen's choice had not been entirely arbitrary. Subsequent royal Sophies tended to be named for the Winter Queen's youngest daughter. (Queen Victoria, usually highly critical of the names bestowed on her grandchildren, was restrained in her disapproval when her daughter, because of the Electress, chose 'Sophie' for the future Queen of the Hellenes.)

The christening at the Klooster-kerke was attended by assorted noble Sophies who sponsored the baby. The States of Friesland stood godfather, and presented their charge with an annual £40 for life.*

---

* They were not complimented in return as had been their *confrères* of Holland, Messieurs les Etats: their godchild, Sophie's sister Louise Hollandine—who had £100 a year—reflected the family's gratitude in her name.

At barely three months, Sophie was carried to the Prinsenhof in Leiden —three hours' drive away—where the Queen sent all her babies as soon as they could be parted from her, and where the children from Brandenburg had since been installed. The establishment was under the direction of M von Pless, once Frederick's own governor, and Anne his wife, who ran it with the help of tutors and sub-governesses. The sisters Quaadt, two old maids 'whose appearance might have been designed with the express purpose of frightening little children', were detailed to care for Sophie. That she survived all childhood diseases and the remedies of her doctors speaks volumes for her constitution and for the sensible, if Spartan, nursery management. This was largely left to the staff, who bundled their charges in manageable groups to the The Hague for occasional parental inspection.

'The Queen,' says Sophie, 'greatly preferred the sight of her dogs and monkeys to that of her children.' Frederick, on the other hand, was a fond papa, and the Winter children, when they were older, never failed to mention his warmth and goodness when discussing his lack of political acumen. He lovingly designed their timetables. Their Royal Highnesses Charles Louis, Elizabeth, Rupert, Maurice, Louise Hollandine, Edward, Henriette, Philip and Sophie variously studied, as they became old enough for lessons, theology, mathematics, history and jurisprudence, besides Latin and Greek, at which Elizabeth excelled and Sophie did not. Rupert, to be on the safe side in case history reversed itself and Bohemia returned to the family, was taught Czech as well.

Sophie loathed all her masters and all her lessons except for the daily hour devoted to dancing. But, rain or shine, her black-robed tutors appeared in her chamber each morning as soon as she was dressed 'unless God in his mercy sent a chill instead', and renewed their onslaughts on her mind every afternoon. Like most of the Winter children, Sophie was very bright. 'I learned everything they seemed so unaccountably anxious for me to know as quickly as possible,' she writes, 'in order to have done with learning the sooner.'

Her day was punctuated by walks and rests, and by long periods of prayer and Bible-reading under the supervision of the hideous godfearing Quaadts. It was their particular duty to make Sophie love the Lord and fear the Devil according to the teachings of Calvin. Consequently she could at an early age give a word-perfect rendering of the Heidelberg

Catechism in German, without, however, enjoying its lyrical beauty: she did not understand a word of it. It was the sense and not the language that baffled her. All the Winter children grew up to speak German, French (the only language that their parents had in common), English and Dutch equally well, and to write all these languages equally erratically.

Sophie regularly practised her French, even if only incidentally, during daily readings of le Sieur Pibrac's precepts for the conduct of man and the *manière civile de se comporter pour entrer en mariage avec une demoiselle*. This book, oddly, was one of the tortures inflicted on Protestant little girls in the 17th century (the future Mme de Maintenon was a fellow-sufferer). Sophie quickly forgot the uplifting moral quatrains, which she read while her governess was attending to her toilette, but she was always to remember the Quaadt's grimaces as she brushed her yellow teeth.

Even at meals, Sophie's mind was not safe from improvement. Every Wednesday and Sunday, braces of professors from Leiden University would appear at dinner, which was served at precisely eleven o'clock at a long refectory table. Sophie's heart sank at the sight of the visitors' learned heads that seemed to rest like John the Baptist's on the plates formed by their old-fashioned goffered ruffs, and was not cheered by the sound of their learned discourse.

Like everything else in the nursery household, mealtimes were subject to the old, rigid, Heidelberg Court ceremonial. Even the number and profundity of the bows that Sophie was obliged to perform were regulated to the last degree. Framed by the door, and wearing gloves as for a call, she would at a given signal bow deeply to her brothers, lined up with their gentlemen behind them. Moving forward to face them, she bowed again. Then came a bob to Mme von Pless as she entered with her attendants, bobs on handing over the gloves for safe-keeping, bobs on being offered ewer and basin for washing her hands, and bobs, interlarded with bows, to the princes before and after grace. Sophie counts nine in all before the sight of food. This was never particularly delicious, and the menus were planned —presumably subject to seasonal variations— 'as in a convent', once and for all for every day of the week.

The Memoirs say nothing of diversions, outings, boating, sledging or skating. There is no mention of holidays at Rhenen, where Frederick had built a summer residence in an attempt to dissipate his melancholic humour. The golden glow illuminating most childhood recollections is absent from Sophie's, where treats seem to have failed to pierce the boredom; in Leiden, the sun might never have emerged from leaden clouds piled up on the low horizon.

The only game that Sophie does mention has a pathetic ring to it. It was called '*Die Reise nach Heidelberg*' (the journey to Heidelberg), and may indeed have been the dressing-up occasion suggested by some of her biographers. Alternatively, it may have been the young Palatines' adaptation of a game as old as the Crusades—'*Die Reise nach Jerusalem*', the ancestor of musical chairs, where one player after another comes to grief during the journey to the Holy City.

While Sophie was still a baby Gustav Adolph of Sweden, who had swept all before him on his triumphant march south, accepted the Winter King's keenly offered services. Frederick, although he still hated leaving the Queen, was glad after years of enforced idleness to have something better to do than to join her in her energetic diversions. For their part, the Dutch were glad to see the departure of their expensive royal guest, who had been known to snap at the republican hand that was feeding him and his enormous family, and who had implored his Maker to preserve him from the *canaille* of Holland.

Elizabeth regretted only that her husband was obliged to present himself to his old friend Gustav Adolph 'like a mean volunteer, having no army to bring with him'. However, when his train teached the Swedish encampment at Frankfurt it numbered no less than forty carriages. Some had been sent by the Landgrave of Hesse, others by the King of Sweden himself: 'his welcome,' said the Queen, 'was cheerful enough'. Gustav Adolph received him with every mark of friendship and full royal honours, as well he might, since political considerations had made full Palatine restoration impossible. A more astute politician than Frederick would have realised that the usurper from Bavaria could not be deposed at this stage. Maximilian, now himself at odds with the Emperor, was under the protection of France, who was also supporting Sweden in her bid to break Habsburg supremacy.

However, Gustav Adolph's Protestant allies required the Protestant Liberator of the North to do something about the Palatinate; Frederick was full of hope when Swedish troops occupied parts of it, and Gustav

Adolph replaced the Catholic priests with Protestant pastors. Frederick's brother the Duke of Simmern—'none of Solomon's heirs', according to the Queen of Bohemia—was appointed Regent. He was too ineffectual to prevent the Swedish forces from raping, murdering and robbing the Elector's former subjects much as the enemy had in the past, and they had little joy of their liberation.

Frederick's visit to Heidelberg, in Gustav Adolph's wake, did not bring him much comfort. The Palatines' rejoicings were too lukewarm to be convincing, and he soon left again, in a black mood, feeling 'like a stranger and a guest'.

On his return to Frankfurt in November 1632 he learned that, while Gustav Adolph had inflicted an all but crushing blow on the enemy at the Battle of Lützen, he had been mortally wounded and had died on the field of battle. With him vanished Frederick's last hopes. His despondency turned to despair. Whether he fell victim to the plague that ravaged the Rhineland, or the undiagnosed ailment from which his doctors had recently pronounced him cured, within two weeks he, too, was dead.

As soon as the sad news reached Holland, the Winter King's eldest surviving son, fourteen-year-old Charles Louis, whose teenage portrait shows a handsome youth already expressing profound scepticism in the motto DOMINUS PROVIDEBIT that surrounds his likeness, wrote from Leiden to his uncle in Whitehall. Committing his brothers and sisters into the King's royal arms, he wondered what was to become of them all. Charles I handsomely replied that 'they had but exchanged a father, I coming into his room', and sent the Garter. He also warmly invited his sister to England. Although Elizabeth had often longed for such an invitation in the past, she now wrote to her brother that she could not obey his command until, in accordance with Frederick's last wish, 'her children were re-established in the Empire, or at least in a fair way of being so'. Though the Palatinate had been retaken and recatholicised, most of the German estates, thinking it wrong 'to visit the sins of the father on to the son', had recognised Charles Louis as titular Elector Palatine. This made it essential for the family to stay on the continent, for all the comfort that returning home would have been to the grieving Queen.

Elizabeth was petrified with sorrow by her husband's death. For three days she neither ate, drank, spoke nor wept, but lay on her bed like an effigy. She rallied only to observe her mourning in minute accordance with Palatine etiquette. Her apartments were hung in deepest black, and there was, of course, no stirring out of the house for some time. Even in her grief, the Queen did not avail herself of what distraction the company of her young children might have afforded her. They were firmly kept in Leiden, except for her thirteenth child, born in 1632 and named Gustav Adolph after the Swedish King on whom so much hope had been pinned. This baby was altogether too sickly to be sent away at the age when she usually parted from her offspring, although it was not long before he too —still ailing—arrived at the Prinsenhof.

On their father's death Charles Louis and Rupert, the brother next to him in age, cut short their studies at Leiden University and joined the forces of Frederick Henry of Orange, the greatest hero of his day, and since his brother Maurice's death Stadholder of Holland. Charles Louis showed 'such spirit as seems fit to command an army, and any great decision may be built upon him'. In addition to this optimistic assessment, his mother's secretary informed England that 'the sweet Elector is willing to jump upon horseback whensoever his uncle shall command him', but no orders came.

The Palatine restitution 'was going like a crab'. Charles I continued to be generous with envoys, but to little purpose, and Elizabeth tirelessly covered sheets of writing paper urging more decisive action. 'Kings of England,' she pointed out, 'never made good peaces by treating.' As a Christian and a woman, she would rather that the issue were decided by peace, but she had lived so long amongst soldiers and war 'as it makes one as easy as the other, and as familiar'.

In 1636, a year after the old Emperor had made his peace at Prague with all but a handful of the Empire's Protestant Princes—the Landgrave of Hesse, some of the Brunswicks, and of course Charles Louis were among the exceptions—he was succeeded by his son, Ferdinand III. Charles Louis, who had reached his eighteenth year and the age of majority as a Prince of the Empire, arranged to visit England to plead the Palatine cause in person.

The Queen of Bohemia hoped that her son's innocent boyish face would work wonders at Whitehall, and warned him only not to annoy the King with 'impatient pressings'. Accordingly, Charles Louis danced attendance

The Queen of Bohemia with her family, by Gerrit van Honthorst. From the next world Frederick V and his eldest son look down on the survivors. *R to L*: Philip, Edward, Gustav Adolph (winged), Elizabeth, Louise Hollandine, Henriette, Elizabeth of Bohemia, Rupert, Charles Louis in electoral robes, Maurice. Sophie is the winged baby with the laurel wreath.

Sophie's brothers, the Princes Palatine, Maurice, Edward and Rupert. All three often sat to Honthorst. The first two portraits are by that master's hand; that of Rupert is attributed to him.

on his uncle for nearly two years, gaining 'much embracings and all signs of love', but neither arms nor men. There was some talk of ships— 'Perhaps he will find the Palatinate at sea?' said his friends in the Empire, put out at the notion of the Elector's adventuring in a borrowed fleet—but none materialised. 'All their comfort to me,' Charles Louis informed his mother, 'is to have patience.' For all that he was careful and calculating even in his youth, he was singularly unendowed with this quality, and he raged and fumed while cooling his heels in the anterooms of power. Unlike him, Rupert, who had followed him to England, had a splendid time. He saw little of the Elector, for whom he did not greatly care in any case, and spent most of his time with Charles I's Queen, Henrietta Maria. He was so great a success with her and her predominantly Catholic Court that Elizabeth, in fear for his Protestant soul, urgently recalled him. She also wrote, pointedly, to the King that rumours of her eldest son's idleness were harming the cause, and some money was finally made available for him.

Charles Louis gladly prepared to depart, but Rupert so hated leaving that he prayed on the last day's hunting that he might break his neck and leave his bones in England. He was, however, even then a fantastically accomplished horseman, and arrived safe and sound back at The Hague, together with Charles Louis, in 1638.

The Queen was hoping to use at least some of the English money to pay her mounting debts, but Charles Louis insisted on using the whole amount for the purpose for which it had been so laboriously collected. He bought a tiny army and a little fortress, and so laid the foundations for the financial arguments that were to characterise his relationship with his mother forever after. The Queen was soon to cease referring to him as 'him I love the best', and Rupert became her favourite. Charles Louis became 'Timon' to his family, and in due course quarrelled about money with almost every member of it. Only Sophie, to whom he was unfailingly generous, was to love him without reservation.

She saw little of him when he returned from England, as he set out at once at the head of his force, which he lost as a result of his first engagement, together with all his supplies, documents, and even the Garter. His fortress was taken by Hanoverian Cuirassiers under the fat Duke of Brunswick-Lüneburg, to whom Elizabeth scathingly referred as 'that tun of beer'. Charles Louis also lost the services of his cavalry colonel, because

B

Rupert—the future 'mad cavalier' of fabulous repute*—ended his début by being taken into Imperial custody.

Soon after this débâcle Charles Louis also became a prisoner, and learnt to his cost that Richelieu, who had ordered his arrest on a technicality, was not unduly concerned about the Palatine problem. It took Charles I's personal intervention to have him released. In 1640, together with his brothers Maurice and Edward, in Paris to learn manners, Charles Louis returned to The Hague. At the end of that year Rupert, too, was set free.

Meanwhile, the Prinsenhof had gradually emptied of nursery occupants. Prince Philip was completing his education by travelling, and the older girls were all at the Wassenaer Hof, from where it was hoped that suitable husbands would carry them off to Courts of their own. Only Sophie and the youngest Prince were still in Leiden. Unwittingly, little Gustav Adolph, fair and angelic looking, was instrumental in badly shaking Sophie's self-esteem. The Queen, who liked to parade her children before guests, had sent for them both. When they had been put through their paces 'like horses in the ring', a visitor remarked with astonishing lack of tact, 'He is very pretty but she is thin and plain, I hope she doesn't understand English.' Sophie, of course, understood all too well, and was convinced that there was no remedy for her condition.

But she was fond of her little brother, and sincerely grieved when he died in 1641 after nine years of agony. At his post mortem 'a stone the size of a pigeon's egg, surrounded by four other, jagged ones' was found in his bladder, and another one in his kidneys 'shaped like an enormous tooth drawn with the root'. So much, says Sophie, for the doctors, of whom formidable quantities had been in perpetual attendance throughout his short life.

Her brother's death left her as the only child at the Prinsenhof, and although at the age of eleven she was scarcely '*hoffähig*'—capable of appearing at Court—the Leiden establishment was closed down, and the Winter Queen's youngest daughter moved to The Hague.

To Sophie, the Wassenaer Hof was the seventh heaven of delight. Her governesses were left behind, 'too old to be able to weather the change';

---

* His enemies thought him to be in league with the devil, and a white poodle called Boy, who until the Prince fell at Naseby invariably accompanied him into battle, was described as 'an enormous black hound' and believed to be his familiar.

there were no more tutors, and it was goodbye forever to the dreary Leiden routine. Instead, there was this infinitely sophisticated adult world in which to make a mark: no easy task for a plain, thin child, who sensibly allotted herself the part of *enfant terrible*.

The Queen, not famous for affection for her children when they were young, had said as they grew older that she loved them 'more because they are the late Elector's than because they are mine'. For her daughters, at any age, she had no understanding at all. They in turn were perfectly immune to her legendary charm. When they later refuted the 'Helen' story by pointing out that their parent had, in her young days, cared for nothing but amusements, they were describing no Queen of Hearts but an unfeeling, frivolous woman. None of them was quite to forgive her for her lack of warmth.

Sophie's horrible practical jokes, recounted with modest pride in the Memoirs, at least attracted the Queen's attention. They involved, for the most part, dogs' turds and close-stools. (The Queen's was handily placed in a cabinet leading from her presence chamber, and dogs' messes were everywhere.) Sophie's inventions discountenanced the courtiers but regrettably amused her mother, who regarded her child's pranks as she might the antics of her monkeys, and she quite enjoyed seeing Sophie teased so that she might observe her sharpening her wits.

Sophie dwells with obvious pleasure on her precocious accomplishments. For a family production of Corneille's *Medea*, after she had been considered too young to be able to memorise a part, she quickly learned the entire play, 'although I only needed to know the part of *Nérine* which they finally deigned to give me'. She performed it, mounted on *chopines* to give her height, coached in her gestures by a professional actress, and 'the Queen was well pleased'.

It was after this triumph that Sophie's sisters stopped ignoring her, and Sophie benefited from their interest, as all of them were more accomplished than she.

Elizabeth, tall and dark, was nicknamed *La Grecque*, not because of her wonderfully even, classical features but for her impressive learning 'in all the languages and sciences'. She befriended René Descartes when he came to Holland; his *Principiae Philosophicae* are dedicated to her and he called her, together with Gustav Adolph's daughter Queen Christine, the most scholarly woman in Europe.

Sophie says that for all her philosophy Elizabeth was unable to rise above the misfortune of her nose, which, narrow and aquiline though it was, often turned bright red. On such occasions she would go into hiding and not emerge even when it was time to appear before the Queen. Her Majesty could not be kept waiting, as her daughter Louise Hollandine, who anyhow did not much care about appearances, knew well. She would urge her elder sister to hurry, and when Elizabeth asked, 'Do you expect me to go with such a nose?', would only heartlessly enquire, 'Do you expect me to wait until you get another?'

Louise Hollandine had no vanity, and was far more easy-going than Elizabeth. Sophie found her less pretty. Louise's portraits by Honthorst, who regularly painted all members of the family singly and in groups, and whose talented pupil she was, show that she was very pretty indeed, with auburn hair and a witty air.

Henriette was the beauty of the family. Ashblonde, with 'that complexion of lilies and roses' longed for by all her contemporaries, she had huge blue eyes, and differed from all her brothers and sisters in being docile and submissive. Fittingly, concocting sweetmeats was her great if sole talent.

Sophie claims not to have been daunted by these three graces—'all more beautiful and better educated than I'. But she was still so dejected about her looks that the first hint of a compliment almost unhinged her critical faculties, which were highly developed at an early age. These surprising words of praise were uttered by her aunt, Queen Henrietta Maria, wife of Charles I of England, who arrived in Holland in 1642. With her was her eleven-year-old daughter Mary, whose betrothal to Prince William of Orange, aged fifteen, had previously taken place in England. Sophie, on her first official engagement, formed part of the reception committee in Honslaersdyk. She was deeply disappointed with the appearance of her aunt. She had expected the vision from the Van Dyck portrait, but saw instead 'a tiny woman on high *chopines*, with uneven shoulders and long thin arms and tusklike teeth that protruded from her mouth'. However, 'from the moment that she was kind enough to say that I resembled her daughter, I found her beautiful'.

'Princess Royal', as Mary always insisted on being called, was a grave little girl with delicate features and a petulant expression. She shared the tragedy of the nose with her cousin Elizabeth, and was a far cry from the pink and white beauty that Sophie admired, but she was surrounded by such an aura of glamour that one could not help being flattered at being likened to her.

England had sent her, reluctantly, to marry William, the eldest son of Prince Frederick Henry of Orange and his wife Amalie von Solms, formerly a lady-in-waiting to the Queen of Bohemia—'one of my maids'. It had been thought that Mary's younger sister would be quite grand enough, in view of Amalie's comparatively humble birth, for which she compensated by extremely superior airs which irritated the Winter children and their mother. But during the long marriage negotiations Charles' position had become very difficult. England was teetering on the brink of civil war, and the connection with the enormously rich Oranges became increasingly important to him. The Oranges' eagerness for the honour had waned in proportion. The ambassador said that the younger princess was unacceptable, since she 'looked sickly and like to die' (which she did at the age of thirteen). So, if there was to be a marriage at all, it had to be 'Princess Royal', and at once. The marriage contract was duly signed, and with it a document promising financial assistance to Charles I. Owing to her youth and her exalted station, the child-bride celebrated the pro-forma consummation of her marriage not, as was usual, in a ceremonial nightshift, but in a sack sewn up on three sides and drawn to her chin, and the placing of the groom's foot on a corner of the bed was altogether omitted. These elegant refinements naturally made her an object of great fascination for Sophie, but precluded friendship between the girls, as the Princess was always to be intolerably haughty.

However, although she did not like her English cousin, Sophie, on overhearing a conversation between some gentlemen in the English suite, who thought that she, the ugly duckling, would one day outshine her own ravishing sisters, conceived 'an affection for the entire English nation'.

After the Princess Royal's proxy marriage to William had been solemnised, Charles Louis, sounding doubtful, wrote to his uncle to express the hope that the advantage which His Majesty expected from his daughter's union with William 'do correspond to the honour you do him by it'. He had rather wanted to marry the Princess himself, for what he needed for an equitable Palatine solution was to be seen to enjoy the support of his uncle in England. He quite saw that the troubled King, lately 'the happiest

Prince in Christendom but for his nephew's business', but now in straits which had caused his Queen to bring the English crown jewels to the pawnbrokers in Amsterdam while delivering her daughter to the Oranges, could send him no financial aid. Charles I, who was borrowing vast sums from France, suggested that Charles Louis should look henceforth in that direction himself. Charles Louis, knowing from his recent experience that France would not lift a finger unless England did so first, promised not to badger his uncle in these hard days, but hoped that the King would remember his poor nephew in better ones.

Remembering that Charles I had once commended him 'for not sleeping upon his business', he proceeded to grasp at straws. Hopefully, whenever things looked up he congratulated his uncle on 'the perfect settlement of Your Majesty's affairs', and continued proposing visits 'without putting Your Majesty to any ceremony or charge'. Since, during one of his many English visits, Charles Louis had been nominated as alternative king by a Scottish member of Parliament who suspected that his rightful monarch had been seduced by the Queen's Papists, Charles I preferred to keep his nephew out of his kingdom.

But Charles Louis did arrive, unbidden, in July 1642. He clearly perceived on kissing hands that the King was as displeased with his coming as he was with the object of his journey, which was to lay the Palatine case before Parliament, with whom the King was now hopelessly embroiled.

Charles Louis did not stay in England long. While Rupert and Maurice sped to their uncle's side to help him in his struggle against the Parliamentarian army, Charles Louis prudently left the country. He indignantly refuted Charles' allegations of disloyalty. Appealing to His Majesty's own knowledge of him, he begged the King to consider whether he had not always been most solicitous in obeying his advice and commands—'though sometimes contrary to my own sense and advantage as I then conceived'. Promising to explain all his actions at the next meeting, he was supremely confident that the King would understand that he was obliged to be Elector Palatine first, and His Majesty's nephew a poor second.

But while Rupert became 'Robert le Diable' for feats of bravery in his uncle's cause, and Maurice was thought loyal though uncouth, Charles Louis blackened his name forever in Royalist circles by referring to the Puritans as 'the children of truth and innocency and, under God, his best friends'. The King never forgave him. Nor did the Queen of Bohemia approve of her eldest son's attitude, 'thinking his honour somewhat engaged in it'. But she allowed her name to be linked with his when, for the sake of her pension and the Palatine restitution, he disassociated himself from his Cavalier brothers. 'It is impossible for myself and the Queen to bridle my brothers' youth at so great a distance,' the Elector wrote to the Parliament, 'and it would be a great indiscretion for any to expect it and to blame us for things beyond our help.' Later, when a letter from the Queen to Rupert containing very different sentiments fell into Parliamentary hands, she allowed herself to be persuaded by Charles Louis to request the Speaker 'to remove all such impressions as might deprive her of Parliament's good opinion'. By 1645 Parliament had all but stopped her pension.

Most of the Queen's jewels went into pawn. 'We often feasted more richly than Cleopatra, dining exclusively on diamonds and pearls,' writes Sophie of the hand-to-mouth existence that followed. But although rats, mice and creditors might plague the Court, tradesmen continued their deliveries and Sophie thought that providence would, presumably, see to the settling of their accounts. The misfortunes of *la maison* did not affect her cheerful temperament. Life at The Hague was pleasant enough for a growing girl. She was now satisfied with her looks to the point of smugness. Besides feet and ankles 'perfectly turned like all those of our family', she lists light brown hair, naturally wavy, a lively *dégagé* air and a good figure, not very tall. Most important, her bossy sister Elizabeth had seen to it that she deported herself *en princesse*. Sophie now had two young maids of honour of her own, the Misses Carray, who fussed about her appearance as the old Quaadts had once fussed about her salvation. They successfully kept her *à la mode* in spite of a shortage of pin-money. 'Youth itself,' Sophie said glumly when her glass no longer reflected anything of the sort, 'is ever *une des plus belles parures*.' She no longer tortured the courtiers with disgusting jokes, but mocked them instead, and was always forgiven, for she proved to have inherited much of her mother's irresistible charm.

Sophie's particular butt at Court was William Craven. Lord Craven, the son of a former Lord Mayor of London, had placed his person and his immense fortune at the disposal of the Palatine family, whom he had come to assist during Frederick's lifetime. He had become so loyal and devoted a friend to the widowed Queen that there were the usual rumours—unsupported—of a secret marriage. It is hard to imagine what would have become of the Palatines without his unfailing generosity, but, ungratefully, Sophie does not spare 'the old Milord' in the Memoirs. She writes him off for a fool, who actually liked being teased, and scornfully reports that he was always ready to offer 'a collation and a thousand trinkets to ingratiate himself with the young, and at his most absurd when he intended most to shine in conversation'.

There were other, more stimulating people about, for The Hague swarmed with interesting refugees seeking asylum from oppression at home. English visitors unfailingly came to kiss the royal ladies' hands at the Wassenaer Court, and were welcomed in the Winter Queen's gloomy presence chamber—still hung in black velvet in remembrance of the Winter King, as John Evelyn noted a decade or so after Frederick's unfortunate decease.

The town itself was cheerful and beautifully kept. The tree-lined streets and cobbled passages were regularly patrolled by the Watch. Disturbers of the peace were immediately dealt with, even if they happened to be the Princes Palatine, whose presence was often marked by halloings and other jovialities which scandalised the solid citizens. No idle vagabond was suffered to loiter in the bustling streets ('There is not a child of four or five but they find some employment for it,' admiringly writes Evelyn), and it was safe for Sophie and the Carrays to walk about the town. Changed from Court clothes into tidy dresses and caps as worn by burghers' daughters, they would chat to farmers' lads who had brought their produce to market. If a fair was in town, they might gaze at such strange exhibits as elephants, and note 'that contrary to vulgar tradition these animals were extremely nimble for their monstrous bulk, and moreover could support two or three grown men on their probosces'. Pliny's film-footed onocratulus—the pelican—might make Sophie shudder in remembrance of her classical education, but to compensate for this there were two-headed cocks, four-footed hens and other monsters. Booths richly stocked with pictures of landscapes and scenes of everyday life, which were attracting the attention of collectors—Evelyn stocked up, noting that these 'clownish representations' were called Drolleries by the Dutch—left Sophie cold. She was never to develop a real feeling for art. But she always had a keen eye for splendour and could feast it at the Stadholder's palace, which, besides being 'filled with modern pictures', was wonderfully opulent, and overlooked gardens full of ornament, statuary and grottoes, and what Evelyn calls 'artificial music', in the sense of skilfully made.

Although 'Princess Royal' had proved too stiff and haughty to be much use as a friend for Sophie, there were others, especially the Portuguese Dorothea Guzman and the Dutch Florentine van Brederode, with whom she giggled and exchanged notes that would be delivered at breakfast each morning.

But if these young ladies ever learned of Palatine family upsets, it was not from Sophie: throughout her life she preserved deep silence on matters touching disagreeably on the honour of *la maison*.

The chain of troublesome events which led to estrangements within the family began in 1645, when Edward, who had returned to Paris, became a Catholic. He took this step in order to marry Anna Gonzaga, sister of the Queen of Poland, and, as a daughter of the Duc de Nevers and Mantua, a relation of the royal family of France.

Eight years older than Edward, Anna had been the long-standing mistress—she said morganatic wife—of the Prince de Guise. When this affair broke up she needed a face-saver, and it seemed to her that Edward, with more than a fair share of the Palatine looks, good birth and a gift for riveting gossip, would make a most presentable husband. She herself had such capacity for intrigue that Edward's lack of any real ability hardly mattered: she had enough for both of them. Bossuet says that the infinite fertility of her expedients gave a secret charm to all her enterprises. Edward's faith was the only obstacle to the match, but she achieved his conversion in record time and eloped with him, creating a scandal.

If matters of religion were of supreme indifference to Anna, they were far from being so to the Queen of Bohemia. Her reaction whenever a religious change had been suggested in the past in connection with any child of hers had been one of pure horror: Rupert in Imperial custody, the subject of much proselytising, had worried her half to death; the idea that Princess Elizabeth might change her religion in order to marry a Catholic prince had been dismissed out of hand; and when Charles I had suggested that Charles Louis might solve the Palatine problem by becoming a Catholic and marrying a daughter of the Emperor she had indignantly replied that she would, with her own hands, strangle any of her children who left the Protestant religion. Henceforth, Edward was to be no child of hers. (She forgave him in a surprisingly short while. Anna's charm communicated itself even by post.)

Charles Louis suffered political embarrassment through Edward's action. His case at the peace conference of Westphalia, assembled since 1644 to bring an end to the Thirty Years' War—with the Protestant powers at Münster and the Catholics at Osnabrück—naturally rested on an unblemished Protestant family record. Sweden, his main Protestant supporter, behaved as though the hassock had been pulled from under her knees. France, having honoured the Elector with a family connection, expected his envoys to give way on various vital points. Charles Louis plaintively asked not to be blamed for what was his affliction, and offended France while failing to mollify Sweden.

Edward sent his brother a long, correctly spelled letter of explanation filled with theological argument. Charles Louis replied in sorrow and astonishment that he recognised his brother's handwriting, but both style and content seemed to be the handiwork of the priests; he could only hope that Edward was not truly persuaded of the fopperies to which he pretended.

Privately, he was convinced that Edward had apostatised not, as he claimed, because his eyes had been opened to the truth, but because he had no desire to exchange the 'soft entanglings of pleasure' at the French Court for the home-life of the Winter Queen. Charles Louis sensibly decided that attempts to retrieve his brother's soul would be so much *peine perdue*. He composed some religious verse, in English, on the back of this correspondence with his brother, which touched on 'foul damps of sensuality' and 'those that fell, from pride and unbelief', and asked his mother to withdraw his brother Philip, Edward's companion in Paris, from so dangerous an environment.

Philip returned to The Hague in 1646, and added to the family's problems by taking exception to the attentions paid to the Queen by the Marquis d'Epinay, a Frenchman visiting The Hague. The Queen was of course an old hand at dealing with admirers, even such notorious ladykillers as the Marquis, but Philip, feeling that stronger measures were required, pounced on the unsuspecting Marquis and stabbed him to death.

As a result the Queen struck another son off her list. The Dutch Estates, who had so far been lenient with law-breaking Palatines, even closing their eyes to the occasional, strictly illegal duel, took such violent exception to this latest deed that Philip was forced to leave the country.

The Princess Elizabeth tried to intercede for Philip with her mother, and was struck off in turn. She departed to Brandenburg, accompanied by Henriette.

Charles Louis shared his sister Elizabeth's surprisingly light-hearted view of the murder. He begged his mother's pardon on Philip's behalf, saying that to do so really needed more apology than his brother's youthful indiscretion itself. The Queen, to his amazement, remained deaf to all entreaties, as did Messieurs les Etats. Only Philip's absence prevented the law from taking its course.

The Palatine envoys at the interminable peace negotiations in Münster and Osnabrück had a hard time of it. They had never been able to cut fine figures, as lack of money, plate and *Verehrer-wein* made it impossible for them to treat their fellow delegates in the manner to which these were accustomed. Objects of derision in their old and shabby clothes, the Palatines often had difficulty in gaining admittance to the conference tables at all. Now, in the face of Dutch displeasure, Charles Louis' envoy at Münster hardly liked to leave his filthy though expensive lodgings, and vainly tried to dispel the suspicion that God's blessing was absent from his enterprise. Both he and his colleague at Osnabrück were disagreeably surprised to learn that the Princess Elizabeth, in Brandenburg, was complicating the difficult situation by bombarding the Courts of France and Sweden with financial claims of her own without first advising them of her intention.

Any hopes for a full Palatine settlement had in any case long been abandoned. Preliminary discussions had clearly shown that there would be no return to the status quo of 1618. Maximilian of Bavaria had no intention of yielding an inch, and was only with difficulty persuaded to return the Lower, Rhenish, Palatinate to Charles Louis, while keeping the Upper Palatinate and the Electorship for himself.

Mazarin continued the ambiguous policy of his predecessor Richelieu, and played off the Empire's princes against each other in the interests of the boy King Louis XIV, who, as the Habsburgs' power crumbled away, was emerging as Europe's new master. Mazarin continued to support Maximilian, who might always be a useful ally, but he also felt it wise to support Charles Louis in his claims. The Lower Palatinate would be a most useful French foothold, much more convenient if ruled by a friend; so Charles Louis had Mazarin's full blessing in insisting on his Electoral rights.

In spite of the ancient Golden Bull that stipulated the mystic number of seven Electors, Charles Louis '*per amore pacis*' agreed to accept an eighth Electorship, specially created for him, together with half his country and a sadly inadequate annual payment in compensation for the loss of the rest of it. He felt shabbily treated: there was no justice, he said, only mercy, for the disinherited of this world.

After the peace treaty was signed in December 1648 to the sound of Te Deums, Charles Louis appointed a Regency Council under his brother Philip. The Elector himself remained abroad until the Palatinate was clear of foreign soldiers, Catholic priests and Bavarian officials.

Among the people who flocked to the Wassenaer palace to congratulate the Queen of Bohemia on the Palatine restitution was her nephew Charles Stuart, Prince of Wales, whose father was now a prisoner on the Isle of Wight, while the Queen of England and her younger children had found refuge at Louis XIV's Court. Charles, too, had been a guest in France, where he had courted, but failed to charm, Anne Marie d'Orléans, the greatest heiress in France. It had been his mother's idea; he himself had not been able to muster enough enthusiasm for Mademoiselle (later La Grande, to distinguish her from the baby claimant of this title) even to make the effort of speaking French. The courtship, conducted through Rupert, who acted as interpreter, had not yielded results, and Charles' arrival in Holland was cheering to mothers of unmarried Protestant daughters.

'We saw,' writes Sophie, 'a prince well-formed in mind and body, but one whose fortunes were in no condition to allow him to think of marriage.' Many of the English Royalists, however, were thinking of it for him, 'especially as it was thought that a marriage to a princess of his own religion would be popular in England.' Of all available Protestant princesses, none was more highly born than Sophie, a few months younger than the eighteen-year-old Charles.

The Queen of Bohemia had long cherished this plan. She had, in vain, built castles in the air for all her girls, but the fortunes of *la maison* were too low to tempt any suitors with the prospect of handsome dowries or political advantages. In dreaming of the palace of Whitehall for Sophie, Elizabeth felt that two birds might be killed with a single stone. Her brother Charles I could only benefit by marrying his son and heir to a princess whose father had died a martyr, so to speak, for the Protestant religion, while her son Charles Louis could not fail to profit from having a sister married to the future King of England.

The idea had already been discussed four years earlier. The Memoirs say that Amalie, with a marriageable Protestant daughter of the right age of her own, had ruined the plan by deliberately setting her son William, as yet 'Princess Royal's' husband in name only, on to Sophie's trail in order to ruin her reputation. The scheme had failed because the Wassenaer Hof had got wind of it, and Sophie had contrived to disappear whenever Prince William darkened the door of her mother's anteroom. She had emerged from this episode with her reputation unstained, but not before William had impertinently sent word that it lay within her power to rule over all Holland if she would emulate the Duchesse de Chevreuse—a lady famous for her amorous adventures.

It is possible that William considered the seduction of Sophie a piquant change from the brothels of Amsterdam, but highly unlikely that the ambitious Amalie should have wanted to double her ties with the Stuarts at such an unpropitious moment. The account of this episode in the Memoirs says more about the Winter family's attitude to Amalie than about Amalie's intentions.

In 1648 there were no counterploys of an amorous nature by William, now Stadholder, and host to his brothers-in-law Charles and James Stuart. The Prince of Wales seemed to be falling in with the Queen of Bohemia's fondest wishes. Daily he was to be seen in Sophie's company during her regular promenade on the Voorhout, and the fashionable world, gathered here in the early evening to see and be seen, drew its speedy conclusions. The Queen was not on sufficiently cosy terms with her youngest daughter to learn 'that Charles always behaved as a good cousin should', and wishfully believed all the rumours which supplied the missing romantic element. She was highly delighted, while Sophie was wryly amused to find herself treated as a person of the utmost importance by all the refugees at The Hague.

The news of Charles I's execution in January 1649 brought an icy chill to every Court in Europe. Not even the members of the Bohemian Court, more aware than most of his desperate situation, had expected so barbarous a stroke. Edward Hyde, lately the King's Chancellor, now in Jersey but well-informed of reactions in Holland (where he was shortly to send his daughter Anne as one of Princess Royal's maids of honour), said that the consternation in The Hague was such that everyone seemed bereft of reason. Even the common people were deeply affected, and he was gratified that a pregnant woman 'of the middling rank fell into travail with the horror of the mention of it, and in it died'.

Messieurs les Etats, in a body, voiced their sympathy in terms of great sorrow, except that there was not enough bitterness against the murderers to satisfy Hyde. But he was pleased with the service during which the misfortune was lamented in a very good Latin oration 'in terms of as much asperity and detestation of the perpetrators as it was possible to express'. He would for once have approved of the Palatine manners which he normally deplored: Prince Edward, in The Hague while his wife was pulling strings during the *Fronde* in France, loudly insulted the Parliamentary envoys in the street.

The Queen threw caution and the last hope for her pension to the winds. Cromwell the murderer became the veriest beast, the Devil incarnate, and she didn't care who knew it. If her sin was to have been the sister of the King of England, she was proud to own it.

Charles Louis, who had been in England during the trial in an attempt to sort out his finances, was painfully aware that Charles I had blamed him to the last. A few days before the execution the King had refused even to see him, accusing him of complying with his enemies. 'He said I did it only to have one more chicken in the dish,' complained the Elector. 'These and suchlike expressions would have moved a saint—particularly in view of the many neglects my person and my public business had received at Court.' As for being blamed for not 'intermeddling on the King's behalf', Charles Louis said that he had better reason than most to know that 'in all governments strength prevailed, be it right or wrong'. However, he was as appalled as the rest of the family.

'My brother the Elector is now here; he cares no more for those cursed people in England,' wrote Sophie in April to Rupert and Maurice, both in Ireland to raise ships for Charles, whom the Scots had proclaimed King in February. The Scottish Commissioners—'full of impertinent proposals'—

were already in The Hague, seeking Charles' signature to the two Covenants which were to assure their religious liberty.

Amalie, making mischief as usual, took pleasure in pointing out that Sophie always accompanied Charles when he attended Common prayer, and could therefore not be an acceptable Queen Consort in the eyes of what she called 'the Brethren'. Indeed, it became obvious to Sophie that Charles himself made a point of ignoring her whenever they were about.

Sophie observed 'further signs of weakness' in her cousin, and especially regretted his treatment of the Earl of Montrose, to whom all the Palatines were devoted. From the time that Montrose had sailed to Scotland on the King's business, only to be abandoned by his monarch and hung, drawn and chopped into tiny pieces in Edinburgh, Sophie no longer trusted Charles.

But the daily walks continued, and she found to her astonishment that his behaviour changed from good-cousinly to amorous. He began by telling her that she was prettier than Mistress Barlow, the courtesy title adopted by Lucy Walter, who had recently presented him with a son (later to be the Duke of Monmouth). It was at best a questionable compliment: few princesses care to be compared to those whom they consider common whores, and Sophie had heard that all who could afford it enjoyed the favours of 'Mistress Barlo'. After so inauspicious a beginning, the end of Charles' speech—'he said he hoped to see me in England'—carried little conviction.

This, she knew, was not the way in which 'the marriages of great princes are made'. Her suspicions were confirmed when she discovered that Lord Craven's fortune rather than her own person had prompted Charles' love-making: his companions were hoping that her old friend's famous generosity would extend itself to them through her influence. She promptly put an end to the promenades on the Voorhout, inventing a corn for her mother's benefit which, she said, prevented her from walking. Although she was to tell Bishop Burnet years later 'that she was once like to have married Charles II, which would not have been the worse for the nation, seeing how many children she had brought into the world', at the time she realised that nothing was less probable.

In October 1649 the Elector Charles Louis entered the city of Heidelberg at the precise moment when the Catholic clergy departed by a different gate. Ironically, the first person to congratulate him on his arrival was the Bavarian Ambassador, who had done nothing to smooth his path. Long delays had been occasioned by Maximilian's demands for compensation for the harvest—a poor one—gathered but not consumed by Bavaria, and for some Bavarian cannons too heavy to move. 'Indeed,' said Charles Louis, 'they seem to begrudge us the very air of our fatherland.'

He could not yet call his country entirely his own. France, an ominous neighbour since her annexation of Alsace (which gave her a voice at the Imperial Diet and powers that reduced the Emperor to a mere figurehead), continued to garrison his wine-growing centre of Bacharach. The Spanish were to remain for years in Frankenthal, the Winter Queen's dower. And the country itself was very different from what he might have remembered it if his memory had stretched that far back.

'The orchard of Germany' was razed to the ground. The population was disastrously reduced, trade was dead, and grass grew in once busy market-places. Heidelberg Castle was too shot up for habitation. While repairs were under way, the Elector moved into one of the government buildings in the town, together with Charlotte of Hesse Cassel, whom he had married six months earlier in order to secure the Protestant Palatine succession. His son Louis von Rothenschild, by an unnamed English girl referred to as 'a lady of quality' by his biographers, was useless for dynastic purposes;* so was Edward, with whom this amiable youth lived in Paris; and the Elector's other brothers were daily exposed to mortal danger: Rupert and Maurice were buccaneering on the high seas in Charles II's service, and Philip was soldiering in the French army against Spain.

On the face of it, the alliance with Hesse Cassel was highly advantageous from every point of view, except that Charlotte's mother, the formidable Landgravine, herself had felt obliged to warn the Elector of his bride's foul temper. However, he became wildly infatuated, and applied himself to the task of procreation with unparalleled gusto which reflected his Stuart ancestry, and his fervour as a husband was matched only by the enthusiasm with which he became the father of his country.

Strict though loving, he deployed his subjects to deal with the ravages. Quarries worked overtime, houses sprang up, free asylum was offered to all made destitute or persecuted on religious grounds, and people came

---

* The Elector was devoted to this boy, and one of his first official acts was to create him the Freiherr von Selz.

flocking to swell his labour force. Vineyards were replanted—and beer brewed while the grapes were forming. Roads were relined with fruit trees, and past the saplings sped the new Palatine express post to give a further fillip to the economy.

Wolves, roaming the countryside until recently littered with cadavers, still threatened villagers and travellers. Charles Louis' subjects were free to shoot over the terrain, although hunting and shooting were by tradition the prerogative of princes, so jealously guarded that any infringement led to horrific punishment. The wolves were eventually dealt with, but quantities of red deer still continued to disappear. Charles Louis cancelled permission to shoot, but his Palatines took to the woods with enormous deerhounds—to protect themselves, they said, from the wolves that remained. The Elector then ordered that each dog was to have a progress-impeding hobble-stick tied to its hind-quarters, but this decree proved understandably unpopular and was quietly dropped.

The Elector's long-term programme included the modernisation of the Palatine school system, the pride of enlightened Electors for centuries. With characteristic attention to detail he ended the long-standing practice of having pupils troop out to sing at every local funeral, and relieved schoolmasters of such domestic duties as sweeping and dusting their classrooms, so that they could concentrate on teaching.

The resuscitation of the ancient university was a project dear to his heart, lending an element of *gloire* to the work of reconstruction. The ruined building was put under repair. The collection of manuscripts, carried off by the Duke of Bavaria and stored in the Vatican, was not to be returned in Charles Louis' lifetime in spite of his protests (and, indeed, was not sent back until 1815). But he set up a new book fund, and looked around for distinguished scholars to attract students.

Princess Elizabeth's friend Descartes, a logical first choice although his books sent Charles Louis to sleep, was, alas, no more. He had left Holland to become resident philosopher to Queen Christine of Sweden, and died soon after his arrival of the northern winter, which her eccentric timetable forced him to face in the small hours of the morning. Spinoza, in Geneva, did not accept Charles Louis' invitation, though it offered attractive conditions and guaranteed religious freedom; in the end Charles Louis appointed Ezechiel Spanheim, who combined sound scholarship with *savoir faire*—he ended his days as a full-time diplomatist—and parents sending sons to study in Heidelberg received letters of thanks in the Elector's own hand.

His efficient chancellery dealt with such mountains of official correspondence that the landlady of the Red Goat, ordered to supply free quills in punishment for a misdemeanour, loudly complained that she was forced to keep a special flock of geese for the purpose.

Making every Reichsthaler do the work of three, Charles Louis achieved something like an economic miracle. His penny-pinching habits, so distressing to his family, greatly benefited his country.

Even with the best will in the world he could not have satisfied his relations, whose combined demands for money exceeded his annual income. The Queen had always understood that once the restoration was accomplished she herself would be properly re-established. She quite saw that while Frankenthal remained full of Spaniards she could not take up residence there; nor did she wish to join her son in Heidelberg. What she wanted, and angrily demanded, was her jointure as laid down in her marriage-contract.

'It afflicts me to see so much evil mixed with so small a beginning of good,' wrote Charles Louis to the Queen in reply to a letter in which she hoped 'that he would soon give her cause to be his affectionate mother', and he invited her to inspect his books 'with your wonted temper towards me'. He pointed out that a diminished country meant fewer subjects and smaller revenues, and expressed surprise that she seemed unprepared to share in the losses he had incurred through the Peace of Westphalia. He would do what he could, and it was unreasonable to expect more.

He could, and did, invite his youngest sister to come to Heidelberg. This move, although easing his mother's desperate situation by reducing her household, proved unpopular with the Queen. Charles Louis wrote that as Her Majesty's letters had never suggested anything but indifference to the plan, he was now surprised to find her 'absolutely displeased therewith'. Had the Queen been pleased to signify her disapproval of Sophie's coming in express terms before her departure, 'I am confident neither of us would have desired the journey'.

Charles Louis spoke only for himself. Sophie had accepted the invitation with alacrity and could hardly wait to be gone. She chose to believe that the Queen, who was still 'flattering herself with the English marriage', had allowed herself to be persuaded that it might be as easily arranged from

Heidelberg. She also deluded herself that the Queen desired her to have the company of the two Carrays, 'of whom I had grown so fond'.

'If Carray says she went with Sophie by my orders, she is much in the wrong,' wrote the Queen after Sophie had gone. 'I think Sophie had as much wit as she to govern herself, this is most true upon my faith, and if Carray say otherwise she does not say true.' She added, for the record, that she had all along been opposed to Sophie's departure, although, 'I will never keep any that has has a mind to leave me, for I shall never care for anybody's company that does not care for mine'.

CHAPTER TWO

Heidelberg
(1650–1658)

Sᴏᴘʜɪᴇ ᴀɴᴅ ʜᴇʀ party travelled up the Rhine in a barge borrowed from Messieurs les Etats. She was anxious to reach her destination as swiftly as possible, and somewhat annoyed when the heads of the states *en route* insisted on paying their respects. Their hospitality failed to impress her, but nonetheless she seems to have enjoyed herself. She was never so pleased as when she had the opportunity of dwelling on the imperfections of others, and clearly still took enormous pleasure in listing them for the Memoirs.

There was the sadly old-fashioned castle of the Duke of Neuburg near Düsseldorf, containing some tapestries that were both beautiful and antique, but much furniture that was only antique and the worse for it. And the Duke himself, trying to dazzle by changing his costume twice during her short visit but only managing 'to look a little smarter than his entourage', bored her to tears. He showed her hundreds of small religious drawings on parchment that were pinned all over his walls—these have the sound of some quattrocento sample collection, and would have struck her as very old-fashioned indeed—and insisted on taking her over his chapel and the adjoining convent. She cheered up on meeting a gaggle of gay and pretty English nuns, and the Duke, who had recently become a Catholic, noted a tiny glimmer of interest in his visitor's glassy gaze. Hoping for her conversion, he archly refused to lead her away. She marched off, unsupported, as stoutly Protestant as ever, and he and his untidy suite were obliged to come puffing after her so that the courtesies might be observed.

The castles by the banks of the Rhine looked spectacular enough on their summits, but on closer inspection proved 'more like private residences than the seats of important people'. Although Sophie noted with approval that princes were treated with enormous respect in Germany, they lacked the requisite grandeur, which should not have surprised her considering the events of the last thirty years.

As for the seatless, strangely constructed vehicle that met her when, on reaching the Palatinate, she disembarked at Oppenheim to continue her journey overland, it defied description. Sophie and her friends arranged themselves as best they could on cushions prudently brought along, but it was soon obvious that the two unmatched, malevolent horses had little intention of moving at all. 'Most of that day was spent walking through thick mud, there being no paving as in Holland.'

Somehow she reached Mannheim, where she was welcomed by her brother and his wife. Knowing her brother to be a prince *avec infiniment d'esprit*, Sophie naturally expected to find her sister-in-law equally charming, but Charlotte's difficult disposition showed itself at once. On boarding the Electress's coach, vastly more comfortable than that in which she had lately crouched on her cushions, Sophie congratulated her on the luxury of its appointments. She was not to know that it had been a wedding present from the Landgravine, and considered by Charlotte less fine than the carriage received by her sister Emélie on her marriage to the Prince de Tarent, but Charlotte's grimaces clearly showed her compliment to have been misplaced.

Except for her cross expression, emphasised by much face-pulling and jet-black eyebrows, incongruously dyed, Charlotte looked well enough to Sophie. She was a tall blonde girl of twenty-three, with long legs and a beautiful bust. Charles Louis could hardly keep his hands off her. 'There were continuous *embrassades*. I often saw him on his knees before her, and her before him, all in full public view.' Sophie didn't know where to look, and concluded that Charles Louis' passion had impaired his intellect.

If Charlotte so much as glanced at any man, Charles Louis suffered jealous torments. Any hint of criticism from her, and the Elector flew into tantrums. The quarrels were made up only at night in bed with audible violence. Not, says Sophie, that Charles Louis had any serious reason for tormenting himself. His wife only loved to be admired, and her behaviour was not so much culpable as stupid.

It seems that Charlotte could hardly put a foot right, so far as Sophie was concerned. Conversation was hopeless. She would only talk about herself, a topic Sophie found to be of limited appeal. The girls shared no interests. Charlotte was a wonderful horsewoman—Sophie didn't ride or hunt. The Elector himself would by choice 'go a-rumbling on horseback' only to cure himself of the spleen, and did not like to see women galloping about. Gambling was Charlotte's passion—Sophie had only occasionally played at The Hague to amuse her mother, who enjoyed watching a game of an evening; Charles Louis considered gambling a plain waste of money.

The more Charlotte tried to impress, the more miserably she failed. She foolishly mounted a fashion-show, 'causing all her fine gowns to be spread out over the tables, and giving the history of each one when it was not even *à la mode* to own a great many clothes all at once'. Sour grapes may have entered into Sophie's reaction. Charlotte's trousseau did credit to the Landgravine, who was as aware as the rest of the world of her son-in-law's stinginess. However, Sophie gives another black mark to Charlotte, explaining that the elegant thing was to own only a few clothes at a time, and acquire new ones frequently so as to keep up with the rapidly changing fashions. She adds that, anyway, she herself had been taught to regard such mundane matters *en bagatelle*.

Matters between the girls were unlikely to improve when Charles Louis begged Sophie to wean Charlotte from her unfortunate affectations. He loyally explained that his wife's airs and graces were due not so much to a flawed character as to her unsophisticated background, which was of course quite unsuitable for one in Charlotte's exalted position.

Heidelberg manners, by tradition, were courtly in the grand manner. Much as the Winter children had disliked their upbringing, all of them regarded Heidelberg as the seat of civilisation and culture. They were proud of its university, the oldest in the Empire, and of its castle, which was the largest and had, before the wars, been the grandest. The Electoral Court had always been conducted with Gallic elegance, long before it became the fashion for German Courts to follow the model of the Court of France—with results that often made Sophie fall about with amusement. To the Winter children, who regarded the Palatinate as a place apart, Germany was a desert from one end to the other, and pretentiousness, amusing when observed abroad, was a source of embarrassment nearer home.

At her brother's desire, Sophie tried her tactful best with Charlotte, but gave up when her sister-in-law committed the ultimate horror: Sophie hardly believed her ears when, in an unbidden burst of confidence, Charlotte revealed that she had married Charles Louis much against her inclination. But for her mother's insistence, she would have chosen any one of a whole stud of admiring young princes—among them Sophie's future husband—sooner than this jealous old man (who had been thirty-three when he married). At The Hague, thought Sophie, such a thing would be considered beyond the pale, and a wife complaining of her husband be laughed at for a fool. Surely no shortcoming in education but only total lack of *esprit* could account for such peculiar behaviour.

This view was confirmed when Charlotte's sister, the Princesse de Tarent—she of the superior coach—came for a fortnight's visit. Emélie, although she shared her sister's background and upbringing, struck Sophie as a very different proposition. Exquisitely turned out, with a wit nicely polished in the blue drawing-rooms of the *Précieuses* which she frequented in Paris, and managing a susceptible husband and flocks of admirers with an iron hand in an expensively scented glove of finest Spanish leather, here was a woman who really understood the art of living.

Unfortunately, Emélie de Tarent had no influence on Charlotte either. Only someone whom the Electress neither envied nor despised would have stood a chance, and no such creature existed in the world.

Sophie herself was rapidly becoming an object of Charlotte's jealousy. The Electress was growing uneasily aware that Charles Louis appeared to be less besotted by the day, and that he seemed most at ease in his sister's company. That Sophie called him 'Papa' might be allowed to pass—this was not an unusual appellation for the head of *la maison*. But that he called her *ma fille* was perhaps exaggerated. Charlotte was of course not actually excluded from their conversations, but she never understood their jokes, and the irony with which they peppered even serious topics left her floundering.

A few months after Sophie's arrival, the Heidelberg Court paid a state visit to the Duke of Württemberg. This occasion confirmed Sophie's suspicion that the art of living was unknown in Germany.

They were met in Stuttgart with full honours, which boded well; but then their host became overexcited by his splendour and paraded the whole procession several times over the same route, lined with his loyal subjects, regardless of his visitors' travel fatigue. True, they were excused from hunting early the next day, but Sophie found that this and every other non-hunting day was spent over gargantuan meals that lasted for interminable hours.

The men drank incalculable quantities of wine in competition, while the ladies cheered them on. It was of no particular satisfaction to Sophie that she caused considerable jealousy among the elderly princesses, who kindly opened crayfish for the younger guests, when the Duke of Holstein sank a bumper to her health, spewed it up again and gallantly redowned it at once, while she sat aghast, deeply conscious of Palatine superiority.

In 1651 the birth of an Electoral prince, Charles, gave joy to his country, his parents and his aunt. The baby, as befitted his station, was born at the ancestral castle. Carpenters, stuccoists and painters had restored much of the old spendour, glaziers had worked wonders in the *Gläsersaal*. The Queen of Bohemia had reluctantly sent some suits of hangings and a few 'movables', but only those from her children's old bedrooms—the rest, she said, she had bought with her own money. 'They have nothing to do with you,' she wrote to Charles Louis, who had put her dotal pact in front of his lawyers and claimed all she owned as his legal property.

She was growing perfectly exasperated with her son, and showed it. Well aware of her grandson's arrival, she refused to take any notice until she was officially informed of the event. Then she wrote with petulance that she might have been told sooner, and regretted not being able to send a present, 'having all my jewels in pawn besides those that I cannot give away'. Charles Louis could appoint whom he pleased to stand in for her at the christening. She only wondered, since he had bidden so many Charleses as godfathers, that he had not included her nephew the King of England. 'I know he would have taken it very well. Besides, his father christened you, and many other reasons besides.'

If her ill-fated plans for Sophie's English marriage were still occupying her mind, she had at least the satisfaction of learning that Brandenburg was engineering a match for her daughter Henriette. The Elector's reinstatement had come too late in the lives of Elizabeth or Louise Hollandine. In their early thirties, they were long past the age when marriage could be thought of, in spite of Imperial dowries promised at the Peace of Westphalia. Even Henriette was cutting it fine at twenty-five, and her betrothal to the highly recommended Prince Racoczci of Transylvania would be something of a diplomatic triumph for the Elector of Brandenburg.

The Princess Elizabeth had been detailed to obtain Charles Louis' consent to the proposed marriage. Messengers sped between Brandenburg and the Palatinate with letters that grew more acrimonious with every post. Charles Louis dithered, unable to warm to the idea of sending a sister at great expense to the back of beyond for a match *si peu considérable* as to be of no political interest to him at all. This attitude struck Elizabeth as the height of ingratitude. She pointed out several clauses in the draft of the marriage contract which she thought most advantageous to her brother. He replied that she appeared not to understand Latin: his interpretation differed from hers. Elizabeth said her Latin had always been excellent and rather better than his, and please to stop prevaricating and to send a clear decision one way or the other.

By the time the Elector had decided against the marriage, all the arrangements for it had been concluded. Henriette sent a bewildered childish note to 'her dear Papa'. She only wished to please him and everyone else, and now hardly knew what to do for the best.

Charles Louis sent her a pair of drop-earrings as a wedding present, and she was carried across the mountains to her prince in a carriage that Elizabeth had miraculously extracted from the Queen of Bohemia. But unfortunately Princess Henriette was to have no opportunity of developing her housewifely talents. A few months after her wedding, she died of a mysterious fever.

Another death had already thinned the ranks of the Winter children. At the height of her quarrel with Charles Louis, Elizabeth received news that Philip, always her favourite brother, had been killed at the battle of Rethel. She took to her bed with grief, and dispiritedly begged Charles Louis to stop vexing himself and his friends as all had afflictions enough.

At Sophie's instigation the Elector did the handsome thing and invited Elizabeth to the Palatinate. When she arrived, they found that she had turned into a bitter old maid, combining her habitual bossiness with an air of martyrdom. Charles Louis, Sophie and Edward—in Heidelberg on one of his frequent visits—were appalled at the change. What had happened to her spirit and her looks? Especially to her beautiful mouth? The Electress turned against Elizabeth on sight. Charles Louis, too, found her disagreeable, and did not, after all, forgive her for her part in Henriette's marriage.

Sophie, who had been longing for a kindred spirit of her own sex, was bitterly disappointed. Elizabeth, in her governessy way, was every bit as hard to live with as Charlotte. Harder, really, for Charlotte now became all honey, determined to gain Sophie as an ally against Elizabeth. The Electress could be very charming when she chose. Sophie responded to her overtures, but blamed herself in retrospect for this sudden, disloyal friendship. The Memoirs, otherwise not notable for self-criticism (not surprisingly, as Sophie wrote them with the express purpose of cheering herself up), say, 'I was much to blame for not forcing myself to submit to my sister, whose judgement clearly was so superior to my own'.

But Charlotte's sweetness soon evaporated. Her temper, always dreadful during pregnancy, hardly improved after she gave birth to a daughter, Elizabeth Charlotte, in May 1652. Liselotte, who was to grow up to be her Aunt Sophie's most devoted admirer, was a fat, round-eyed, energetic baby. Unlike Charles, her dull and pasty elder brother, she thrived under the care of the ugly Quaadt sisters, winkled out of retirement to take up the careers they had been thought too old for when Sophie had moved to The Hague as a girl.

Visits to the nursery became a regular part of Sophie's days, and a welcome escape from domestic rows. She also had the run of her brother's library and became very well-read, though never a true blue-stocking intellectual like her sister Elizabeth, who was spending most of her time at the university. Sophie found that her mind grew rusty without physical exercise, and went for mammoth walks which her ladies dreaded. They were pleased that she took up playing the guitar, and rested their legs while she practised.

In the evenings there were frequent theatricals in the wooden structure used during the day as the ball-court. These entertainments might be home-made or given by the students, but often there were professional performances by strolling players.

Charles Louis loved the theatre, particularly English players,* and felt that the expense involved was perfectly legitimate for a reigning Elector who had to see to his magnificence. Nervous of appearing to indulge himself at the expense of his creditors, he insisted on absolute secrecy in any

* Troupes touring the Empire with Shakespearean repertoires were much in demand.

contractual arrangements with visiting troupes. He insinuated them into his country one by one, disguised as unlikely-looking scholars, or mounted soldiers in search of employment. The party of Jesuits whom he once persuaded to play comedy for him, however, was genuine.

For the sake of economy, he himself provided the costumes, and these remained his own property so that, tall, short, fat or thin, Shakespeare's princes, kings, maidens and gentlemen who trod his boards inevitably resembled their counterparts by, say, Corneille to a degree that would have astonished the creators of these characters.

Plays took the strain off entertaining visiting nobles, who naturally called at the castle when passing through the Palatinate. Among them were the inseparable Brunswick-Lüneburg brothers, George William and Ernst August. The two young men first visited Heidelberg in the spring of 1653 on their return journey from Venice, where the famous Carnival, the largest and most festive in Europe, extended from Christmas to Lent. The Empire's princes flocked to its spendours, and none attended it more regularly than these two pleasure-loving dukes.

Elizabeth, noting their arrival in Heidelberg, denied the rumour that this year the Brunswick princes had been in Venice in search of brides. For one thing, she said, people went to Venice for whores, not wives, and for another, the young men had spent so much good money abroad that they could not be thinking of marriage.

Sophie found Ernst August better looking than when she had first met him about five years earlier at The Hague. Then, as now, she was taken with him, and admired his high Guelph complexion and his prominent sky-blue eyes—'he was considered so handsome that everyone liked him'. Besides, he danced with elegance and spirit, and when he played guitar duets with her he displayed the most beautiful hands in the world.

After his visit Ernst August sent her more music, arranged for the guitar by Corbetti from Hanover. Enclosed was a letter so larded with compliments and hand-kisses for the Elector that courtesy forced her to reply in order not to appear proud, which would have been a '*gros crime*'. But as soon as she decently could she dropped the correspondence. Ernst August, youngest of the four Hanover brothers—the *cadet des cadets*—was without prospects and unthinkable husband-material. There was no sense, Sophie felt, in prejudicing a more *convenable* match by giving rise to unnecessary gossip.

With astonishing self-possession for someone on the wrong side of twenty, she calmly awaited more eligible suitors. Dorothea Guzman's suggestion of her compatriot the Duca d'Aveira was hardly worth thinking about. Sophie's old friend painted the Duke, his riches, and indeed Portugal in glowing colours, but 'although I had lost much of my beauty in an attack of the smallpox, I could not stoop to marry a subject after thinking of marrying a King'.

The Queen of Bohemia no longer mentioned Sophie's English marriage. For the next few years her letters to the Palatinate were to be filled with more pressing matters. She was in worse straits than ever. Her kitchens were without turf, bread or ale; she was obliged to swelter in the city while 'Princess Royal', newly widowed and longing for company, spent the summer in the country with her baby son William III. The Winter Queen told Charles Louis that the discontent and grief of being left behind in The Hague were hers, but he 'would have the dishonour of it that I don't have the means'. Her jewels were with the pawnbrokers, even the diamond chain that had once belonged to Queen Elizabeth I. There was no money with which to retrieve them. Would he please expedite matters? What she needed was cash. She was of course grateful to receive boatloads of grain and wine, but the grain got mouldy in transit, and the wretched boatmen, a crew of rogues, tapped the barrels *en route* and the wine always reached her watered down. She required money for her daily needs and for the upkeep of her summer-house in Rhenen, which Charles Louis claimed as his property. 'You would be surprised if I told you for whom your father built it,' wrote the Queen, adding that it was now in sad disrepair. 'Princess Royal had been like to cry to see the place so spoiled': all the palisades broken, and the hangings rotted. The caretaker had turned out to be the veriest knave, and had stolen the gold trimmings of the Queen's own bed.

As for coming into Germany—a subject that was periodically discussed —she would be willing enough to make the move if only she knew how to satisfy her creditors, or what houses she would have to dwell in.

The Spanish had at last departed from Frankenthal with great reluctance, which the garrison commander Frangipani illustrated by kissing the ground he had bled white, 'so that the dust clung to his lips'. Clearly, much work would have to be done there before her dower-house was fit to receive the Queen. At times, she thought that she would meanwhile live at the castle. Detailed plans for the allocation of rooms in the Otto Heinrich wing went off to The Hague, with assurances that an Italian architect had greatly added to the convenience of the building. The Queen examined them carefully and asked for additional cabinets for this or that deserving person, notably her chaplain, who preached extremely well but was too old to go abroad at night in case his services were required. In the end, to her children's relief, she decided that two households under one roof would not answer—'humours being so diverse'.

She also declined an invitation to take a house in Heidelberg itself, and demanded money instead. She hoped that the compensation for Frankenthal, when it arrived, would be sent straight to The Hague. In the meantime, a traveller from Holland to Heidelberg, nervous of footpads, had left a few thousand Reichsthalers with her on the understanding that the Elector would reimburse him. Heidelberg might also expect a visitation from her butcher's wife, who was planning to collect the Queen's outstanding debts direct, but a firm promise would do. The Queen would much prefer to receive the money into her own hands.

Sophie wrote that what money there was would reach her shortly, although it was less than she had asked for. But money was 'a rare commodity in a country as ruined as the Palatinate'. The Elector of Brandenburg was demanding the repayment of ancient debts, and his wife was writing 'nothing but injuries on the subject'. Everyone was complaining that Charles Louis was not doing enough, but he had to pay out so much to maintain himself in his rights and to acquire those due to him that he could not do more.

In the autumn of 1653 Charles Louis hoped to be able to settle at least some of his dues at the Electors' Diet in Prague, where a meeting had been arranged between him and Emperor Ferdinand III. Charlotte was outraged when Charles Louis left her and his sisters at home, and wept furious tears as he rode away. Sophie sadly missed him, and supplied him with reports from the domestic front. Afraid of boring her most illustrious and Serenissimus brother with her scrawl, she suggested he might read it 'during his playtime'—*Spielstunde*. He might then find it tolerable to learn that everyone lived for his letters, and all were eagerly looking forward to going with him, as promised, to the Diet of Ratisbon in the spring.

The entire household was punctilious in carrying out his orders, and for fear of contravening them 'good nights' were said at nine o'clock. During the day Charlotte, who had quite got over her fury, busied herself with *petites affaires*, like cutting out linen for herself and the household, and making a wig with evident, if surprising, enjoyment. Elizabeth, who had hurt her leg, was making perfume-sachets. Sophie was practising her guitar. A new arrival at Court, Louise von Degenfeld, so tall that she wore no *chopines*, seemed neither pretty nor *de bonne mine*. But her eyes were nice, and if she looked rather naïve, Sophie thought it suited her as she was only sixteen. No one believed that the newcomer knew enough Italian to instruct them all, as was hoped, but there had been no time to examine her yet. Few visitors descended on them, and only one or two calls on suitable noblewomen had been paid in the town. A consultation with the local soothsayer had proved unprofitable. The crystal ball reflected nothing but its owner's death, and sadness had prevented the wretched woman from concentrating on anyone else's future.

Charles Louis was apparently not too occupied with affairs of state for violent reactions to innocuous communications from home.

'Charlotte would not have gone a-gossiping with foolish women if she had known the Elector didn't like it,' wrote Elizabeth in a huff. (Her leg, said Sophie, had been so inefficiently treated by the surgeon-barber that the evil humours were now rising to her head.) As for the visit to the prophetess, Elizabeth had been under the impression that it had been expressly ordered by Charles Louis as a diversion for his wife. Such entertainments as there were had in any case taken place only on Sunday afternoons. For the rest of the time, Charlotte had diligently 'acted the *hussif*'. Yes, she had toyed with the idea of trying out the Elector's bay gelding and had him brought into the paddock, but she had not liked him and there had been no riding after all. No, he need not worry about male visitors. Charlotte spoke but rarely to any man. As for her general conversation and 'mending her discourse', he knew very well that there was nothing anyone could do, least of all Elizabeth, whose leg anyway obliged her to keep to her chamber for most of the time.

Charles Louis' meeting with the Emperor was considered a great success by most members of his family. He was received with gratifying pomp at the White Mountain, where Frederick V had once lost his kingdom *in absentia*; and no one who observed the warmth of the parting hand-clasp between Emperor and Elector doubted that Charles Louis had gained more than his father ever lost. The Queen of Bohemia said that it remained to be seen whether the realities would equal the ceremonies. They did not, but for the time being honour was satisfied.

The Elector returned home bearing a new title, that of Imperial Arch-Treasurer. Edward reported that Mazarin had been glad to hear that the Empire now possessed such an officer, and had only wondered about the treasure. But for Charles Louis a great wrong was amended, for the hereditary Palatine arch-office had gone to Bavaria at the same time as the premier Electorship.

In a spirit of optimism, the Palatine Court prepared for the journey to the Diet of Ratisbon, for which the Diet of Prague had been a preliminary event. Charles Louis was looking forward to his official investiture. He took his Elector's bonnet of purple velvet, surmounted by a golden arch, and the rest of the regalia out of storage, where they had lain for over thirty years, and hoped that the ceremony would finally mark the end of his struggles.

No expense had been spared for the Electoral train that triumphantly entered Ratisbon. The carriages were, if not brand new, at least refurbished, and did not threaten to disintegrate like those of which the Palatine ambassadors were unceasingly complaining. The horses were burnished to a high gloss and *en embonpoint*, a far cry from the envoys' old and tired hacks that were in constant danger of collapsing never to rise again. Barrels of *Bacharacher*, the *Verehrer-wein* with which the Elector was usually so mean, followed the procession, which was flanked by Charles Louis' mounted guard and his foot-soldiers, all in resplendent new coats, and led by drummers drumming and buglers blowing fanfares.

The Elector was duly installed, and although as eighth member of the College he sat at the very end of the table and not, like his ancestors, on the Emperor's right, he was highly satisfied with his usage.

The Empress made a point of being particularly gracious to the Palatine ladies. She offered an armchair to Charlotte—an unheard-of honour—and Elizabeth and Sophie had armless chairs instead of the tabourets to which they were entitled. It was most gratifying.

There was no end to the ballets, comedies, concerts and parties. The

Imperial couple gave a *Wirtschaft*, a much favoured kind of entertainment where the hosts played the part of innkeepers and the guests could move freely, uninhibited by the protocol that stifled more formal social occasions. Instead of the stately pacings of the saraband and the pavane, everyone stamped and jumped about in rural dances. 'We danced our feet off,' wrote Elizabeth, whose leg had fortunately mended. 'I never saw such leaping about.'

Rumours that Sophie's charms caught the eye of the Emperor's eldest son, the Archduke Charles, unrecorded by their owner though referred to by her niece years later, date from this social whirl where everyone had an enjoyable time except for Charlotte.

She had confidently counted on being the belle of every ball. She had sent to Paris for masses of finery and a French hairdresser, and now none of her dresses would do up at the waist. A third pregnancy was ruining her figure. The waste of it all made her so furious that she was in a continuous tantrum.

It was more than Charles Louis could bear. He avoided her apartments and was constantly seen in those of Sophie. She was now taking singing lessons from the Emperor's star soprano, Domenico del Pane, and soothed her brother by singing to him in a small but pleasant voice.

'Incredible as it may sound,' says Sophie, 'Charlotte thought that my brother had become my *galant*.' She adds that she was well known to honour him like a father and that he was old enough to be just that. Since he was only thirteen years older than she, and in writing to him she often insisted that the difference between their ages was minimal, this was a poor argument. But given her temperament and the fact that such things, then, were not discussed in terms of Freudian insight but as matters of actual fact, it was a monstrous allegation. Elizabeth, who should have known better, used Charlotte's jealousy of Sophie to create a bond between herself and her sister-in-law, and encouraged the Electress in her unfortunate belief.

The atmosphere was strained when the three ladies accompanied the Elector to the *Kaiserwahl* in Augsburg, where the Archduke Charles of Habsburg was nominated as his father's successor and was crowned King of the Romans during the Emperor's lifetime. However, he never became Emperor himself as he died a few months after his election.

The Palatine ladies were prevented from travelling to Charles' corona-

Elizabeth, Princess Palatine, by Gerrit van Honthorst.

Louise Hollandine, Princess Palatine, by Gerrit van Honthorst.

tion in Frankfurt, because Charlotte unexpectedly went into labour. Elizabeth wondered whether she had simply miscalculated with typical inefficiency, or whether the baby, who died after only a few hours, had arrived prematurely because there had been too much dancing and riding at Ratisbon. Or had the baby succumbed because Charlotte had watched a gory Good Friday procession of twitching flagellants streaming with blood? Whatever the reason, Charlotte was very ill and could not be moved for weeks.

The Court returned to Heidelberg in the summer of 1654. The great event of that season was the arrival of Rupert.

His career as Charles II's Lord High Admiral had been no less spectacular than it had been as Charles I's Diabolical Cavalier. He returned from the West Indies like a conquistador of old, and entered Heidelberg with a train that included parrots, monkeys, three quarrelsome negroes and a docile, tiny, black child.

Maurice, his Vice-Admiral, was, alas, not with him. Missing, believed 'swallowed up by the sea' in a hurricane off Anguilla, he was variously reported as having been offered for sale at a slave-market in Algiers and planting sugar in Barbados. Enquiries were still being conducted, but discreetly in order not to raise the ransom-demand in case he had been captured by pirates or buccaneers. Rupert was not hopeful, and indeed Maurice was never found again.

The loss of his alter ego, and the strange hardships he had endured, had apparently much 'decayed Rupert's fire'. Sophie's long-lost brother had changed during the last twelve years.

He had formerly been the greatest hero and the greatest *beau*—the way he had tied his lace handkerchief around his neck is said to have set the fashion for the jabot that followed the Van Dyck collar. Now he was ungracious, hard, and stern even when he most wished to please.

Rupert had arrived to claim what he considered his patrimony—the county of Simmern. But Charles Louis had no intention of further fracturing his diminished domain. He offered his brother alternative accommodation, but Rupert refused first Laubach—'too watery to be healthy'—and then Umstadt as being unsuitable for a peaceful life because it was subject to constant border disputes with Hesse. Months of wrangling caused him to accept an annuity in compensation, but he felt ill done by, and showed it.

C

His visit was dismal in every respect. Even sport, which usually dis-
persed his worries, was disappointing. To return from a day out with a bag
of twenty larks was ridiculous for a shot of his calibre, although he fared
better than Charles Louis, who fired so wildly that he singed his own wig.
Rupert bitterly complained that the signal '*tirez*' invariably came too early,
and found the Palatine hunt servants so hopeless that he offered to replace
them with a pack of English hounds to be kennelled at his own expense.

The brothers did not agree on this or any other point, and their relationship, never warm, grew barely cordial. Sophie did what she could to
smooth things over, but achieved little. The Queen had warned Rupert
that anything he said to Sophie was bound to be repeated to the Elector,
and also warned him to beware of Elizabeth, whom she believed to be too
great a hypocrite to be trustworthy.

Charlotte, however, was a willing recipient of Rupert's complaints,
particularly as Charles Louis was making her own life a perfect misery.
Recovered in health, though not in spirits, at the time of Rupert's colourful entry, she was greatly cheered by his arrival. Regardless of what his
friends described as 'diminished sparkishness and sprightliness' in him, she
set out to charm him. Led by vanity to misinterpret his fellow-feeling for
her—were they not both victims of Charles Louis' tyranny?—for warmer
sentiments, she encouraged him for all she was worth. She was therefore
surprised to find, on opening a book, a note in Rupert's hand complaining
of coldness on the part of the object of his affections. She tried to reassure
him with the broadest hints and displayed all the coquetry that Charles
Louis detested. Strangely, Rupert failed to respond, and it finally dawned
on Charlotte that the letter had not been addressed to her at all. She had a
rival, whom a little sleuthing soon revealed to be Louise von Degenfeld.

Louise was no longer gawky or naïve, but a good-looking young woman
with pretty manners. Far from flirting with Rupert, she seemed to be
avoiding him. Just to make sure that there could be no nocturnal assignations, Charlotte said she was afraid of sleeping alone, and had the girl's bed
moved into her own chamber, which Charles Louis had hardly entered
since Ratisbon.

Her attempts to nip Rupert's affair in the bud blinded the Electress to
what she otherwise might have noticed: Charles Louis had fallen in love
with Louise, deeply and forever.

He too posted *billets doux* to his beloved in books. It was as well that

Louise was known to be a great reader, for the traffic in books was truly prodigious. The communications tucked between their pages were addressed, in Italian, to the *dolcissima Rosalinda*, and signed by *Montecelso*, who soon stopped making jokes about being *il vecchio* and begged her to commit her *persona*, *volontà* and *contentezza* into his care.

Louise's linguistic skills, perfectly adequate despite Sophie's earlier doubts, failed her at this point. She was a well brought up girl from a good family, and wrote to Charles Louis in her native language that this latest suggestion was incompatible with her honour. What else, she asked, would she have to fall back on when he tired of her?

Her virtuous scruples did her nothing but credit in the Elector's eyes. In spite of his passionate nature, he was by temperament a husband rather than a lover, and desired a permanent attachment rather than a passing fling.

What he needed was a divorce. All his accusations against Charlotte's conduct, which she loudly refuted, giving him further welcome evidence of her foul temper, were designed to build a case. A little book on 'La coquetterie', printed in France, went off to her brother in Hesse; Charles Louis innocently hoped it would amuse and enlighten, as he himself might have failed to explain the exact meaning of the term at their last meeting. The Landgrave must have profoundly wished to have been left in ignorance, because Charles Louis made coquetry the basis of a confession which he prepared for Charlotte's signature. He would gladly have substituted actual misconduct, he told Louise, and only regretted that 'no man had been discovered between her legs'. Charlotte not unnaturally refused to sign—and Charles Louis could point to yet another instance of wifely disobedience.

Meanwhile, his attentions to Louise grew more and more pressing. Charlotte awoke one night to find the tall figure of a man hovering near Louise's recumbent form—not, as she had feared, Rupert's, but that of her own husband. According to Sophie, she found him in bed with Louise; according to Louise, he was standing by the bed; but whether he had been in or by, horizontal or vertical, the Electress leapt up to pull out hanks of Louise's hair and almost bit off her little finger. 'She would have killed me,' wrote Louise to her brother the Freiherr von Degenfeld, 'had not the Elector protected me and called in the guards to restrain her.'

On the following day Charles Louis installed Louise in a cabinet directly above his own, and instructed his workmen to cut a hole in the ceiling so that he could visit her by means of a ladder brought in for the purpose. The Electress discovered this arrangement, and it was not long before she herself ascended, a knife in her hand and murder in her heart. Luckily, her servants pulled her down before she had done any damage.

A letter, allegedly from Charlotte to the Emperor, says that she was virtually kept prisoner in her apartments, prevented from setting foot out of doors and from sending or receiving letters. Nevertheless, she managed to make her way to Louise's old room. There, by her own admission and everyone else's reports, she broke open Louise's jewel-case. She found not only unfuriatingly *grands cadeaux* and the Italian love-letters which she thought to be in Latin, but, worse still, a draft document suggesting that Charles Louis intended 'to keep house with the whore who was to pass for the wife', while the lawful wife was to be sent away.

Charlotte's screams shook the castle to the rafters. Sophie and Elizabeth arrived on the scene as the Elector was once again shielding his beloved from his wife's blows.

Between bouts of kicking and scratching, Charlotte marched up and down the room clutching Louise's presents. 'Princesses,' she cried on becoming aware of their presence, 'this is the whore's reward. Should it not be mine?' Sophie thought this an odd way of putting it. Her giggles increased the Electress's hysteria; then Charles Louis demanded the return of Louise's property and Charlotte flung the jewels across the room, and while everyone scrabbled on the floor for rings, at least a dozen diamond poinçons and quantities of loose pearls, she swept out to complain to her brother the Landgrave in a letter which she managed to smuggle out to him.

Louise, too, wrote off to her brother. Not that there was time to wait for his advice 'on how to extricate myself from the labyrinth in which I find myself'. Should she return home? But if she left the Court the world would say it was because she was pregnant, which she was not, 'nothing dishonourable' having occurred. Should she stay where she was? But then, she said, she would have to yield to the Elector's desires, 'for his patience is wearing thin'. On the whole, this seemed the wisest course. 'He is my only refuge, and without him I should be entirely lost and all alone.' In a post-script, Louise dealt with the great obstacle of her 'honourable copulation': the Princess Sophie, whose marriage prospects might be adversely affected by her brother's divorce and the unpleasantness expected from Hesse in consequence.

Sophie had longed to get away ever since Charlotte had broadcast her *médisances* at Ratisbon about Charles Louis and herself. They had come to the ears even of the Winter Queen; she had dismissed them, but Sophie felt uncomfortable in a place 'where the world had no way of judging my conduct'. Besides, Charlotte had made no bones about wishing to rid herself of her imagined rival, and Charles Louis, though less outspoken, was anxious to settle his sister so that he could rearrange his own life.

Thus a proposal from his cousin Adolph of Zweibrücken, whose brother Charles X had succeeded Queen Christine of Sweden on her abdication, seemed to solve a great many problems at once. Sophie decided to overlook the Prince's enormous chin, except for which he was presentable enough. Charlotte took care not to tell her that Prince Adolph, a widower, was a famous wife-beater. Charles Louis, passionately devoted to the new King of Sweden, said he could not bear to disappoint any member of his friend's family and accepted on Sophie's behalf. The match was perhaps less grand than might have been hoped, but the Queen wrote from The Hague that she could hardly be against it 'seeing the condition we are all in'. Charles Louis sent a long list of stipulations regarding Sophie's income and dower to Sweden. Adolph, carrying her portrait, set off for Venice, which attracted him as magnetically as the Brunswick-Lüneburg brothers, George William and Ernst August, although he could afford it less.

His likeness went up in the *Gläsersaal*, where Sophie had ample opportunity of forming 'an aversion to the original that only a sense of duty would have enabled me to overcome', while the negotiations of her marriage contract proceeded at snail's pace.

Heidelberg had reason to rejoice that Sweden was slow in agreeing to support Sophie in the style to which she had not so far been accustomed, for she was still unbetrothed when George William of Brunswick-Lüneburg pointedly enquired how far, if at all, the matter had progressed. Charles Louis, who had just informed his mother that 'our copulation is in the hands of the King of Sweden', replied that it was up to George William 'to make or break it', and awaited developments.

There could be no doubt that George William would be a better catch than Prince Adolph. His forefathers—unlike most German princes, except for Electors—had for generations avoided dividing their dominions into as many parts as they had sons. His own father, the Winter Queen's 'tun of beer', had followed in the family tradition.* Only two of his four sons had succeeded him as reigning Dukes: Christian Louis, the eldest, and George William. Christian Louis, excercising the senior's right of choice between the domains of Celle-Lüneburg and Calenberg-Göttingen, had picked the former, which he governed from Celle. The lands of Calenberg, which were greatly superior to Prince Adolph's tiny Zweibrücken, went to George William. Neither the third brother, John Frederick, who had appalled first his family and then the Estates by turning Catholic,† nor the fourth, Ernst August, had inherited land. Both might, however, succeed to one or other Duchy, as might their eventual male heirs, if either of the elder Dukes died without founding a dynasty of his own. In this event, the senior survivor would be entitled to choose once again between Lüneburg and Calenberg; and since neither Duchy wished for a Catholic system of government, both were anxious for their sovereign Dukes to provide them with heirs for the succession.

Christian Louis, the only one of the brothers who was married, had so far remained childless, and there was nothing to be done but hope that the prediction which said that he would be the father of sons would sooner or later become true. George William, who reigned from Hanover—too fond of amusement to have much time to spare for ruling, too gallant to take kindly to the thought of marriage—would have to be persuaded to take a wife, particularly since John Frederick had lately announced his intention of marrying. Not that the Catholic Duke had anyone specific in mind; he had merely enquired what provision the Estates planned to make for him once he had found a suitable bride.

Horrified at the prospect of a long line of Catholic Dukes, the Estates had been galvanised into action. An urgent, if respectful, petition asking

---

* Duke George, the sixth of seven brothers, had become the only 'marrying duke' among them, after they had drawn lots to determine who should carry on the line. All the others had signed covenants to remain bachelors.

† Snatched more than once from the brink of Catholicism, John Frederick had after all changed his faith in 1649, when during a Mass at Assisi the Cross had turned black and the Host petrified, owing, it was said, to his heretical presence. This miracle led to the canonisation of the officiating monk—he became St Joseph of Coperta—and was used by Rome for propaganda purposes, so that the secrecy with which the family had tried to shroud the Duke's conversion became impossible to maintain a few years after the event.

George William to marry had gone off at once, and since it was well known how highly this extravagant Duke valued his freedom, an offer for a handsome increase in revenues had accompanied the request. Not nearly enough, said George William, if his subjects seriously expected him to take such a distasteful step. Confident that they wanted a duchess at any price, he demanded more and meanwhile wrote to Charles Louis to ask after Sophie.

Soon after receiving the Elector's message he left Hanover in the company of Ernst August for his customary Venetian holiday, and on the way called at the Elector's castle. Sophie thought him more agreeable than Prince Adolph, and extremely polite. 'He told me a thousand obliging things, and frankly, my reply was not too unfavourable. At last he spoke the great word, and unlike a heroine in a romance, I said yes straight away.' The Elector, she thought, loved her well enough to approve her choice, especially as 'this marriage would be much more *considérable* than the other'.

No time was wasted in drawing up the marriage contract, which was formally signed by Sophie, George William and Charles Louis. Everyone agreed to keep the betrothal secret in order to give George William greater bargaining power with his Estates, and the Dukes moved on to Venice, promising to write and to return after Easter.

George William's portrait was hung in the *Gläsersaal*, and contrasted pleasantly with that of the shoehorn-chinned Prince Adolph. He, meanwhile, showed Sophie's portrait as that of his fiancée to the assembled nobility in Venice. Both George William and Ernst August were invited to admire it, but their lips, of course, were sealed.

Secrecy also suited Charles Louis, as it enabled him to extricate his sister more gracefully from her engagement to Adolph. He wrote to Charles X of Sweden that rumours had reached him of His Majesty's doubts regarding the couple's future happiness; he was in honour bound to bow to the King's superior judgement, adding that although his sister might not have the honour of marrying his brother, she would be his devoted servant as long as she breathed.

He was equally tactful with M. Lasalle, Charles X's envoy, who had arrived to settle Sophie's Swedish marriage. He left, his mission unaccomplished, but so laden with honours and presents that it was hoped his love for the Elector would prevent him from being too explicit at home.

Sophie feared that he had guessed the secret: on his stately exit through the *Gläsersaal* he had paused before George William's portrait and performed an exaggerated bow, declaring himself the Duke's most humble and obedient servant.

M. Lasalle's terror of his monarch and his love for the Elector appear to have prevented him from reporting at all clearly, for in the spring Prince Adolph arrived with all his relations, insisting on celebrating his nuptials. He refused to listen to reason, wept, made scenes and cried affront, and was only with difficulty persuaded to go away. His brother the King was fortunately too occupied with Poland to pay much attention. Lasalle was dismissed, but to Charles Louis' relief the affair fizzled out.

If the Hanoverian contract was still a great secret, the Hanoverian project was of course nothing of the sort. Shortly after the Queen of Bohemia had offered to ask the King of England's permission for the Swedish match, which courtesy she rightly assumed to have been neglected, she wrote to say that she had heard of the Duke of Hanover's offer for Sophie, 'though I of course deny everything'.

It was as well, because, on reflection, George William had changed his mind. Marriage, after all, was not for him, and he was busy with the construction of a new plan to lay before the Estates. Against a further increase in his allowance to enable him to raise his youngest brother's apanage, Ernst August would take over George William's bride, and the future progeny from the union would succeed to George William's possessions. This, he hoped, would satisfy all concerned. The Estates would be able to look forward to a Protestant dynasty. The Elector Palatine would still gain a brother-in-law, and not be able to make trouble regarding any breach of contract. He himself would give an undertaking never to marry and to retain his liberty until the day he died, and there was no reason to think that Sophie would object to such a change of detail as he was now suggesting. Ernst August, the only person not to have been delighted with the earlier arrangements—not because he wanted Sophie, but because he hated the thought of sharing his brother with anyone—had agreed at once, and left Venice for discussions with the Estates and his brother John Frederick, without whose consent the matter could not be taken further.

Easter came and went, and while Sophie waited in vain for a sign of life from George William, that Duke was himself anxiously awaiting letters from his brother, who should long since have arrived in Hanover.

In fact, Ernst August had fallen ill in Vienna, and had been unable to proceed. George William, receiving this news in Venice, saw only the word 'death', and tore up the letter without reading on that Ernst August had been snatched from its jaws and was slowly recovering. Almost sense-less with grief for his brother and concern for his own future, he calmed himself only when the fragmented letter had been stuck together again.

Ernst August's illness caused the first long delay in Sophie's matrimonial affairs; John Frederick's disinclination for his brother's scheme caused the second. He did not see why, if George William was dispensing largesse, Ernst August instead of himself should benefit. He was aware that his youngest brother's prospects were already better than his own: by the Treaty of Westphalia, youngest princes of Brunswick-Lüneburg would succeed to the bishopric of Osnabrück turn and turn about with Catholic churchmen. As soon as the present incumbent died, Ernst August would become a secular bishop with a handsome palace of his own. John Frederick had no such pleasant expectations. And now he was being asked, as it were, to give up his place in the queue for the succession. He said that he was perfectly willing to take on George William's riches along with his fiancée—a suggestion that could not seriously be put to the Elector Palatine because of John Frederick's religion—and it was months before he agreed to be bought off. All these long delays, unsatisfactorily explained, were a great trial to Sophie, but the Memoirs say, 'I was too proud to be affected'. However, in a spirit of revenge she pretended seriously to con-sider a proposal of marriage from the Duke of Parma, delivered by a self-appointed messenger who could hardly believe his luck. For reasons of religion alone it would have been an unthinkable match, but the offer did wonders for her *amour propre*. When the messenger realised that he had failed after all, and was found floating in the Neckar shortly afterwards, she says with grim satisfaction, 'Perhaps he drowned himself from disappointment.'

Meanwhile, matters had come to a final break between Charles Louis and Rupert, who still insisted that 'Simmern was ever an elder brother's portion'. Charles Louis wished to discuss the matter no further, and one day, when Rupert returned from a trip, he found the great castle-gates closed against him. On being challenged, the sentry produced the Elector's handwritten orders debarring him, and Rupert tore off his hat and swore to God never to set foot in the Palatinate again.

He went to Mainz in search of support, and among the letters he wrote to make the Elector's shabby behaviour known was one to the Landgrave of Hesse Cassel, to whom he mentioned that Charles Louis was hatching some very curious plans, boding no good for Charlotte or himself.

The Electress was now living in a state of persecution. Her servants, whom she beat black and blue when they did not do her bidding, were dismissed out of hand by the Elector when he found them spying on her behalf. All of them were spied on, and most of them were employed to spy on her. Her antechamber was, she said, filled with Swiss guards whose rattling armour prevented her from sleeping. Every move she made was watched. She was not allowed down to meals even when her own brother was among the guests. All who came into contact with her— Elizabeth frequently; Sophie as rarely as possible; her children, whom she cursed to damnation when they refused to let her caress them—were cross-examined by Charles Louis when they came away. He made sure of never setting eyes on his wife. By his orders her walks and drives were carefully routed so that there were no chance encounters. If one happened to occur, Charles Louis would stare straight through her as if she did not exist.

All Europe pitied Charlotte and blamed Charles Louis for his high-handed behaviour. It was common knowledge that he desired to rid him-self of his lawful wife and legalise his union with Louise von Degenfeld, but not known that his strongbox already contained the parchment proclaim-ing that he had ended his marriage, according to the powers vested in him. His wife, the document states, had for years been shrewish, foul-mouthed, stiff-necked and undutiful, in spite of frequent promises to improve. He was now giving up hope. Because formal divorce proceedings might endanger the peace of the Empire, he had searched the Bible, and found enough precedents honourably to '*adjunctieren and beilegen*'—'adjunct and lie with', a phrase that Louise detested for its explicitness—the Freyin Louise von Degenfeld.

This document was not to be published until Sophie was safely married, and meanwhile Charles Louis' explanations satisfied no one. Edward thought that he must have taken leave of his senses. Surely one wife was enough to exasperate any man? He was in duty bound to point out that the Melancthon/Luther correspondence on the subject of such irregularities, which the Elector considered an absolute godsend, had clearly required that old bigamist Philip of Hesse to sleep with both his wives in turn—had Charles Louis read it carefully enough? What a pity he should be so much less continent than his *trèshumble frère*.

Louise, too, had needed jollying out of her scruples. Again Charles Louis resorted to biblical argument. He invited his *dolcissima signora* to consider Ahasuerus. 'He had convinced Esther that, in spite of legal obstacles, he had long been divorced from Vashti. *Inde hinc* Esther was living with him. Query, would not Esther feel free to practise her Christian religion and take Holy Communion even before the stumbling block was removed?' He answered in the affirmative, and Louise felt less sinful for most of the time in spite of his evident confusion of the Old and the New Testaments.

Charles Louis firmly regarded himself as a happily remarried man. Louise was moved out of harm's way to Frankenthal. The house, now ready for occupation, was still vacant, as the Queen's debts had prevented her from leaving Holland. To Charles Louis' relief, the sum that his mother required for linen alone ('I have not a smock but is broken and my servants are naked') seemed generous to Louise; it covered her pin-money and the board and livery for her household of ten indoor servants. Her coach and six horses, as well as her outdoor servants, were paid for out of a different budget. So were rather more than the customary number of guards, necessary because threats were beginning to issue from Hesse, but a worry to Charles Louis in case their frequent cries of '*Qui va*' kept his beloved signora awake at night.

Louise brought out all that was kind and loving in Charles Louis' nature. She did not transform him: he remained uxorious, careful about money and as suspicious as ever, but he was able to joke about it now. 'Are not we forty-years-olds peculiar folk?' he asked after sending her an account of a fellow prince's jealous behaviour. 'Prince, philosopher and man', who, he complained, were usually at odds within his breast, made their peace when he was with Louise, who satisfied all his needs both physical and spiritual.

He sent her loving gifts whenever he could not come in person. 'Happy Easter-eggs' says a letter accompanying the first spray of orange-blossom from the Heidelberg greenhouse (one of the first to be built). It was followed by the first oranges, the first lemons, a striking clock, ribbons from Paris, and a dozen or so pairs of gloves 'which unfortunately have

been in evil company', having passed through the '*Padrona's*'—
Charlotte's—hands.

The statues in Louise's newly laid out garden became 'our beautiful
white children', and Charles Louis was overjoyed when Louise became
pregnant. He was full of solicitous enquiries. Were her stays still comfortable? Would she be careful not to eat too much of the first melon he
was sending her, especially at night? Would she please substitute the
sombre hangings of her chamber with gayer ones—green ones would be
best—and would she rest her eyes on as much green as possible?

The Queen of Bohemia was deeply shocked by the rumours about the
Elector's home-life. She had first heard them from Hesse and paid no
attention, 'knowing how they love to embroider the truth'. To her, he
was 'openly avouching sin. It was no use quoting the Bible at her, she had
read the scriptures too well.' Nor was it any good citing John of Gaunt,
who, contrary to the Elector's view, had never married at all, let alone
kept two women at the same time.

She chose to blame her eldest daughter: without Elizabeth's interference
everything might have blown over, although the Princess would, of
course, deny this, 'taking vanity in her sufferings as usual'. She had best be
sent away now, but not to Holland. 'I will not have her with me for many
reasons.' While Elizabeth made her arrangements, Charles Louis might
try ignoring her completely—'nothing would annoy her more'. Had he
known her humour sooner and got rid of her earlier, it would have been
better for Sophie, for him and for Charlotte. But why must he persist in
making mountains of the molehills that were Charlotte's little faults?
Maybe Charlotte was flirtatious, but hardly more so than her sister Emélie,
and the Prince de Tarent seemed to be bearing up. 'And Charlotte would
have had to be a patient Grizelda indeed (which I hear she is not) to have
held her peace over Louise.' On the whole, the Queen of Bohemia pitied
her daughter-in-law—'all persons in misfortune should pity one another'.
But if he was serious about sending Charlotte away, what about Sophie?
'She cannot in honour stay with you. To be with your wife would be best,
except that the business about Arsace and Berenice were ended would be
best of all.'

Characters from the romances of which the Queen had been so fond
peopled her correspondence when she discussed family matters. Berenice
was Sophie, but Arsace was still George William. As the Queen had said,

The Hague gossips were convinced that Hanover was sending for Sophie, but there was now talk about the very youngest Duke. She thought they had got it wrong. 'But I carry my body very swimmingly,' she assured her children, 'and take notice of nothing'. She did, however, think it a good idea for Charles Louis to cancel his plans for attending a new *Kaiserwahl*, occasioned by the death of Ferdinand III, and to stay at home to treat about Sophie.

This *Kaiserwahl* was more strongly contended than the last one. Mazarin, intent on reducing the Habsburgs' power, even put Louis XIV forward as a candidate, while Maximilian of Bavaria, who had designs on the Imperial Crown, was also supported by France. In addition, Mazarin hinted that he might be prepared to back the Elector Palatine, and Charles Louis ordered a very expensive Imperial crown from a Paris jeweller. On arriving in Frankfurt he received a letter from Sophie, who wrote of 'a man arisen from the dead at Heidelberg who prophesied that the next Emperor would bear the name of Charles Louis'. Despite this the Imperial diadem, not yet paid for, turned out to be an unnecessary luxury. The next Emperor, elected in July 1658, bore the name of Leopold I, and was a Habsburg after all.

Although long discussions in Frankfurt took up a great deal of Charles Louis' time, he did not neglect his family. Louise received regular letters with gossip about the attending dignitaries. The Elector of Saxony's living hot-water bottle caused amusement; his wife had thoughtfully sent along a buxom peasant girl whose only function was to lie on top of him when the colic, from which he suffered, prostrated him. Charles Louis took the opportunity of assuring Louise of his undying fidelity. He also despatched bibelots and jewels from the fair, and two parrots—'my Indian ambassadors—one green and silent, the other blue and talkative'. She might like to pass on the green one, likely to amuse her less, to Liselotte. But no, as it grew more familiar, it developed the habit of singing psalms for its supper; perhaps she had better keep them both: Liselotte would never know. Also, Charles Louis had managed to obtain some powdered rhinoceros horn which he had heard highly spoken of. It would arrive in the same shipment as the parrots, but as he was not quite clear about its purpose, perhaps she would consult the doctor who was attending her during her pregnancy.

Of Rupert, also in Frankfurt for meetings with the Emperor, there was nothing to report other than that his negroes had stabbed each other to death, but there was good news about Charles Louis' upholding the family honour: he had flung an inkwell at the Bavarian Ambassador for making derogatory remarks about the Winter King. This led to a flurry of activity. Charles Louis had to ply so many gentlemen with Bacharacher 'to remove the inkstains with wine' that he had no time to visit the theatre, and missed Master George and his English troupe; but he said it was a small loss, for the comedy enacted daily by his colleagues was funnier.

Sophie, too, received news from the Elector. George William's envoy, Hammerstein, had arrived in Frankfurt with Ernst August's formal proposal of marriage, and the document in which George William renounced all dynastic privileges and solemnly promised to live *in coelibatu* for the rest of his life.

Charles Louis voiced his doubts about the constancy of George William's resolution in view of recent evidence to the contrary. Hammerstein met this point by assuring him that his master's excesses with a Greek whore had rendered him not only unfit for marriage but also incapable of fathering children. Nor was there anything to fear from John Frederick for all his declared intention of marrying: he was clearly far too fat to accomplish the production of heirs.

Understandably anxious to get on with his own life, the Elector told Sophie that Ernst August appeared to be even *plus considérable*, more sensible and altogether more amiable than George William. She replied that *cher Papa* would, as always, know best. She would do with pleasure whatever he considered to be to her advantage. Her only desire was for a decent establishment. If this was to be found with the younger brother, very well, she would feel no qualms at 'leaving one for the other'.

Ernst August and Sophie exchanged gifts and letters, and she embraced with joy the suggestion that Hammerstein would personally inform her mother, only wishing that this embarrassment might be over as the Queen 'gives the *démenti* to all who speak of it and it is the talk of all The Hague'.

Sophie was the last of the Winter Queen's daughters to settle her future. Elizabeth was arranging what Sophie called 'her canonisation' by becoming the Coadjucatrix of the Protestant Abbey of Herford. Such religious establishments were recognised boltholes for unmarried princesses, and needed not so much a vocation as noble birth and a reasonable dowry.

Even then admittance was difficult to arrange. Louise Hollandine's application for membership to such a Protestant order had been turned down despite Elizabeth's assurances to the governors that all sixteen of her sister's quarterings were impeccable, and that 'we have nothing to do with any commoner, being descended not from Anne Boleyn but from Henry VII who married a King's daughter'. Louise Hollandine made secret enquiries elsewhere and vanished in the winter of 1657, leaving a note for her mother. She went into France, to be received into the Catholic Church before taking the veil. In due course she became the Abbess of Maubuisson, an elegant convent under royal patronage, not far from Paris. The gossips in The Hague said that she had disappeared because she was pregnant— quite untrue. In the eyes of the Queen of Bohemia this added gratuitous insult to the injury she had sustained by her daughter's action. She went to endless trouble to deny these *médisances*, and was understandably upset when the gossip about Sophie, which she denied just as firmly, turned out to be perfectly true.

'About the change in Sophie's marriage,' she wrote acidly to Charles Louis, 'it was secret only from me, for to all at Cassel and everywhere it was known before I knew it. I do not at all dislike the match concerning the person for whom I have a great esteem, which is all I will answer as neither my opinion nor consent has been asked. I have no more to say, but wish that it may prove for Sophie's content and happiness.'

Other congratulations poured in. Charles II wrote in English to the bride and in Latin to the groom. Louis von Rothenschild, Charles Louis' natural son, in the habit of sending Sophie pretty poems for her birthday— one was addressed to his *Adorable Princesse, vraie déesse de sagesse*—said that on this occasion he hardly knew which line to take. Was he to produce hymns and epithalamia in celebration of Hymen, or an elegy because she was leaving Heidelberg? After three false starts, he solved his problem by writing in prose.

CHAPTER THREE

The Holy Trinity
(1658–1665)

Sophie's wedding took place in Heidelberg four days after her twenty-eighth birthday. Ernst August had suggested a quiet ceremony in Hanover, but Charles Louis refused to hear of it. He was no friend of ceremonial himself, but his sister's marriage was to be celebrated with all the pomp and circumstance due to her station. He reminded Ernst August that a former King of Sweden had once come all the way to Heidelberg for a great-great-aunt princess Palatine; but he suggested that, if Ernst August wished to keep his expenses down, he might travel by the regular post, and he himself would send his sister to Hanover in proper style. Ernst August said that, once she was his wife, Sophie would naturally be his responsibility as soon as she crossed the Palatine frontier; and he duly arrived by public transport on the eve of his wedding-day.

He was led to the altar by the seven-year-old Electoral Prince Charles and one of the Zweibrücken dukes, a brother of the spurned Prince Adolph but no grudge-bearer. Charles Louis and Edward, the only members of her immediate family to attend her wedding, escorted Sophie up the aisle. She wore a dress of white silvery brocade, with a prodigious train carried by four of her maidens *à la mode d'Allemagne*. Her hair, once her pride for its natural waves and now her despair despite frequent applications of ointment to make it grow, failed to cascade over her shoulders in the approved fashion; but it hung loose about her neck in becoming tendrils, surmounted by the great diamond coronet of *la maison*. Twenty-four noblemen carried torches decorated with coloured taffeta ribbons, blue and white for the Palatinate, red and gold for Brunswick, in front of the procession, which poor Charlotte watched with streaming eyes from an upstairs window.

The castle cannons boomed out across the Neckar valley as Sophie and Ernst August were pronounced man and wife. They were then placed on canopied thrones opposite each other, and during the ensuing Te Deums Sophie contemplated the man she had decided to love for the rest of her life. She found that she would not be called upon to do violence to her feelings, and sent up a private prayer of thanks that her husband, a vision in cloth of silver, with a wreath of diamonds to symbolise eternal love, still looked handsome and likeable.

After Sophie had formally renounced any claim to the Palatinate, as was the tradition for marrying Palatine princesses, supper was served. Charles Louis' daughter Liselotte was allowed down for the occasion, but could not look at Sophie's duke without bursting into floods of tears. This prevented her from enjoying the unusually festive menu. Normally plenty of home-grown green and root vegetables were served to take the edge off appetites before the grander meats, venison and poultry appeared, but on this evening no expense was spared. Nor did Charles Louis practise his pet economy—beloved of all princes, before or since—in the lighting arrangements. His usual instructions regarding pitch, tallow, or even tar were waived, and only tapers and flambeaux of finest beeswax illuminated the great rooms.

The traditional *Fackeltanz* opened the ball after supper. Nobles and princes, carrying blazing torches, walked in pairs before and behind the couple, who solemnly marched around the room to the strains of the Elector's band. Before the band made way for the orchestra which opened the ball proper, Sophie had paced around the room with every princely member of the party in turn, according to the custom which was long to survive her, and was still followed almost unchanged when Queen Victoria's children married.

Before going to bed, Charles Louis wrote to Louise. She was now nursing a baby son, named after his father and called Carllutz for short. That Sophie's marriage was an accomplished fact, the Elector said, was a weight off his mind, although his pocket was now lighter by 30,000 gulden. He could hardly wait for the remaining festivities to be done with, but the celebratory outing and another dance for the *Frauenzimmer* of Heidelberg would soon be over, and then he would be able to fly to the bosom of his *carissima Signora*, 'our Pantagruel permitting'.

On the following day he wrote that the bridal pair had not emerged from their apartments until it was time for afternoon church, and wondered with uncharacteristic archness what they had found to do for all that time. Sophie herself says of her wedding night that it transformed her feelings from the esteem that the Duke's merit had always excited to love inspired by sincere passion.

A few days later Ernst August left by the regular post chaise 'much as he had come, unless in his heart he felt more than he had expected'. When the time came for Sophie to take her leave, the Elector and his entire court accompanied her, as promised, to the frontier at Weinheim, where the Duke's suite was awaiting her. She shed some tears at parting from her brother, but not many, 'my heart being elsewhere'. There would, Charles Louis hoped, be many opportunities to meet. 'Moreover, he did me the honour of promising to write' (and faithfully kept his word: Charles Louis and Sophie exchanged letters at least once a week).

In return Sophie promised to see, in the event of his death, that Louise and Carllutz would 'suffer no *tort*'. Edward had made a similar promise before leaving on the previous day, although neither he nor Sophie had seen the beautiful new baby. Sophie could not be invited for reasons of etiquette, and Charles Louis considered that 'brother Ned is too full of *raillerie*' to make such a visit desirable.

As soon as Sophie had crossed the border Charles Louis, without reference to any court of law, published divorce documents, duly sworn before the Imperial notary and carrying the official Electoral seal. Reaction from abroad was predictable. Everyone questioned the legality. The Queen of Bohemia washed her hands of it. Edward was furnished with copies of the Luther correspondence to appease French Protestant critics. For the Catholics he had an old letter from the Pope condoning Philip of Hesse's earlier bigamy. Mazarin, said Edward, was *bien fâché*, and Charles Louis had better write to him directly if he did not wish to endanger his French subsidies. But the Elector had the satisfaction of pointing out to Louise that Sophie's Duke, on whose account the publication of his home-made divorce had so long been delayed, had only alluded to it by wishing him luck. He was less enchanted by the fact that Charlotte disregarded the whole affair and firmly remained in the castle.

Sophie's wedding-journey was punctuated by such entertainments as Courts usually provided for distinguished travellers. Hesse-Darmstadt regaled her with fireworks, specially prepared by the eldest prince, whose hands still bore the marks of his labours. Later that evening he performed a ballet together with his aged mother and all his brothers and sisters. Hesse-Cassel, mercifully, did not mount any special diversions. On reaching Minden, near the border of Westphalia—'the land of Pumpernickel'—Sophie was dismayed to find that even the white bread was stone-hard. She wished she had brought the Heidelberg baker along, but at Oyn-hausen the bread was delicious again.

On the outskirts of Hanover she was met by the four ducal brothers at the head of a splendid retinue. She descended to greet them according to protocol, happy to see Ernst August and not to feel any embarrassment at meeting George William. John Frederick was indeed quite horrifyingly fat; his own mother said of him that if she were a young lady she wouldn't take to him—and Sophie didn't. Christian Louis, showing signs of the alcoholism that his mother feared would sooner or later 'calcify his heart', was sober, and delivered the speech of welcome. Then all four Dukes squashed into Sophie's carriage and entered the city to the thunder of cannons and the pealing of church bells.

All the ladies of Sophie's new family were assembled in the forecourt of the Leine Palace. Sophie immediately formed a great liking for her sensible, long-suffering mother-in-law, who handed her out of her carriage. This Princess, she was pleased to report to the Elector in her first letter, found nothing odd in Charles Louis' behaviour. Indeed, she thought that he had been a model of restraint: had she behaved like the Electress, her own husband would have killed her at once.

Sophie's determination to make a success of her marriage prevented her from finding fault with the Leine Palace. Unlike the dramatic stage-set castle of Heidelberg overlooking scenery that was positively theatrical, her new home, built on the foundation of an ancient monastery, stood squarely in a narrow street. It overlooked the Leine at the back, but there was no panorama, only a view of dyers' shacks on the opposite bank. But then, 'views' were a concept of the future, and whenever Ernst August gazed at the river it was with the object of potting low-swooping swallows with his crossbow. Sophie declared great satisfaction with her apartments, through which her husband led her by the hand. She was highly delighted with her ante-room, hung in yellow, her darkish presence-chamber and her bedroom, well-appointed with the usual offices such as dressing-rooms and the secret cabinet for her close-stool. Two windows led out to a small balcony where orange, jasmine and myrtle grew in gilded tubs.

Her suite lay directly over her husband's, with which it was linked by narrow stairs. Another set of wooden stairs led right into the Schlosskirche. Highly convenient, as frequent church attendance was obligatory. Sophie, who used to get on with her correspondence during the sermon, once dated a letter 'as from Paradise, where time has no meaning', but complained that writing was difficult because Ernst August, reading a burlesque by her side, was laughing so loudly that it disturbed her concentration. But the first service, the great *festin de cérémonie* that marked the marriage, was a solemn affair. There could be no secondary activity as she sat on a dais under a canopy of gilded copper, listening to the Hanoverian Te Deums.

Sophie took pleasure in speeding the departing wedding guests on their way, happy to be alone at last with Ernst August. Had she liked him less, she would still have professed to idolise him, and was perfectly prepared to find him indifferent towards her, for his motives in marrying her had been no less self-interested than her own. She was mature enough to face facts, and to enter married life determined to give satisfaction, in return for an establishment of the sort to which her rank and upbringing qualified her.

Confident though she was of her attractions, dewy-eyed brides who enslaved husbands tended to be nearer fifteen than thirty. Luckily, at twenty-eight Sophie was wearing well. She was admirably thin, small-waisted and graceful. Her colouring was still pretty in spite of smallpox, her teeth still perfect—a rare attribute of beauty in the days of barber-surgeons all too quick on the draw—and her eyes, always bright and intelligent, were beginning to acquire their chiselled lids which later gave them their hooded look of wisdom. Her trousseau—Charles Louis had been unstinting for once—put her at a further advantage; but it remained to be seen whether she would succeed in holding Ernst August's interest.

It came as an agreeable surprise that the Duke appeared to feel and display such passion that, Sophie wryly observes, one might have thought he would love her forever. And in a way he did: he was never to stop assuring her that he much preferred her to every one of his numerous mistresses. Any jealousy she might have felt she kept to herself—she was far too cool to make scenes.

Not so Ernst August: ridiculous though it seemed to Sophie, he became frantically jealous of his own favourite brother. Quite soon after Sophie's arrival in Hanover, George William showed regret at having bartered his bride. Ernst August, after years of contentedly playing second fiddle—both in official matters and in those of the heart, which in any case occupied George William more—was so sure George William was in every way more desirable than himself that he mistakenly thought Sophie shared his opinion. Prevented for the sake of fraternal harmony from tackling his brother on the subject, he concentrated on watching his wife with hawk-like attention.

George William left Sophie in no doubt about his sentiments. If this was balm to any feelings of injured pride that may have remained, it created a most difficult situation, requiring all the tact and diplomacy she could muster. She could neither ignore the Duke in whose palace she was a guest, nor avoid him. If she suggested spending the day *à deux* with her husband, George William would berate her for 'alienating his brother and robbing him of the best friend he had in all the world'. Although often feeling like the crowd-making third in the company of the two insepar-able Dukes, Sophie could not act with the friendliness of a sister-in-law because Ernst August would make jealous scenes as soon as she was back in her apartments. So that he could not accuse her of making eyes at his brother, Sophie evolved a technique of averting her gaze from George William's ever-present countenance, and so perfected it that she says in her Memoirs 'for years I only saw his shadow'. She was safe from one Duke's amorous advances and the other's jealous sulks only when her husband settled down for his after-dinner nap, with his feet firmly anchored either side of her as she sat on a facing chair. It must have been a strain but she took it for flattering proof of sincere love, 'although he often slept for hours and many would have thought it tiresome'.

Anything was better than Ernst August's oppressive silences when he believed he had reason to doubt her affection. She would weep bitter tears and wish that she was dead, while he morosely refused to open his mouth. On one such occasion, when he finally spoke, it was her turn to be speech-less with surprise: she had said to George William, '*Quand on n'a pas ce qu'on aime, on aime ce qu'on a*'—a tag which she frequently quoted, and which admirably summed up her attitude to life. Ernst August had chosen to refer this remark to himself, and peace was made only when she ex-plained that Venice, and not he, had been the subject of the conversation.

George William, on being asked whether he was not longing for Italy, had declared that since her arrival in Hanover he had no wish to be anywhere else. Her reply had been intended to deflect this compliment.

It was an extravagant one, in view of both Dukes' passion for the south. Venice was their favourite topic. When they were not discussing their last visit they were planning the next one; Ernst August claimed that his humour improved when he 'merely contemplated the construction of a gondola'. His greatest wish was to enjoy, simultaneously, his *Sérénissime Duchesse* and the *Sérénissime République*.

Sophie had only been married for a short time when Charles Louis learned that the 'Holy Trinity'—never a hint of the tricky triangle—was setting out for Venice. Sophie, firmly stating that she would gladly have followed her husband to the Antipodes, does not explain why she turned back to Hanover after only a single day's journey, and merely states in the Memoirs that the brothers proceeded without her.

From the Leine Palace she wrote to Charles Louis that she must be 'the miracle of the century, a woman who loves her husband', but supposed, reasonably enough, that this affliction would soon be cured if Ernst August did not love her in return. 'But as he writes a million *belles choses* with every post, I remain *prise*. My people spare no effort in trying to amuse me, but they fail because he is not here.' When the Dukes returned in April she was so delighted to see Ernst August again that she entirely forgot to salute George William, and had to be nudged into politeness by her husband. That in itself, she thought, might have shown him where her true affections lay, but Venice had not diminished Ernst August's jealousy, nor, it seemed, George William's passion.

All should have been well on a hunting trip to Hummlingen. There, the brothers and their parties met only for sport and supper, retiring for the night in separate villages. George William, however, could hardly stand the thought of his brother's bed 'containing a wife while he himself was unprovided for'. His advances grew more ardent, and the Holy Trinity was in perpetual danger of exploding. Sophie was delighted when he began to console himself with one of her ladies, but not displeased to be asked to find her a husband: she says that the girl's reputation had somewhat suffered by 'this flash-in-the-pan affair'.

Fond though she was of the open air, Sophie did not triumph at Hummlingen. After her first day in the saddle Ernst August charitably decided that the wooded, hilly terrain was too dangerous for his wife. She was reduced to playing at cards with her ladies and hawking for heron in her *calèche*, while nursing her leg that had been rubbed sore by the pommel.*

She wrote off to Heidelberg for some of Joost the tabledecker's ointment, which had cured her sister Elizabeth after the barber had failed. She also asked, urgently, for more pomade to make the hair grow; the last batch, although religiously smeared on two fingers thick, had yielded no results.

Such domestic requests were addressed to Katharina von Uffeln, who had originally been a member of Charlotte's entourage from Hesse-Cassel, and had recently been drawn into the Elector's service. Liselotte had become too much of a handful for Sophie's aged governesses. After she had kicked one of the Quaadts' brittle shins so that the old lady sank lifeless to the ground, rallying only to pack her boxes and retire in earnest, Jungfer Uffeln was asked to fill the vacancy. Charles Louis, trusting nothing that came out of Hesse, would have much preferred to find another person for the position. He had desired Sophie to help, 'but where,' she asked, 'do we find bread in the desert?' She would do what she could, 'but here,' she told her brother, 'the ladies are very homely.' (These words are in English—'verrey homley'.) Besides, for the kind of salary he offered, not even the very plainest would take on the job, and there were his curious domestic arrangements, which ruled out anyone of reasonable birth. Uffeln, whom she rather liked, would have to do, even though it meant having both daughter and governess under constant surveillance for symptoms of disrespect and disobedience to papa.

Sure enough, Charles Louis saw signs suggesting that Liselotte had inherited her mother's unfortunate disposition, to say nothing of 'grimacing, just like Charlotte'. Sophie thought that the child would never improve while her mother's example was before her eyes. Why did not Charles Louis send Liselotte, together with Uffeln, who was clearly devoted to her, to Hanover? She would be more than welcome, and loved and cared for 'as though she had been drawn from my own body'. Ernst August, too, was all for the plan, and in any case he owed her a favour in return for her

---

* Later on heron-hunting was to involve no exercise at all: hunters retired into square wooden pavilions for their card-games, and rushed out only when the look-out men reported sightings from the doors that opened from all four sides.

complaisance in letting him go gallivanting in Italy without complaint. That much said, Sophie added a word of warning: 'Of being coquette or familiar, Liselotte will learn nothing here. But for learning the art of civilised conversation with all manner of people, that I can't answer for, unless it please God to give us a Court of our own which we can arrange according to our *fantaisie*. To tell you the truth—"under the rose"—there is little *grandeur* here. Months pass when we don't see anyone but the *domestiques*, of whom we have vast numbers.'

Liselotte's arrival provided Sophie with a much needed interest. The child's tendency to burst into tears over every trifle was soon cured, as was the dreaded grimacing. Liselotte regained her *bonne mine*. Jungfer Uffeln also found happiness in Hanover. She married Sophie's Master of the Horse, M von Harling, and continued to be a model governess, of whose firm, kind methods Sophie thoroughly approved. Together, they invented a system of prizes for Liselotte's progress in her lessons. Both agreed to check the Elector's ambitious plans for making his daughter more learned.

'French she can learn from the ladies-in-waiting,' wrote Sophie, and referring to a female sage—'the star of Utrecht'—who was attracting attention at the time, 'you do not want *ma fille* to become a Schurmann.' Sophie was delighted with Liselotte's progress, especially since she thought her niece would remain 'my only child'. Sometimes she would hopefully note that 'Jungfer Katharine'*—a Heidelberg euphemism for monthly periods—was absent, but to her disappointment it would unfailingly appear, if belatedly. Mme von Harling was asked to provide 'preparations to help a person to conceive', but all was in vain, as was Charles Louis' advice to take it easy and 'conserve her energies for greater exertions'.

'Fertile or infertile', Sophie wrote to her brother in the autumn of 1659, she would go to Holland to show Liselotte to her mother while Ernst August was in Italy. The Queen was longing for the visit. Sophie had become her best daughter, and the letters exchanged between the two sound positively affectionate. The 'Holy Trinity's' visit earlier in the year had been cut short because the Dukes' mother had unexpectedly died, after warning her sons for a long time that they were worrying her to death. Then, the Winter Queen had hardly had time to remark that Sophie appeared quite unchanged 'except for a few marks through the smallpox',

* From Catharr: Flux.

but had made up for her disappointment by using the extra money which Charles Louis had made available for the entertainment of her guests by travelling to Brussels, where Charles II was planning his restoration. Now she wrote to the Elector to ask for more money, and expressed joy at the opportunity of meeting her grand-daughter, as well as having Sophie to herself, unencumbered by her Duke.

Sophie's journey went off well, marred only by George William, who had not gone to Venice on this occasion, but turned up like a jack-in-the-box as she passed through part of his possessions, and then again in Holland where he said he had some business. She believed that he had followed her, and begged him to leave her be unless he meant to bring ruin on them both. George William's unwelcome attentions, which feature prominently in the Memoirs, have sometimes been taken for wishful thinking on Sophie's part to make up for having been jilted earlier. Rumours of his devotion to his sister-in-law had, however, reached The Hague even before Sophie herself. The Winter Queen, positive that Sophie would never allow scandal to touch her, wrote to this effect to her son, adding, 'It looks as though you will be an uncle some six months hence. But God forbid that it should be believed, as her ladyship herself does not believe it.'

Her ladyship, who had written to Charles Louis 'if part of being pregnant is being sick, then I'm not', was in little doubt about her condition, but deeply averse to discussing it. In order to persuade Hanover 'that she was doing her best to make them a prince' she retired to her bed, and all The Hague gathered in her chamber to observe the interesting details. Only the Princess Royal did not call—'*quel crève-coeur!*'—as she had hastened to Breda, where her brothers were waiting to set sail for England —a journey which in the event did not take place until the following year.

After Mary's return, the Queen took Liselotte to call on her. 'Little William is making love to my niece but she is *fort cruelle*,' said Sophie, who was passing the time by making wedding plans for the child. On the whole she was more anxious to make her Queen of Denmark than Princess of Orange—the situation of that family had, since William II's death, become too precarious. Liselotte had made them all laugh by references to Cinderella when she was teased on the subject; this did not prevent her from romping about with her cousin, and Anne Hyde had to gather her up from a turkey carpet where she was rolling about in his company when the Queen of Bohemia ended her visit. When Sophie learned that the child had run up to haughty 'Princess Royal', firmly pulled her back by the skirts and preceded her through the door, she laughed so much that she almost did herself an injury. 'Liselotte', she said, 'has avenged us all.'

The presence of her grand-daughter brought a great change over the Queen. Sophie was astonished to see her imperious mother wait patiently while the child's *mouchoirs* and *coiffes* were pinned about her in preparation for outings, and with her own hands move Liselotte's chair closer to her own. 'Her Majesty,' she told Charles Louis, 'no longer speaks of hounds and guinea-pigs but only of Liselotte.'

Sophie had never shared the Queen's enthusiasm for her menagerie. Although she always owned the fashionable quota of little dogs, and had been known to send dutiful greetings 'to all the puppies in Heidelberg', her interest had been at best polite. There is no record of tears when fatal accidents befell them, as when a young lynx got one of them by the throat or a careless page dropped another to its death. Liselotte, however, had inherited her grandmother's lifelong passion for pets, and the only time she did not gladly obey her aunt Sophie was when she was bidden to give a much loved dog to Christian Louis' wife as a present. When her fond grandmother decided to have her painted, the mortification of having to sit still was lessened by the presence of Celadon . . . 'one of the prettiest beagle bitches that was ever seen,' wrote the Queen of Bohemia to Charles Louis when announcing the portrait. When it was finished she sent it to Heidelberg, saying that Celadon was 'not as small as she is painted but proportionate and even prettier', while Liselotte's likeness went without comment. But the child could not complain of lack of admiration. 'She is not like the house of Hesse, she is like ours,' said the Queen, who was, presumably because of her grandchild's fair colouring, reminded of 'my poor Henriette, the prettiest of my daughters'. Sophie grew afraid that she would become intolerably conceited. But when Liselotte overheard speculations as to whether her brother, whose likeness in wax had arrived at The Hague, might not have the better forehead, and wept, both ladies firmly declared that hers was prettier, 'which much joyed her'.

Although the shared interest in Liselotte created a new and pleasant bond between mother and daughter, and although it was altogether a comfortable visit, Sophie became so bored in Holland that she decided not to wait to be collected by her husband. 'The climate here is more conducive to the well-being of the body than of the spirit,' she wrote. 'It is not the place for such a muse as me.'

She had heard more than enough about the art of housekeeping, about cleanliness and about her *ventre*. Even the French Ambassador did not ignore the subject, and the Danish Ambassador talked 'like an old midwife'.

Sophie wanted to go home. She boarded her carriage, acquired in Holland and 'made after the new fashion, all glass and gilt, lined in velour and curtained in damask—finer than any of the Princess of Orange's', with whose establishment, Sophie noted, her own compared well: 'not bad for the wife of a *cadet*!'. In spite of the dreadful roads, she was confident that her coach would prove *fort commode*, although springs were still in the future.

She had several spills but remained unhurt, bearing physical discomfort with stoicism. As for danger, she faced it—according to Liselotte—'with the courage of a man'.

'Did you hear that Sophie was like to be burned to death?' wrote the Queen of Bohemia to her son a few days after her youngest daughter's departure. While the travellers were spending the night in Cloppenburg the thatched and timbered village had seemingly burst into flame. The fire, starting in the stables over which Sophie was lodged, consumed fourteen houses in less than half-an-hour. By the time she had put on her dressing-gown and slippers, her windows had been pierced by the flames. 'A page carried Liselotte to safety,' she wrote to her mother, 'and the village idiot performed this service for me.' Liselotte's cries, 'Where's *tante*, oh, where's *tante*?', rang out above the noise of terrified stampeding horses, frightened villagers and rushing servants—'wonderfully prompt and *soigneux*'—who rescued Sophie's *vaisselle* and all her clothes. The child was always to remember her aunt's impressive sangfroid. 'Highly pregnant, escaping only when the very room was alight, she remained calm and cheerful.'

Safely back in Hanover, Sophie settled down to await the return of Ernst August and the arrival of her baby. Charles Louis was appalled at the Duke's absence at such a time, but Sophie took it philosophically. 'People are different, and made more different by upbringing and diet,' she wrote to her brother. 'What if Ernst August is not expressing his affection as we should expect? As long as a husband behaves in accordance with his own notions of love, no sensible wife has reason for complaint.'

George William seemed to have taken her hints, and had stayed in Holland to conduct his *galanteries* at the Princess of Orange's Court. Attractive to women though he was known to be, Sophie chose to attribute his triumphs to the success of his latest mining operations in the Harz mountains rather than to his magnetic charm. The *'affamées'* at The Hague, she was sure, languished not so much for his embraces as for 'mountains of pure gold and rivers of pearls'—too bad there was only silver.

This, however, was found in such large quantities that many new shafts had recently been sunk both in his and in Christian Louis' concessions. That Duke's loving subjects had wished to name one mine after his wife, and to add the suffix *'Landesmutter'*, mother of the country. In view of the absence of children, he had ruled against it. The Duchess, Sophie heard, was frantically trying to amend her condition. Doctors, quacks, taking the waters and medication with every known concoction failed, and she was said to be so jealous of Sophie that there were rumours of plots against 'the burden I am carrying'. Sophie said that she would gladly exchange it for all Christian Louis' country and revenues, and only regretted that this was not practicable.

Hanover, on the other hand, was deeply grateful for the prospect of an heir. True, in the absence of both Dukes the Council was unable to agree on precisely who was to have the honour of delivering a loyal address to this effect to the Duchess, or what protocol to employ for the ringing of church bells to celebrate, belatedly, the baby's stirring in the womb. Both courtesies were therefore omitted, but Sophie remained calm. When the cats are at play, the mice will squabble. There was nothing she could do about it; she could only wait and pass the time by doing needlework.

On 29th May 1660, the birthday of Charles II, lately restored and on that very afternoon entering his capital amid cheers, Sophie wrote in an unsteady hand, '*Me voici*, returned from the dead'. George Louis, future King of England, had arrived after a labour so arduous and protracted that his life, and his mother's, had been despaired of.

For three days and nights horrifying noises had issued from Sophie's chamber, and had so terrified Liselotte that she decided to investigate for herself. She was not the child to be fobbed off by Mme von Harling's stories of babies, in the shape of cleverly made rag-dolls, growing under shrubs in gilded tubs, and had earlier informed one of her friends that 'aunt is becoming so fat that I think something young must be on the way'.

She was discovered in her hiding-place behind a screen in Sophie's room, when the real-life baby, enormous and pink, with white eye-lashes, was being given his first bath. But she was not punished for naughtiness; in the universal joy, all was church bells and congratulations.

Ernst August was delighted. George William, 'much joyed', left the amorous ladies of The Hague and made for home. Christian Louis said it was a *bonheur* for the entire House, and tales of his wife's jealousy had only, said Sophie, in English, been malicious 'tittle tarttle'. Charles Louis wrote that he was crying '*victoire, victoire*', and Sophie replied that she was adding a private '*ma-i, ma-i*'—the sound of wailing from the Litany. If it depended on her alone, she would never go through such torment again, but rest content with the little creature gurgling in his cot by her side. She thanked the Elector for the gift of a coral teething ring—'guaranteed to make his mouth more beautiful still'—and for wishing her son the combined good fortunes of St George and St Louis; as soon as the baby became more eloquent he would express his own appreciation, and he was certain to follow the Elector's catechism to the letter, 'unless, God forbid, he grows up to be a disobedient son'.

Sophie was so pleased to be out of danger that she did not stop talking from morning till night. Ernst August and John Frederick both took their usual robust meals by her bedside. Sophie herself took no nourishment besides the *sel de vipères* prescribed by her physician Dr Tachen. For all the Palatine dislike of doctors—'those charlatans'—she had great faith in her dear Dr Tac, or Tictac, and was soon strong enough to sit up and sing trios with the brothers, which she herself accompanied on her guitar, and to plan diversions for the time when her 'six weeks' penitence was over'. 'A journey into the blue—no more than two carriages, just the Duke, *mon fils* and *ma fille*, and only very few attendants', unless the Elector thought that this might be considered eccentric? Alternatively, since the Queen of Bohemia was now making preparations for returning home, she toyed with the idea of taking her little family to England.

None of these delightful plans materialised. Instead, Ernst August departed without her to Pyrmont, a watering place in Westphalia, in the company of George William, whose arrival in Hanover had failed to transform the pleasant trio into a harmonious quartet. In spite of frequent references to a lady in The Hague with whom he claimed to be in love, Ernst August continued to suspect him of designs on Sophie. This so upset George William that he fell ill, and was advised to take a cure. Ernst August decided that he, too, would benefit from the health-giving waters, and Sophie quite understood—'after all, one does not hate to see the people one loves'. She regretted only that at this rate '*ma fille*' was unlikely to become 'a much-travelled lady and learn how to live *en princesse*', for which Hanover offered no opportunities; she herself was becoming positively '*stupide* from sitting *au coin du feu*'.

In December Ernst August said that no man of his constitution could be expected to face the bleak Westphalian winter, and went to Italy, while Sophie paid her first official visit to Heidelberg.

She arrived with sixty attendants and as many horses, and her arrival was marked by formal addresses from both town and gown. Conditions at the Castle were much as she had left them. She was shocked to find her nephew Charles, Liselotte's older brother, looking neglected and miserable. What spirit he had was crushed by the combined efforts of his celebrated teachers, Spanheim and Pufendorf, and by his father, whom he could please only by behaving badly to his mother.

Sophie did not call on Charlotte. Nor could she call formally on Louise to see 'the progeny', which had been increased by the birth of a little girl. 'I had to be careful in showing my friendship for her, so as not to embarrass the Dukes,' she writes. But if a formal visit from the Duchess of Lüneburg was impossible, an informal one from the cousin of the newly restored King of England was a different matter.

The Palatinate had celebrated the restoration with a day of thanksgiving. 'It will be well-liked in England,' the Queen of Bohemia had written approvingly, complaining only of the quality of Charles Louis' envoy to London—'a mere handicraftsman', worse even than M Rubens, sent by Spain in an earlier reign, or Gerbier, the miniaturist, sent by the King of France. But then, Charles Louis' behaviour to Charles had never pleased her. At least, now, she had the satisfaction of learning that her children remembered their English blood. For on St David's day Charles Louis and Sophie drove to distribute posies of leeks, 'as is the custom', to all their astonished Heidelberg acquaintances. This patriotic gesture became the pretext for Sophie's call on Louise, where she admired the children—

'the prettiest I have ever seen, with the exception of my own'. In what she knew to be the tiresome way of all proud mothers, she said that to her eyes at least 'George Louis is as beautiful as an angel', and promised to show him —'*mon guenon*', my little monkey-face—to her mother before the Queen of Bohemia set sail for England.

In May 1661 Sophie—pregnant once more—travelled from Heidelberg to Rotterdam to wave goodbye to her mother from the quayside. Although the Queen had firmly declined Sophie's offer of accompanying her, the letters between the ladies had remained warm and friendly. Often they were accompanied by acceptable gifts—'I am loaded with gloves and perfumes from the Duke, who is delighted to be of service to Your Majesty'—and filled with family gossip. Mother and daughter were keenly following Charles II's plans for marriage. 'I hear the King of England is marrying Mazarin's niece,' wrote Sophie, knowing all about the beautiful Hortense Mancini from Ernst August, and it was a great relief to hear of Charles' Portuguese marriage to Catherine of Braganza—'much better like that'.

And what of James, Duke of York? Inconceivable that he should indeed have married Anne Hyde, especially as Sophie knew on good authority that 'Nan', finding herself pregant, had begged her doctor for the strongest possible purge. This had been administered, and only when she asked to have the prescription repeated had the good man recognised her design and refused her request. In Sophie's opinion, had there been a secret marriage Nan would have had no reason for wishing to destroy the child. When this marriage was finally revealed, mother and daughter disapproved in unison.

So certain was the Queen of her welcome in England that she embarked even before she had received her nephew's official invitation. She had long taken pleasure in pointing out that the King always treated her like a mother rather than an aunt, unlike her own son, who she believed was trying to starve her out 'as they do besieged cities'. Even when she left Holland he did not help her to get her jewels out of pawn because 'he does not think he deserves well enough of me to have them after my death. But I will leave him my debts and that will trouble him more.'

Soon after her arrival at Whitehall the Queen died, within a short time of the death of 'Princess Royal' and of poor Louis von Rothenschild, for whom a post had been found in England, and who had been the first to catch the smallpox that killed them all. The Queen's will enraged Charles Louis, as she had planned. Although he was chief heir, she had added a codicil leaving everything of any value to Rupert, who had planned to settle in England but not till after the Coronation—'so wise, it will save a great deal of expense'—but in the event had attended it after all. Even before the Winter Queen's funeral at Westminster Abbey he had her apartments sealed, and prevented the Palatine envoy from taking an inventory. This added fuel to the smouldering quarrel between him and Charles Louis, but this time it was the younger brother who remained adamant.

Edward and the Queen's daughters, except for Louise Hollandine whose name was not even mentioned, received token pieces of jewellery. Sophie inherited the Queen's everyday pearls, which cannot have spent much time with the moneylenders because, in the Dutch portraits, they adorn every Palatine lady's throat in turn, and probably made the rounds of the sitters.

In October 1661 Sophie's second son, Frederick August, a dark-skinned, dark-eyed baby, whom she called 'my Palatine' in contrast to 'my Brunswicker'—the pink George Louis—leapt out into the world after his mother had retired to bed after supper and a large quantity of good Palatine grapes. This time there was no six weeks' penitence afterwards. Within a fortnight she was out of her own and in Ernst August's bed, where she 'caught a cold which prevented me from producing living children for some years'.

Two months after Frederick August's birth the old Bishop of Osnabrück fell ill, as he had many times before. So far, Charles Louis' fond wishes for his speedy despatch had remained unfulfilled. Sophie was given to predicting darkly that he would live on for ever, ridding his system of poison '*en caquant* (by your leave) *des paternosters*'. This time, however, he did not recover. Ernst August, the new secular Bishop, and his lady thanked George William for his hospitality and gratefully set up house on their own—not a moment too soon for Sophie, for life in the Leine Palace, where Virgil and Seneca remained unopened ('We only read comedies and chatter, all day long'), was beginning to pall.

'*Tout va ici d'un autre air qu'à Hanover, Dieu merci,*' wrote Sophie from Iburg, where Ernst August installed her in the Bishop's palace. All was

Sophie, Princess Palatine, from the studio of Gerrit van Honthorst, *ca* 1648.

Charles Louis, Elector Palatine, anon, *ca* 1650.

suitably magnificent, from *vaisselle* and furniture to the halberdiers who lined the passages; and when she wrote that her indoor servants bedded down in the stables on palliasses of straw it was not in a spirit of complaint but to ward off a threatened visit from her sister Elizabeth. She was happy to be able to create a Court of her own on the lines of Charles Louis' 'Parnassus at Heidelberg, where knowledge and reason flourish'. If, for the time being, Iburg did not reach those intellectual heights ('We play at nine-pins, tric-trac and run for the ring'), Sophie was able to say with satisfaction, 'Things go well for a little bishop who can live in peace and rely on his brothers in case of trouble'.

In a congratulatory letter from Heidelberg, addressed to *Sainte Sophie*, Spanheim said that all that remained was for the bishop's mitre, so becoming to *la princesse la plus spirituelle du monde*, to be exchanged for the triple tiara. But things could hardly be better if Ernst August and she were *pape et papesse*, wrote Sophie to Charles Louis, and by way of touching wood added that she only hoped they would not find '*de la merde au bout du baton*'.

Liselotte hugely enjoyed herself in her new home. She drove about the countryside in a little cart drawn by two large dogs, presents from Ernst August, played with a small dog which owned a wardrobe of clothes and walked on its hind legs when it was dressed up, fired arrows from her cross-bow at the bottoms of the maids, and got drunk, once, on the vintage wine that made the neighbouring abbot's excellent collations so pleasant. Her only regret was being a girl, a condition which she had heard might be altered by jumping from unprecedented heights. When she had to spend an uncomfortable period in an orthopædic bodice because the doctors said she had rickets, she did not believe them, and blamed the jumping.

Sophie had assured the Elector over and over again that, were she to have twenty children, she would not care any the less for her niece, but Charles Louis conceived the idea that Liselotte was no longer welcome at her Court. Sophie believed that he wished his daughter to be brought up in a more polished environment than Iburg was able to provide. She agreed that if Charles Louis insisted on having his daughter at home, go she must, especially since Charlotte had finally departed from Heidelberg. Accordingly, Liselotte was removed in the summer of 1663, and was always to remember the years with her aunt as the happiest of her life.

D

Sophie wept to see her go. She hated being parted from any of her *poupons*. 'I am a fool about my children,' she said, and although 'my Palatine' was growing so handsome and full of fire that George Louis seemed plain by comparison, she said that her eldest 'always touches my heart more', and never quite liked to admit even to herself that her second son was becoming her favourite. Whenever possible she took her children with her on the short journeys which made a pleasant change from her daily routine. But she left them behind when, in the company of Ernst August and George William, she inspected the ducal silver mines in the Harz mountains. She was the first woman ever to descend into a mining shaft, and felt positively reverent as she walked by the light of a mining lamp over 'miles of pure silver'. 'If you knew how much trouble it takes to make a medal,' she told her brother, 'you would hold your coins and medals in higher esteem'; but it was unnecessary advice as Charles Louis was building up a collection of coins and medals which he cherished above all his possessions.

In February 1664 Sophie's journey to Italy, discussed every year but never so far accomplished, was to become reality. At Ernst August's request she collected a bevy of beauties as her travelling companions. No plain lady-in-waiting was to spoil the effect. Of her Hanoverian ladies only Ahlefeld, Keppel and Landas were judged to be presentable, and the Duke desired her to poach on the preserves of the Princesse de Tarent, whose pretty ladies his brothers had admired in Cassel.

Accordingly letters of invitation went off. Mlle de la Mothe, a young Frenchwoman who had caught John Frederick's eye, accepted. Eleonore d'Olbreuse, captivator of George William, declined, preferring to travel to Holland with her employers, and George William discovered a sudden preference for the canals of Amsterdam over those of Venice.

Ernst August preceded his wife to Italy, and when Sophie set off she paid a visit to her brother and deposited her two boys at his Court. It was thought to be safer for them to stay with their uncle, as the neighbouring Bishop of Münster, close to Osnabrück, was making war-like noises, although not loudly enough to keep the Dukes at home. 'Lord give us peace in our time,' prayed Sophie, reluctantly preparing to say goodbye to her pretty babies.

She had meant to travel on at once, but she and her enormous suite, which included an orchestra of French violins, remained in Heidelberg while she suffered a miscarriage of twins from which it took her some time to recover. 'As thin as a beanpole and as dried up as a mummy,' she departed in April.

Impatient to join her Duke, she complained about the delay in Augsburg, where visitors to Venice had to obtain clean bills of health before being admitted into the republic, at the same time obtaining certificates of ill-health to enable them to eat meat on fast days. There, also, the under-carriages of coaches were narrowed to enable them to negotiate the mountains. This did nothing to steady them. More than a dozen spills so terrified her ladies that they walked most of the way, but Sophie travelled on, coolly playing cards. That she did not look out at the scenery meant that she saw none of the yawning chasms over which her coach danger-ously teetered, two wheels at a time. In the end she allowed herself to be transferred to a litter, and occasionally to a sledge, provided and pulled by the local peasantry.

Near Trento the Duke, accompanied by Italian nobles and their suites, Dr Tac and his attendants, and his own large retinue, met Sophie and her suite, which was infinitely larger. 'Never can there have been a more public incognito,' she observed, and indeed in Verona all the quality assembled to greet her, and a new bridge spanned the river to enable her more quickly to reach her quarters in the Casa di Brunswick, a house built entirely with money which its owner had won at cards from the Dukes.

Sophie, conditioned to think of Italian ladies as angels incarnate, admired only the rich clothes, which mitigated their hideousness, 'but as soon as they talked to me, I was enchanted by their spirit and their obliging behaviour'.

The Giusti gardens and the Arena were duly inspected and elicited no comment from her beyond *'fort ancien'* or *'fort beau'*, whichever was appropriate. The ravishing Palladian Piazzas delle Erbe and dei Signori became in her description 'a sort of market place where they promenade every afternoon, finding more pleasure in conversing with gentlemen than displeasure at ruining their complexions', and when she arrived in Venice as night was descending her impression was one of overweening melancholy. Although she did not admit this to Ernst August, 'I saw nothing but water and heard no sound beyond the gondoliers' *"peni"* and "*stali*"', and her husband's beloved gondolas with their black velvet upholstery and gleaming steel fittings looked to her like so many floating coffins.*

It took her some time to get accustomed to the amorous climate that palpably enveloped this strange, sombre city. The very churches appeared to be places of assignation. Embracing lovers could be discovered even under the altar, and the nuns seemed to think only of men, except at one convent where the senior sisters—some bearded—made love to the younger, prettier ones, who looked as though they had been painted by Titian. As for the ladies of quality, each with her *cavaliere servente*—Charles Louis would find the sight of them in their gondolas as unbelievable as she did herself.

Sophie's hand-picked ladies attracted flocks of admirers, although, in fact, her palazzo—the Ca'Foscari on the Grand Canal—resembled a hospital: Landas was still in looks, but turned out to be pregnant (until she came to be delivered of a dead premature baby in the carriage taking the party to Milan); Ahlefeld, suffering from a fever, looked like death; while de la Mothe had fallen off her horse and been dragged some way in the stirrup—and no gentleman would come to her aid because she was wearing no drawers and 'displayed the symbol of her *pucelage*'. It was a wonder she had not broken her neck, and she was now purging to preserve her health. Keppel was in a worse state than her colleagues, but according to Dr Tac was ill only from love. Although she denied it for all she was worth, she was spending every night in the chamber of M de Sandis, one of Sophie's gentlemen, who ungallantly admitted the fact as soon as he was asked. Had they been in Iburg, Sophie would have packed Keppel off to her mother at once, but here Ernst August pleaded to let it pass.

The Dukes were evidently in their element. John Frederick, who was living at Ernst August's expense in the Ca'Foscari, hired a separate casino especially for assignations, and Sophie judged that Ernst August, too, was drawing solid profit from the general air of *galanterie*.

His female friends of earlier visits called on her in droves. Her tolerance stretched further than she would have believed possible, and she only drew

* In anticipation of Byron, who says of the gondola in *Beppo*
'It glides along the water looking blackly
Just as a coffin clapt in a canoe.'

the line at his suggestion of appointing the Marchesa Paleotti from Bologna, by whom he had a son,* to her own household.

'In a land where every woman had a lover,' Sophie wrote, 'I should have felt out of place without one of my own.' The Duke chose one for her, a harmless one, and in the evenings Sophie and her ladies would laugh about the follies that had taken place during the day. Venetian society was astonished to see the Brunswick party dance in the street '*alla moda francese*', and a crowd of two thousand gathered to see them tilt for the ring at the Lido, driving chariots clad in panels of coppergilt, and wearing plumes and glittering costumes from the wardrobe of the Opera. Mlle de la Mothe caused surprise by being unable to reveal how Frenchmen made love. 'Why, were you so young when you left France?' asked a perfectly respectable Marchesa—as if unmarried girls were expected to answer such questions.

Sophie reflected that Italian customs were, after all, as unsuited to her temperament as the climate was to her physical well-being. She, too, fell ill, 'contracting a disorder frequently suffered by visitors from abroad. Everything I ate passed through me at once.' She felt weak and feverish, but took care not to spoil the sport of her Dukes and attended every concert, *conversazione* and *ridotto* to which she was bidden.

The highspot of the season came on Corpus Christi day with the Doge's ritual espousal of the sea. The ceremony opened with a gigantic civic procession that threaded its way from the Doge's palace around the square of San Marco to the sea front, interwoven by a second religious procession emerging from the entrance of San Marco itself. Guards, banners, trumpeters, nobles (each with a pilgrim on his right to indicate humility, so that, said Sophie, they don't need to bother with it for the rest of the year), intermingled with the effigies of saints carried shoulder-high by priests whose hats reminded her of 'omelets with half-oranges stuck in the centre'. The Doge himself was followed by all the ambassadors accredited to the Republic, and beside him were carried the emblems of his dignity: his chair, his cushion and his umbrella of gold brocade.

He boarded his vessel of state, the red and gold Bucentauro, and when he and his party had settled under the fringed canopy of damask, supported on fine gilt pillars, two painted, gilded boats, each manned by a

* Liselotte later heard that this young man was courting the daughter of Ernst August's official mistress, and wrote, 'Disgusting—they're probably brother and sister'.

dozen oarsmen, pulled the unmanœuverable craft out to sea. There the patriarch of Venice said a blessing, and the Doge committed a golden ring to the waters. His departure and return were marked by incessant salvoes and by peals from all the bells of Venice, the sound of trumpets, horns and fifes, and cries of admiration from the crowded, flag-lined shore. 'Nothing could be more beautiful than the Doge's boat and the confusion of gondolas that take part in the fête,' wrote Sophie, estimating that the *argenterie* alone must be worth at least twenty million.

Her own finances, always a subject of concern, were augmented by money she won at cards during the evening parties, although, she complained to Mme von Harling, her most considerable win came from the pocket of her own Duke. She wrote with great regularity to '*la gouvernesse des jeunes*', who had stayed with her when Liselotte returned to Heidelberg, and was already unofficially the Mistress of her Household, and despatched a stream of presents for her sons: glass from Murano, gloves, silk stockings, George Louis' first suit with breeches—he was growing so fast, she heard, that it was time for him to come out of skirts—clothes after the Spanish pattern, and a set of cups in a case. She chose some diamonds for herself in the Merceria—Evelyn's 'sweetest shopping street in Europe', which was tapestried in cloth of gold and silver hung out of upstairs windows for display, sweet with the smell of perfume from apothecary shops, and echoing to the song of nightingales in suspended cages. When she discovered that the merchants shamelessly overcharged foreign princes she promptly returned the stones—there were better ones in Amsterdam at half the price.

She was careful in her private expenditure and positively unostentatious in her presents to friends and acquaintances, but generous with her beautiful boys, who were never far from her mind. She would sooner, she said, see their antics than all the plays of the Commedia del Arte, and their faces rather than all the works of art in Italy—'if my Lord only liked being at home half as much as he loves being here . . . but what the husband wishes, the wife must also desire.'

When the stench of the canals in the summer's heat became intolerable, Ernst August desired to visit Vicenza. There Sophie learned to dance, or rather walk, to the sound of fiddles, while her partners in turn entertained her with the wittiest epigrams they could muster. Vicenzan wit sparkled also on the Campo del Mars, where the ladies drew up in a long line of carriages in the afternoon and the gentlemen, on foot, recited sonnets to them. At the amphitheatre—'very fine'—two couples 'took the trouble of dancing the *montande* and the *marionette* to cries of "*brava, brava*" and "*bene*".' Sophie thought that the ladies of that city had the good fortune of being able to please with very little.

Her party clothes—domino and mask as later painted by Guardi—began as time went on to cover features that grew more and more emaciated. 'I am as thin as a baton . . . but Dr Tictac promises to make me as round as a kettledrum. If he succeeds, he deserves to be canonised when we reach Rome.' It would, indeed, have been a miraculous achievement, for her diet as prescribed consisted exclusively of lemonade, the milk of melon-seeds and *sel de vipères*. Her faith in her physician nevertheless remained unshaken. Even his long-distance remedies for the princes' ailments were religiously passed on to their governess. 'Boil live quicksilver in milk, strain the liquor and serve'; alternatively, 'rub mercury on a sugarloaf until the sugar turns black, and sprinkle on their gruel and the worms will disappear never to return' reads one of his prescriptions. But when the boys fell victim to the smallpox, there was nothing even Dr Tac could do. Sophie almost died of shock at hearing the news. Luckily the attack was a light one, but there was always the worry of disfiguring scars. 'I had looked forward to loving pretty boys. Now I'll have to love ugly ones. . . .' Sadly, she travelled on to Rome.

This too was both '*fort ancien*' and '*fort beau*', but Sophie found that to enjoy this city one would 'have to be a courtisane'. Honest women were quite excluded from society, and rigid adherence to etiquette made for difficulties. There was to be no rendezvous with the ex-Queen of Sweden, in spite of Christine's express wish to meet Sophie, and Sophie's curiosity to see this strange lady with 'a *gigue* in the head'. Edward had met her in France 'wearing a wig such as the Duc de Guise wears in the country, and men's clothes with a lady's *bourret* attached to her *derrière*'. He had sent graphic descriptions of her amorous grapplings with peasant girls. He had concluded that if she was not a hermaphrodite, '*enfin* she must be *clitoriste*, loving women too well for someone not wishing to be one herself'. To her sorrow, Sophie was unable to judge for herself until she saw the Queen, disappointingly dressed in ordinary clothes, some years later. Protocol made it impossible for her to be officially received in Rome, and Cardinal Azzolini, who ruled Queen Christine 'as though she were married to him', would not hear of a carefully arranged accidental meeting in the Queen's garden.

It looked as though Sophie's meeting with the wife of the Connetable di Colonna, formerly Marie Manzini—the first love of Louis XIV and now Ernst August's great and good friend—would be beset with similar difficulties. But a spontaneous visit was finally contrived. Ernst August's mistress received his wife at a party given while she was recovering from an *accouchement*. Sophie found her sitting up in bed, wearing an odd-looking blue and silver Neapolitan jacket fastened down the front with flame-coloured ribbons, and an unflattering lace cap that only just reached her forehead and failed to cover her ears. She wondered where Mme Colonna's attractions lay, and grew no wiser because it was too noisy for conversation. She just made out from the movement of the lady's lips that she was being addressed as *Altesse Sérénissime*, which pleased her. The only words she actually caught were '*un poco di berlan*', which signalled the start of play and brought the mute interview to its end.

Mme Colonna, when she was mobile again, became Sophie's guide to the churches of Rome. St Peter's, in the process of being embellished by Bernini, greatly impressed her, but the Pope, hurriedly bestowing his blessing from every altar in turn, seemed to her lacking in dignity.

Her supremely reasonable Calvinist soul remained unseduced by the mystical powers of the Catholic Church. At Mme Colonna's instigation, the Pope's chaplain himself tried to achieve her conversion. But, attempting to argue in her own terms, he was hoist on his own petard, and did not convince her that the Catholic faith was the best in the world because the Jesuits, known to be the cleverest people in the world, said so. She replied that men who believed in the miracle of a bleeding wax relic, when anyone knew that it was bound to melt in the heat of the candles, must be gullible regardless of reputation. People who accepted that a black cat, streaking out of a church during an exorcism, was the devil himself would believe anything.

Had she ever felt the desire to change, she said, it would have left her for good in Loretto, where the house of the Holy Virgin was believed to have been brought from Jerusalem by angels. In this holy shrine her look of astonishment had been misinterpreted as the radiance of imminent conversion. The tears that filled her eyes, however, were caused by the fumes from all the oil-lamps and candles that blackened the statue of the

Virgin, sculpted, it was said, by Saint Luke himself. Sophie thought that he could not have been a very distinguished artist, and did not admire the statue with its broken nose rubbed white by rosaries and offerings from supplicants. There was little evidence of the treasure of Loretto, famous and said to be richer than that of Saint-Denis. Noting a man-sized angel of solid silver from the Queen of France and a heart of diamonds from the Queen of England, but not much else, Sophie learned that pieces were periodically sold off. She reported, 'The Virgin is a good manager, and owns fine estates, many mansions, twelve coaches and six, and large numbers of lackeys and other servants. However, she shows no more inclination to leave her modest home now than she did when it was still in Jerusalem.'

Sophie's disgust with the cupidity of the clergy was surpassed by her outrage when a touting priest solicited a donation from her in Santa Maria della Vittoria. This was the church where the Te Deum had been sung by the Pope himself after the Catholic victory at the White Mountain. Captured Palatine colours hung in tatters above the daughter of the defeated King even as she gazed upon the Imperial crown and sceptre that Ferdinand II had sent to the Holy Virgin in gratitude for his signal victory. Sophie took satisfaction in telling her guide that the Virgin Mary, having been on the wrong side, could expect no contribution from her, and was confirmed in her low opinion of the intelligence of priests.

After spending a month in Rome, 'like a young man on his grand tour', Sophie was delighted to hear Ernst August talk of returning home. That she was to travel alone, awaiting him in Venice, while he went to Mme Colonna's villa in the country, pleased her less; but 'Mme Colonna is mistaken when she prints in her memoirs that he left for his visit to her when I arrived in Rome. Her wit may be better than mine, but her memory is worse. He only went after I had gone.'

The Duke and his mistress were obliging enough to accompany Sophie to the Porta Flaminia, driving back alone in one and the same carriage, 'contrary to the custom', while Sophie travelled north.

The Grand Duke of Toscana had arranged for her reception at all his fine palaces. Twelve Rosicrucian knights with candles in their hands helped her out of her litter and into the ducal palace in Siena. His brother, the Prince Cardinal Leopold, did the honours in Florence, and Sophie was so spendidly lodged that she feared she would never feel the same about

Iburg again. Mme von Harling received full descriptions of her bed, hung in cloth of gold in a vast room of gleaming marble, together with urgent requests to have all the Iburg mattresses restuffed without lumps, and the table-napkins washed 'so that they do not stink as they usually do'. And would she please see that the servants looked to their tasks? From the ones that had come to Italy little was to be hoped. They had all forgotten how to wield their brooms, and Sophie only wished she could send them to Holland on a refresher course.

Contemplating the splendours of the Florentine palaces, Sophie was able to quell any stirrings of envy with the reflection that the Grand Duchess of Toscana's married life was less satisfactory than her own. If she regretted that Ernst August 'tired of what he possessed', she accepted that mistresses were a fact of life. The Grand Duke, however, was said to be so terrified of over-excitement that he hardly slept even with his wife. When he did, it was under medical supervision, his doctor taking his temperature immediately both before he entered the Grand Duchess's bed and after the ten minutes or so, carefully timed by the physician, that he spent there before retiring to his own rooms. Sophie would not have thought such hypochondriac behaviour possible, had she not received an enormous, well-filled medicine chest from the Duke as a parting present. She planned to pass it on to her friends at home—'I never take such things'.

Ernst August arrived in Venice a few days after her. The Carnival took its accustomed course, and Sophie, pregnant once more, celebrated it disguised as a noble Venetian lady in enormous furs, which enabled her to walk about in the daytime without being recognised. She enjoyed herself, and gladly agreed with Ernst August's suggestion that she should travel to the Carnival in Milan by post-chaise, dressed in a man's coat and wig. There, while he waited in vain for Mme Colonna, Sophie 'danced the galliard for fourteen days and fourteen nights, until I was so exhausted that I could hardly stand up'.

The return journey over the St Gotthard Pass terrified even her, and she was glad to reach Heidelberg, where her children looked as pretty as ever, and the fruit trees, 'tended by happy peasants', pleased her more than all the orange and lemon groves 'planted by papal sweated labour'.

On arrival in Heidelberg at the end of February 1665 the travellers had been greeted by rumours of Christian Louis' death. These were confirmed in Frankfurt, and caused Ernst August to rush to Hanover by post-chaise in order to look after the interests of George William, still absent. Sophie, following in day-stages, learned that her husband was too late: benefiting from George William's disinclination to leave The Hague, John Frederick had appropriated the Duchy of Lüneburg without waiting for George William, now the eldest Duke, to decide whether he wished to retain Calenburg-Göttingen or take possession of his brother's dominion, as he was entitled to do by his father's will.

Sophie had long wondered how George William managed to maintain himself *en puissant prince* while thinking of nothing but his amusements. She was sharply critical of him for attending on Mlle d'Olbreuse in Holland instead of on Christian Louis on his deathbed, especially as his brother had expressed a wish for a business talk before he had become too occupied with the business of dying.

By the time the dilatory Duke finally arrived, naturally wishing to exchange his own for the richer estates, John Frederick had put men under arms to consolidate his *coup d'état*. Ernst August had raised troops to depose him, and foreign powers began to take an interest in the affair. Sweden regarded the quarrel between the brothers as a popish plot. Brandenburg sided with George William, and there was a real danger that France might come to the aid of John Frederick in spite of representations from the two others.

Sophie was desired to enlist the support of the Elector. Would the Palatine Resident in France, she requested, acquaint the French crown, in the Elector's name, of the justice of George William's case? She doubted that her brother-in-law deserved such kindness, having in the past not responded to requests from Charles Louis as she might have wished. But 'you will be able politely to rub his nose in that,' and surely anything was better than that it should come to fighting. 'It will be like the Palatinate. All those not concerned in the affair will be able to rejoice . . . and the country will be ruined.'

Civil war was avoided by a hair's breadth. In August George William moved Courts, and was henceforth known as the Duke of Celle. He handed over some mining concessions and land to John Frederick, who became the Duke of Hanover and imported Franciscan friars into the town and works of art into the Leine palace. *Le gros duc*, more cultured than his brothers, created an extremely handsome library, and the learned men, whose absence Sophie had so often regretted, at last began to make their appearance in Hanover. Queen Christine's scholarly one-time secretary, M Urban de Chevreau, came between engagements in Copenhagen and Heidelberg, to be followed by Leibniz, who came for good.

Ernst August received the County of Diepholz from his grateful brother George William. 'Not bad,' wrote Sophie to Charles Louis, 'merely for raising a regiment.' She was pleased to be able to say that a detachment of Lüneburgers would shortly be despatched to the Elector by her husband in order to help him in a little war which he was fighting with his neighbours. Not very many, because the Dukes had decided to retain a standing army in case of emergencies. She hoped, however, that the troops would be more welcome than the usual offerings of Pumpernickel, sausages and cheeses from the Harz. Charles Louis, she said, might have given his *fille* to a prince more powerful than Ernst August, but hardly to one more generous, honest and good-natured.

The recent troubles had restored the old intimacy between Ernst August and George William, and the Duke of Celle was a frequent guest at Iburg, where he dangled his nephews on his knee and called them the heirs to all his worldly goods. He was often seen in the company of Mlle de la Mothe, not for purposes of lovemaking but to chat about Eleonore d'Olbreuse, for whom he was so visibly pining that Ernst August asked Sophie to invite her to Iburg, together with her friend Suzanne de la Mansilière. She gladly agreed, hoping that George William's ancient passion for herself would 'pass into oblivion when he was provided with a exciting *passe-temps*', and Mlle de la Mothe set off in a coach and six, carrying Sophie's invitation and presents and proposals from George William, to collect her former colleagues from Holland.

CHAPTER FOUR

Mme d'Osnabrück
(1665–1679)

E LEONORE D'OLBREUSE was a daughter of Alexander II, Marquis de
Desmiers, Seigneur d'Olbreuse, an impoverished Huguenot of the minor
nobility of France. She had been discovered by the Princesse de Tarent,
who, during a visit to Poitiers, had been much struck by the girl's beauty
and by the grace with which she performed regional dances for the
entertainment of her exalted visitors. The Marquis, glad of the opportunity
of launching his daughter into high society, had gladly accepted the
Princess's offer of a post in her household for Eleonore.

Eleonore was a great success at her patroness's Court, and much admired
by the Court of France. But before the great marriage that everyone
confidently expected her to make materialised, the Prince decided to leave
France. Eleonore dutifully, if regretfully, accompanied him and the
Princess to Holland, and continued in her role as special pet. The other
girls in Emélie's entourage did not share their employers' enthusiasm for
Eleonore, but it may have been jealousy that prompted them to gossip
about her, and to describe her as flirtatious, haughty and false.

George William, meeting her at the Court of the Oranges, saw only
beauty and decorum and, as ever, grew more entranced upon being re-
buffed. Of all Eleonore's numerous suitors he was by far the grandest, but
inevitably his reputation had preceded him, and he was known to be
unreliable, irresponsible, and the last man in the world to have honourable
intentions. Eleonore, however, was twenty-five, penniless, and more than
a little attracted by this fascinating older man. She decided to take her
chance, and, disregarding the advice of her friends, accepted the jewels,
proposals and invitation that Mlle de la Mothe delivered.

At Iburg Sophie received her at the top of the stairs, an honour usually reserved for equals but accorded to Eleonore as a compliment to George William. To her pleasant surprise, and contrary to Mlle de la Mothe's warning, the young woman seemed *fort aimable* as she gravely responded to Sophie's words of welcome.

Even when Sophie composed Eleonore's pen-portrait for the Memoirs, long after the original impression had turned sour, her account does not contradict the rhapsodic description of Eleonore by an anonymous author who, by his own account, venerated his heroine. In *L'Aventure Historique*, written 'by order of Mme X'—identified by the historian Koecher as Eleonore herself—the account of 'The Illustrious Clorinde whose Fortune caused such a Stir in the World' matches Eleonore adventure by adventure and feature by feature. Clorinde owned every attribute of beauty, from her figure, 'majestic though supple', to her face and especially her mouth, 'garnished with extremely white teeth'. She personified perfection by being vivacious but capable of gravity, fond of teasing but never giving offence, and impressive in conversation not only by what she said but in the way she said it. 'Tall, slim, pretty and well mannered,' is how Sophie puts it.

In the beginning Eleonore played *la sérieuse*, and she continued to behave with becoming modesty when she accompanied the Osnabrücks to Celle for the State funeral of Christian Louis. George William was so wildly in love that he did not even wait to bury his brother before entering into his *mariage de conscience* with Eleonore. In what Sophie called an 'anti-marriage contract', drawn up by Mlle de la Mothe who 'acted the notary', he solemnly promised lifelong fidelity; in return for 'having resolved to live with him' Eleonore would receive an annual income enabling her to appear *en princesse*. After his death the sum would be tripled, and she would be free to live on either of the two estates made over to her, or abroad if she did not wish to remain in the Empire.

Ernst August, Sophie, George William and Eleonore all signed this agreement, and each signatory was highly satisfied. George William was happy to have gained the woman he loved; Eleonore delightedly described herself as the happiest creature in the world, perfectly content to be 'a wife in the eyes of God'; and since it was the dread of George William's marriage 'in the eyes of man' which had haunted Ernst August and Sophie for all the Duke's promises to the contrary, they too had every reason to be pleased, for the anti-marriage considerably lessened the risk. It is true that Sophie, later, felt that she had been over-generous in complying with this arrangement, but 'what else could I do for a duke who had promised all his earthly possessions to my own children?'

Eleonore, however, laid greater store by the world's opinion than she was prepared to admit, and her public relations campaign (of which both *Clorinde* and a subsequent slim volume were a part) began at once. On the very morning after the union had been consummated '*à la sourdine*', without candles or witnesses, she emerged in tears. (Crocodile tears, thought Sophie, designed further to enslave the besotted George William.) Weeping bitterly, she observed that she was still no more than Mlle d'Olbreuse when she had in fact become Mme de Celle, and nothing would do but that she should be styled accordingly.

This Sophie rightly considered as the thin end of the wedge. Both she and her husband vigorously objected, on the grounds that it would be an insult to Christian Louis' widow if a person of inferior birth bore her name. George William, who had been perfectly prepared to humour his beloved, decided not to quarrel with his relations over so trivial a matter as a name, and Eleonore adopted the title of one of her new estates and became Mme de Harbourg.

In Sophie's letters to her brother she becomes *la dame d'Harbourg* or George William's signora. Sometimes she is even 'our signora', to distinguish her from Charles Louis' Louise, who was always 'la signora' and of course most highly spoken of, so that to refer to Eleonore in this way was cordial in the extreme. But all show of cordiality vanished in the spring of 1666, when Sophie heard rumours that Eleonore was trying to get her connection to George William legalised because she was expecting a baby.

Who, the Elector desired to know, could be responsible for this pregnancy? 'Who but George William?' replied Sophie. No one she knew had ever believed a word of the story that he was incapable of having children.* It had been invented in order to make Ernst August appear more desirable as a husband, at the time when George William's envoy had offered him as his brother's substitute. Lies were told everywhere—the better the Christian, 'the more lies could he cram into a quarter of an hour'. No doubt tales of Eleonore's *agrandissement* were being

---

* In her Memoirs, however, Sophie repeats the story of the Greek whore.

carried to Heidelberg at this very moment in order to incite Charles Louis' humble signora to rebellion. If so, here was the truth: in spite of delusions of grandeur, which prompted Eleonore to offer the hem of her gown to be kissed by her own brother, her entourage was modest. Besides her sister Angélique, a gossipy, disagreeable girl—soon to marry the Prince of Reuss—it comprised the wife of George William's valet and two disreputable maids who slept with all the Court. Sophie had never seen more than one footman and two lackeys. As far as she could say, the only good things in that household were the *cuisine*—owing to the importation of a French chef—and the signora's manners. These were, of course, perfect: beautifully trained by the Princesse de Tarent, she never put a foot wrong with people of quality. Her influence on George William surpassed all expectations, as did the couple's mutual caresses, which were and remained *forts violents*.

In September Eleonore gave birth to a daughter, Sophie Dorothea, and almost died of it. George William looked after her with the assiduity of a trained midwife. Although she emerged from her ordeal 'all skin and bone except for her *embonpoint*', and, according to Sophie, never regained her former beauty, he remained as devoted to her as before.

In December Sophie produced her third son (the survivor of twins, Sophie's second pair—the previous ones had been stillborn in 1664). She called him Maximilian for the Elector of Cologne, and William for the Elector of Brandenburg. By this she celebrated a short-lived alliance between these princes and the House of Brunswick in the face of Louis XIV's expansionist policies. During her pregnancy she had been 'as large as the Round Tower at Heidelberg', and although her bloated face reassumed its normal proportions and her wedding ring again fitted on her finger soon after her confinement, it took her a long time to regain her strength.

Ernst August did not nurse her as his brother had nursed Eleonore, but spent as much time as possible with George William in Celle. Sophie joined him for the Carnival festivities, which necessitated a recuperative visit to Pyrmont in Lent. From there she accompanied him to Glückstadt and a meeting with the Danish Royals. While Ernst August joined the talks that were to result in an alliance against France, Sophie befriended his sister, the Queen of Denmark, and did some useful spadework on behalf of the Electoral Prince Charles, her Palatine nephew.

Nothing but glum reports about this angular, repressed boy had been reaching her ears. Although she always credited her brother with having inherited their father's fondness for his children, she must have been dimly aware that Charles Louis' love was reserved for his progeny by Louise, and that his children by Charlotte were more criticised than doted on. Sophie had long made it her business to speak up for Liselotte and Charles. Would not Liselotte's heart—'always in the right place, a pity that you think her changed'—break at being given an old monster of a stone-deaf governess when she needed young, cheerful people about her? Was it on the Elector's orders that Charles, at seventeen, still had his knuckles rapped with his governor's ruler as though he were a child? And was it not time to think of marriages for both? For Liselotte she again suggested the Prince of Orange, more eligible again since his recent adoption as *enfant de la république* and Stadholder by Messieurs les Etats. Sophie, having already taken soundings at The Hague, would be glad to pursue the matter. Perhaps Charles Louis would prefer the Electoral Prince of Brandenburg? There, too, she could be helpful.

As for the miserable Prince Charles, on whom the Protestant future of the Palatinate rested, he could hardly do better than look to Denmark for a wife. The youngest Danish Princess, Wilhelmine Ernestine, would, in Sophie's opinion, fill the bill admirably. Simply brought up, modest to the point of never opening her mouth, god-fearing in the requisite creed and extremely proper, she appeared to have every quality which Charles Louis required in a daughter-in-law. If the girl's enormous hips and bosom fell short of his exacting standards of feminine perfection, they at least suggested an almost unlimited capacity for producing babies. Telling Lord Craven of this plan, Sophie added, surely rather ominously, 'the sight of the Palatinate may always make her thinner'. Since Sophie was probably equally enthusiastic in describing Charles to the Danish Queen, marriage negotiations began soon after the Glückstadt party had disbanded.

This was only the first of many unsuitable matches in which Sophie had a hand. Match-making—if the making or blocking of marriages that heralded or sealed dynastic alliances can be given such a pedestrian name— was the only field in which princesses like her made direct contributions to the course of history. Unlike Anna Gonzaga, who spent her days plotting, and at night rested her head on pillows made lumpy by bundles of secret documents, Sophie was no true *femme politique*. Her influence was, at best, oblique. She wished occasionally that her husband—and later her son—would listen more attentively to her views and act more frequently in accordance with them; she wished, often, to be able to be of greater service to Charles Louis; but on the whole she was content to leave state affairs to the men.

When it came to the making of matches, however, she displayed great skill in sounding out Courts, winning allies in the shape of ladies-in-waiting and ministers of state, and putting forward propositions with such diplomacy that, should anyone demur, no face was lost on either side. Unsentimentally, like any *honnête homme*—the *beau idéal* of the Age of Reason not famous for kindness or compassion, which she embodied more than many of her male contemporaries—she largely ignored the feelings of the principals. These generally knew better than to spoil the arrangements by idle displays of excessive sensibility, and meekly reinforced Sophie's frequently mistaken notion of the delight with which they viewed their prospective partners.

When Charles and Wilhelmine Ernestine met informally, according to Sophie's plan, she happily reported that it was love at first sight, although both young people were quite silent, apparently struck dumb by their mutual disappointment. Each was plainer than the other had expected. Wilhelmine Ernestine was as white as advertised but more billowing even than her portrait, which had been no more than mildly admired in Heidelberg. Charles was as tall as promised, perhaps even taller, but still bright red and pitted after an attack of smallpox. However, no marriage in which Sophie had a hand was ever allowed to be less than a love-match. If tears were shed—and there is no record of any on this occasion—they were firmly described as tears of joy. Possible signs of emotional turmoil were ignored. What Sophie expected was a high degree of self-control, such as she herself was to have ample opportunity of exercising in her married life.

Much as he admired his brother, Ernst August was far from emulating him in his new character as a faithful husband. He still needed his love affairs, and had lately been paying court to Suzanne de la Mansilière. She was pretty and well-mannered like all the Princesse de Tarent's trainees, but unlike most of them she was also religious, and suffered tortures from fear of falling into sin.

Whores Sophie had learned to take in her reluctant stride. La Mansilière, however, with her virtue and her piety, was so respectable that Ernst

August might come to love her, and have less regard—and less *bonté*—for his wife. She was a definite threat. Having lived through Charles Louis' affair with Louise in Heidelberg, Sophie could hardly help being aware of the possible consequences. Benefiting from Charlotte's mistakes, she treated la Mansilière as kindly as possible. She took no notice of the girl's regular evening walks in the Duke's company on the terrace, and also pretended to be unaware of her distress, displayed in dramatic fainting fits, after which she went about her duties with red eyes. Poor la Mansilière, hoping that promenades in full view of the Court would demonstrate the innocence of her friendship with the Duke, found that they had the opposite effect. She wept more than ever, and handed Sophie her notice in order to save her honour. But her sensitive conscience did not allow her to depart without baring her heart. She appeared in the bedroom where Sophie was lying in after the birth of her daughter Sophie Charlotte in October 1668, apologised in tears for having caused grief, sobbingly protested innocence and devotion to Sophie, and dissolved on the floor while Sophie delivered a kindly-meant harangue about Caesar's wife, weakness and regrettably incorrect behaviour. 'I kissed her several times to show that I had nothing against her. I gave her two bracelets to prove my affection, but the greater my expressions of friendship the more she blamed herself,' says Sophie, who was disgusted by the gulps that turned into screams. Finally, she was horrified to see the girl lying apparently senseless but still screaming on the floor, and there was nothing to be done but to jump out of bed and call for people to carry the hysterical creature away.

La Mansilière's departure was not the end of the affair. Rumour—of course—said she had gone into hiding to have a baby, which was 'the greatest lie in the world', said Sophie, blaming Eleonore for this particular piece of gossip. To disprove the rumours she sent la Mansilière her portrait *en miniature*, and started up a correspondence with the girl, 'with whom I was united through the sympathy of loving the same man'. When the Duke did the same, Sophie pretended not to notice. But when he suggested a year or so later that she might be re-employed, adding that Sophie 'was well aware of her virtue', she refused to think of it. Indeed, although later she was to joke about it, this was the only one of her husband's affairs over which she admitted grieving. Mlle de la Mansilière's soul might be beautiful, she said, but her physical presence was too inconvenient; and Ernst August was forced to find a new *amourette*.

Clara von Meisenbug caught his eye when her father brought her home from France, where she and her younger sister Maria had disappointingly failed to make their fortune. Their Paris clothes and the elegant new way in which they dressed their hair in bunches of curls over their ears made these pink-and-white girls the toast of Hanover, Celle and Osnabrück. They were clever and rapacious, and knew exactly on which side their Pumpernickel was buttered. Ernst August decided that Westphalian ham with French dressing was just the dish to console him for la Mansilière, and Clara responded in the proper spirit. Since the only manner in which unmarried girls could live at Court was as maids-of-honour, and the endless jokes about *filles d'honneur* and their *déshonneur* survive to demonstrate the inconvenience of this arrangement, Ernst August arranged her marriage to the Freiherr von Platen. A man of low birth but high ambition, Platen was very handsomely rewarded for being a *mari complaisant*, and was to rise to greater heights than his talents would have immediately suggested. Maria von Meisenbug also eventually found two husbands as well as illustrious lovers at Court, but since she married first and slept with princes afterwards, her career was less meteoric than her sister's.

Ernst August's choice suited his wife as well as it suited himself. When Sophie spoke of Clara she was occasionally acid and only rarely bitter, and that in private. Clara, in due course, rose from *amourette* to the kind of *maîtresse en titre* who was mentioned in the despatches of foreign envoys. Vienna learned, a decade hence, that she governed the Duke entirely, and the French ambassador wrote home that she had '*beaucoup de pouvoir sur l'esprit de ce prince*', while Sophie herself was described as having '*aucun crédit sur l'esprit de son mari*'. The English envoy described her as 'out of humour' with her husband's infidelities', but 'well beaten to such usage', and a contemporary *roman à clef* correctly suggests that she was far too sensible to risk antagonising her husband by any show of jealousy.

This is not to say that she did not suffer whenever Clara, politically more astute than she, made her influence felt in affairs of state in a way that seemed, to Sophie, detrimental to her younger sons. She once complained bitterly at having her name mentioned in the same breath as 'that woman', but on the whole she shared her sons' jokes about *cette Venus* and her well-known charms, especially when Clara's looks coarsened and she herself remained handsome and elegant.

If Ernst August's extra-marital affairs left her relatively unmoved as long as there were no scenes, those of her brother-in-law John Frederick, the Duke of Hanover, gave cause for concern. He had for so long been talking about taking a wife that Sophie had good reason to hope he would die a bachelor. However, in 1668 he acquired a duchess: Sophie's niece Benedicta, the eldest daughter of Edward and Anna Gonzaga.

Sophie rather supported the idea at first: Edward, dead these five years, had left the task of marrying off his daughters to Anna, whose task was eased by an understanding with her sister, the childless Queen of Poland: the Queen's personal fortune would go to Anna's girls, and the elective crown of Poland would if possible be shuffled in the direction of one or other of their husbands.

John Frederick had announced himself as a candidate for the Polish throne—recently abdicated by Anna's brother-in-law—at one of the regular formal conferences at which the House of Brunswick-Lüneburg settled its affairs. Sophie, who attended when her own Duke was otherwise engaged, heard the conference agree to this plan, with the proviso that John Frederick's eventual heirs would thereupon renounce the succession to Hanover. Since her children stood to gain by this arrangement, it seemed an excellent scheme to her, and she applauded John Frederick's approach to Anna Gonzaga, who liked to be thought of as the power behind the Polish throne.

Yes, said Anna, it might be arranged, but '*il faut commencer avec le mariage*' between John Frederick and Benedicta. This duly took place, but failed to bring with it the Polish throne. (Anna Gonzaga was to have no better luck with another son-in-law, the Prince de Condé, who was so confident of his chances that he had the arms of Poland prematurely engraved on his table silver and painted on his carriage doors.)

Since the crown of Poland had gone elsewhere even before Benedicta had arrived from France, it was clear to the disappointed Sophie that the fat Duke and his bride were in Hanover to stay. Not that she disliked her niece, even if the girl could only talk of her pet dogs and her sisters. Like most daughters of gallant mothers, Benedicta had been strictly brought up in a convent and was a model of virtue. She was an incongruous Duchess for the Duke, who was not only about three times as old but certainly more than three times as large, and looked to Sophie 'like a woman about to give birth, God forbid'. Mercifully, Benedicta was as yet showing no sign of becoming pregnant—nothing was less welcome to Sophie than the thought of a Hanoverian heir, especially as she was once again about to increase her own family.

She gave birth to Prince Charles Philip in 1669, after a visit to Heidelberg with Ernst August, who had been asked to act for his sister the Queen of Denmark in the proposed Danish marriage. Typically, Charles Louis insisted on so many advantages for his son—chiefly financial—that almost a year had passed before Wilhelmine Ernestine finally set out from Denmark and the Prince Palatine could nervously look forward to losing his virginity.

Sophie, imminently expecting yet a further baby, accompanied Ernst August and George William to Altona to receive the Danish Princess from her mother, and promised to conduct her to Heidelberg. George William, planning to make the most of this occasion, desired to present Eleonore to Her Majesty of Denmark. At first the Queen refused to see her, but, in view of the irregular household which her daughter was about to join, changed her mind. Eleonore received a royal dinner but no royal kiss, and revenged herself by complaining about the food. Sophie, whose dislike of her had increased on hearing that she too was pregnant again, thought that to pine for fricassées showed baseness of character: 'the gods of this world eat to live—not the other way about,' like some she could mention, whose cooks drew higher salaries than their senior ministers.

The enormous Danish wedding cortège, consisting of over four hundred people and five hundred horses, set off for Hanover, where John Frederick had all the streets illuminated to fine effect, and revealed that he too was an expectant father. Naturally, he and Benedicta were hoping for a son, as was Eleonore, who again informed all who wished to listen that in this event George William would legalise his attachment to her.

As the procession took to the road once more Sophie was almost too preoccupied to mind, too hot, too uncomfortable and shaken about by the motion of the carriage which she shared with the Danish Princess, who, according to her habit, hardly opened her mouth. In Hesse-Cassel she felt so ill that she could only with difficulty respond to Charlotte's civilities, and Wilhelmine Ernestine, vast and silent, did nothing to help. The Electress, meeting her future daughter-in-law for the first time, took immediate offence, and blamed Sophie for causing coldness.

Sophie was beyond caring. To sit in her coach was agony, and she placed herself in a litter, instructing her bearers, the Duke's Italian musicians, to avoid the crowds lining the official route. Her detour brought her within range of the Cassel cannons, and when they were fired in honour of the departing Princess cannon-balls fell to the right and left of Sophie, causing her frightened Italians to break into an uncomfortable trot. Sophie was badly shaken up, but suffered no harm. She safely reached the Palatine border where a message from the Elector begging the party to delay their entrance to Heidelberg as his preparations were behind schedule was the last straw. Sophie knew that she could wait no longer. She organised sedan chairs, mobilised Frau von Harling and the midwife she had brought along, and hurried on.

Charles Louis was pleased to see her. She looked well. The heat had given her a high colour, and Charles Louis thought nothing of keeping her standing while he chatted for an hour or so. Respect for the Elector prevented her from complaining. She managed to excuse herself from supping with him, but as he sat by her bed for a couple of hours' conversation after his meal she longed for her midwife's company instead of her brother's. In the morning, when he sent to ask at what time she would be ready to receive Wilhelmine Ernestine, he learned with surprise that she was otherwise engaged, having just been delivered of a prince, whom she called Christian after the bride's brother, the King of Denmark.

She had been hoping for another daughter, while Eleonore and Benedicta, both praying for sons, produced little girls. Eleonore's died at once, and the birth of Benedicta's caused John Frederick such disappointment that he had all the French fireworks, with which he meant to celebrate the birth of an heir, packed up again for use another time. (Sophie hoped that he would have to wait as long for the event as the Jews for the Messiah.)

Poor Prince Charles, whose wedding was celebrated for almost a week —the speeches alone, in Latin and German, in rhyme and in prose, took days on end—begged Ernst August to instruct him 'in matters which he did not understand'. Sophie judged that he was an inept pupil, as Wilhelmine Ernestine never became pregnant at all, and there was later some doubt whether the marriage had been properly consummated. But by the time the celebrations were over Ernst August was no longer at hand with good advice. He had gone on to Venice, while Sophie remained with her brother and helped him to decide Liselotte's fate.

France's interest in the Palatine had not diminished. Having annexed part of the Spanish Netherlands, Louis XIV was again preparing to do battle with the United Provinces of Holland. A friendly Palatinate would be extremely helpful in this design. And more efficacious than French money or French bribes—all Charles Louis' senior officials were by now the owners of elegant French watches, gifts from hopeful French envoys—would be a close family connection between France and the Palatinate.

Louis XIV's sister-in-law Minette—whose brother, Charles II of England, had already promised to support France in the forthcoming struggle—had recently died, and the widowed Philippe d'Orléans was once again free to be used for the *gloire* of France. That Philippe, called Monsieur, had little use for women—not even for Anna Gonzaga, said to have seduced him once, though she remained his confidante and friend—was a matter of no significance. It was Anna herself who made it her business to secure a friendly Palatinate for Mazarin, and a new wife for Monsieur.

She wrote to Charles Louis offering to make Liselotte the new Madame, very properly saying nothing of the allegation that Minette had died by poison—some thought at the hands of Monsieur himself, others at those of his favourite courtiers, whom he much preferred to his wife. Instead, Anna dwelt at length on the advantages which Charles Louis would enjoy from a close relationship with France, and on the fact that any decision regarding his daughter's dowry would be left to himself; and if the only French stipulation was that Liselotte should be received into the Catholic church—well, it would be a pity if the whole design were to founder on such a bagatelle.

It was, of course, a dazzling offer, and too good to be missed. The Elector's idea of having Liselotte secretly instructed so that he himself might remain uninvolved for reasons of state seemed a brilliant solution to the entire family, with the exception of Liselotte herself. It was left to Sophie to persuade her to be a dutiful daughter, a fact which later elicited the only criticism of her aunt that Liselotte ever uttered. 'I don't know why you're complaining,' she wrote in reply to Sophie's regrets that a relation had apostasised. 'You're no mean Papist-maker yourself.'

Urban de Chevreau, now Charles Louis' new resident thinker and secretary, was bidden to prepare Liselotte for her conversion and, only four weeks after Sophie had brought one princess into the Palatinate, she accompanied another one out of it. With Charles Louis she took Liselotte to Strasbourg and handed her over to Anna Gonzaga, who was to witness her reception into the Catholic Church before delivering her into the bosom of her new family.

Before Liselotte set off for Châlons, where the Royal Court of France was assembling to receive her, she sent a stilted epistle to her father. Only fear of displeasing him, she wrote according to the instructions he had given her, had prevented her from informing him of her religious change, and she hoped that he would find it in his heart to forgive her. Charles Louis replied that he could only marvel that a daughter, brought up to love only truth and honesty, could be so deceitful; but since his paternal feelings were unchangeable, he would continued to wish her well. It was odious, hypocritical behaviour, but Sophie observed her brother's brimming eyes when Liselotte, convulsed by sobs, had been carried away, and gave him full marks for tenderness. She always stoutly maintained that he had acted for the best, even though the French connection was to ruin his country and his life, bringing happiness to no one.

The couple were quite remarkably incompatible. 'How am I supposed to sleep with that?' the horrified Monsieur is supposed to have enquired at the sight of his great hoyden of a wife, who was bursting out of an unsuitable sky-blue silk garment in the middle of November. The late Madame had at least been elegant, which had made the business of fathering two daughters, if arduous, not impossible. But this? Only by gritting his teeth and passing his holy medals over his vital regions did he, in time, manage to father three further children, of whom a son and a daughter were to survive the perils of royal infancy.

Ernst August, in Venice, was longing to know how Liselotte's wedding night had passed. Had the bride pleased her husband as Sophie had delighted him? Not that she did not delight him still, he hastened to add; he only mentioned the first night *à cause de la nouveauté*. Nothing could alter the power that she had over him, and would continue to have, *jusqu'à la mort*. But although the felicity of his life depended on proving his love for her, now he must fly: the opera was beginning. She would have all other news from the pen of Mme von Platen, who, together with her husband, formed part of his retinue. He only had time to thank her profoundly for giving him leave to make love to such Venetian blondes as might come his way, for, regardless of Mme von Platen, he was as susceptible as ever.

In the spring of 1672, when the Duke returned from Italy, France was massing men and guns in preparation for the invasion of the Dutch Netherlands. French diplomacy and French money had secured for Louis XIV the alliance of various German princes, among them the Bishops of Münster and Cologne—Sophie's 'mitred warriors'. John Frederick, too, signed a treaty with France. French agents were doing their best to persuade George William and Ernst August to do the same, and while the bargaining was in progress Ernst August thought it prudent to move his Court from Iburg to Osnabrück, which was garrisoned and could be more easily defended.

The Bishop's Palace of Osnabrück, begun when trouble had threatened a few years earlier, was nearing completion. Like the Palais de Luxembourg in Paris, it was constructed on the pattern of the Villa Madama in Rome, and promised to become pleasingly grand. Sophie, settling down to embroider acres of furniture coverings in tapestry stitch, wished that the painters would hurry and be done, instead of making the garlands that swathed her ceilings and walls even thicker and more floral than the designs she had originally approved. She was appalled that a few extra flowers should take so long and, moreover, raise the price. Would it not be much simpler just to have everything gilded, and send the Italian stuccoists home?

For the gardens Martin Charbonnier, pupil of the great Le Nôtre, came from France. He laid out a marvel of geometry, like his master's scheme at Versailles on a smaller scale. Together with him Sophie pored over plans and drawings, and took pleasure in visualising sheets of water, *parterres* and *avenues à perte de vue*. She was glad to see that Lord Craven's old orange trees, transported from Heidelberg, did well in their square tubs, but the shrubs that she had imported from Italy, where the cool and shady gardens had pleased her more than anything else, died on the journey. Even Dr Tachen, at present engaged in a series of experiments 'to grow things from seed, even minerals', failed to put new life into them.

The doctor was enjoying few triumphs these days, although Sophie gave him full marks for his readiness to admit, unlike his *confrères*, that he had no idea what was ailing his patients. Certainly he could do nothing for her husband. The strain of raising troops and levies, organising the defence of Osnabrück and attending family conferences to decide the House's attitude in the war had made him ill. He was coughing and wheezing, and his headaches never seemed to leave him. Even a few days' hunting at Diepholz did not improve his condition, although Sophie was glad to get away from the smell of plaster and turpentine that hung about the palace. The holiday must have restored the invalid's humour a little, for a letter from Sophie to Mme von Harling suggests that he regained some of his old spirit. 'Our Duke wants to become a farmer, and means to buy a little croft near Osnabrück. He plans to wield the plough himself, I am to lead the horse, and you are to milk the cows. We shan't need anyone else. So please ask around and find out how much we should have to spend; we want to drive over soon to look at our corn.'

These rural delights never materialised. Ernst August would hardly have had the leisure to enjoy such an idyll, and besides, there was his wretched health, which worried Sophie even more than it worried him. If he died her boys' future would be quite uncertain. No one was sure what George William and his Duchess were up to even while Ernst August was alive, and Sophie shuddered to think what would happen if he died. So it was with her whole-hearted approval that he set out to consult Dr von Cranenberg in Clèves.

This was a quack who once saved the life of the infant Electoral prince of Brandenburg after the professional doctors of that Court had given him up for dead. The great Elector had gratefully ennobled him and settled him in Clèves, a Brandenburg possession, where he built up a flourishing practice. Illustrious invalids from all over Europe flocked to be cured of their ills and usually returned home the better for their visit, since their faith in the 'Aesculapius of Clèves' was boundless. His methods were practical rather than miraculous: all the overweight princes were instantly put on to stringent diets, and any man not renowned for chastity was subject to a cure for syphilis whether or not that disease was diagnosed. Cranenberg, who also ran a free clinic for the poor, never made any extravagant claims. This did not deter M von der Bussche, governor to Sophie's eldest boys, from seeking a cure for his blind eye, or Mme von Harling for her catalogue of ailments, though neither did so successfully. Nor were there any spectacular improvements in Ernst August, but perhaps that was because he would not stick to the prescribed starvation regimen.

Sophie's own health was excellent. She attributed this fortunate state of affairs to her 'finest heritage from my mother, the late Queen'.

But in spite of her frequent congratulations to her brother the Elector for his own share in the legacy of the Queen of Bohemia's good health, Dr Tachen's long-distance services were often enrolled on his behalf. None of the powders and drops that travelled to Heidelberg, however, relieved the Elector's recurrent fevers, eye-troubles, gout and haemorrhoids. Sophie felt sure he must be exaggerating, but at fifty-five he described himself as bordering on senility and often wondered if he would live to see fifty-six.

Charles Louis' ailments tended to flare up whenever his affairs went badly, and since Louis XIV's Dutch war had begun they had gone from bad to worse. The Elector viewed the French successes of the early campaigns with a jaundiced eye, and taking Palatine neutrality, which had been stipulated in Liselotte's marriage contract, more literally than Louis XIV had intended, refused to allow the orderly French investment of strategic points in the Palatinate. By doing so he drew the army of his cousin, the great Turenne, into his country, and, like all soldiers obliged to live off the land, the French ruined Charles Louis' vintages and crops and held his subjects to ransom. 'I shan't incommode you further with my troubles,' he closed a letter to Liselotte. 'The dust raised by Turenne . . . is making my eyes smart.' When the French finally moved away—not before Charles Louis had personally challenged Turenne to a duel, 'having no army to do my fighting for me' (a challenge that was not accepted)—they were followed by Imperial troops, sent by Leopold to drive the French from the Rhine. Charles Louis wrote to Sophie that for practical purposes it made no difference whether his country was gobbled up by friend or foe. He was glad that Ernst August and George William were at last declaring against France, but the Brunswick detachment on its way to the Palatine in order to stem a new influx of the enemy would, he feared, be too little, too late, and too indisciplined to do much good even if it ever arrived.

Sophie deeply sympathised with her brother, but allowed no criticism of the Brunswick soldiers. She granted that their commander was not all that might be wished, especially as he had gambled away the money entrusted to him to pay for his men's quarters, but he was brave and popular. No wonder, said Charles Louis when the troops finally arrived, since they were permitted to do exactly as they liked, but he agreed that they were '*les plus beaux du monde*'.

In May 1675, when French troops had reached Trèves in the Rhineland, George William and Ernst August themselves rode out to fight them at the head of an army even more beautiful and brave. George William employed rather more French officers than Sophie thought compatible with the objective of the campaign, but then, his household was almost exclusively French. (The French envoy once remarked to the Duke, over dinner in Celle, '*Tiens*, this is very cosy. Your Highness seems to be the only foreigner here.')

Ernst August's army was wholly admirable, and he himself was the very picture of martial elegance, even though the sash of gold filigree that Sophie had ordered from Holland as a going-to-war present never arrived. The citizens of Osnabrück were so keen to fight for their Duke that any man able to put one foot before the other had marched away. Except for the militia, the very old and the very young, there was hardly a man left in the city.

To his sorrow George Louis, at fifteen, was considered too young to go campaigning. Soldiering was his passion; as a tiny child, wearing the gilt breastplate and helmet that Sophie had bought him on one of her jaunts, he had drilled troops of Court children. As a schoolboy he had steamed over his Latin and Greek because the boy who did best at the weekly examination was allowed to fire the cannon at Iburg as a reward. Now he was in despair at missing the excitement, and his disappointment was sad to observe. Always reserved to the point of sulkiness, he ceased to utter, eat or sleep, and only cheered up when Ernst August promised that he would be sent for in six weeks' time. Sophie's feelings were torn between pleasure at knowing her eldest to be safe at home, and misery at seeing him so morose. She half-wished that the Elector was right when he said that Ernst August had no intention of keeping his word. Meanwhile, she took good care not to tell her son that his Palatine cousin Carllutz had been given a captaincy and was *fort glorieux* in a swashbuckling sort of way, although he would have preferred more gold braid and more colourful facings than Charles Louis and Louise would countenance. In the end Ernst August was true to his promise. Sophie, reminding the Almighty of his well-known practice of extending special care to drunkards and children—with special reference to the latter—hoped for the best as her son departed to face the enemy.

Since Turenne's death, of which his brother had informed Sophie in a letter accurately addressing her as '*cousine*', which she had hesitated to accept because of the familiarity, the French Rhine army had been placed under the command of the Maréchal de Crequi. It was over this Marshal that the Brunswickers achieved a great victory at Conz-Saarbrücken in August.

'You have reason to be proud of your Benjamin,' wrote Ernst August after this engagement. 'He never stirred from my side although the musket-balls were raining about our heads. He is a son worthy of his mother.' Every soldier from the highest to the lowest had acquitted himself well. Ernst August's casualities were light, far lighter than George Williams', and the best news of all was that Marshal de Crequi himself had been taken prisoner. All his baggage, guns and ammunition were captured, together with quantities of French colours and standards. The relief of Trèves was now in sight, and with it perhaps the end of the war.

The happy news had to be shared. '*Victori, victori, victori,*' wrote Sophie to Charles Louis, who, rightly, was less optimistic of the battle's effect on the war. Eleonore, too, received a letter from Sophie's hand. With righteous indignation the Memoirs say, 'I told her all I knew, and observed that my Duke's men had done well, but those from Celle not so well, which was the reason why so many of them had been wounded.'

She was amazed when Eleonore took this to mean that she was attributing the glory exclusively to Ernst August, 'just because I had not mentioned her Duke, when it was up to her to send me his news!' She deduced from Eleonore's reply, which contained several *choses bien piquantes*, that Mme de Harbourg was about to make trouble. To anticipate her, she sent Eleonore's letter straight on to George William and grudgingly accepted the subsequent apology, composed at his command. She did not trouble to answer it. 'What is the point of writing to people who misconstrue what is said to them?'

Louis XIV considered the Brunswicks' victory a blow—not as heavy, perhaps, as the Dukes and their ladies hoped, but a blow nonetheless. 'What is particularly galling,' he said, 'is that we have been so shamefully beaten by people who know nothing except how to play *bassette*.' (Neither Eleonore nor her fifty-one-year-old Duke would have been pleased to hear the King, fifteen years younger, refer to George William as 'the young Duke of Celle, who has been extraordinarily fortunate'.)

When the Dukes returned home after the relief of Trèves, the festivities at Osnabrück outshone even the celebrations after the battle at Conz-Saarbrücken. Fountains flowed with wine and beer, the streets were filled with music and the sound of bells, and bonfires blazed on the ramparts where Sophie and her ladies had lately scanned the horizon for couriers bringing news from the battle.

While the conquering heroes made their entrance to the town through the huge triumphal arch—a happy concept of M Jemme, the children's French dancing master, who had also arranged a ballet to mark the occasion—M de Crequi escaped from captivity. This was thought extremely ungentlemanly, as he had promised in writing to remain where he was. He was still to inflict much suffering on the Empire until the war finally ended in 1679; nevertheless, the Emperor was highly pleased with his brave Brunswick Dukes. He sent a handwritten letter to George Louis which, Sophie feared, was probably all that he would do for *la maison*, gratitude being virtually unknown in the House of Austria. But George Louis was basking in the glow of Imperial graciousness, and seemed to Sophie much improved since he had gone campaigning. She found that her son could be quite entertaining when he chose, and although she took with a pinch of salt a panegyric by Spanheim, who had been at the front, she was clearly proud of him. She was always to think of him as one of the great soldiers of his age—a view not entirely shared by contemporary military men or by future historians.

Owing to her relations' signal victory over troops whom the French liked to regard as invincible, Liselotte had become something of a celebrity at Louis XIV's Court. The King had gallantly congratulated her, and she responded by weaving their names into her conversation, reading Sophie's letters in public, and boring her audience with endless references to *ma tante* of Osnabrück. It was therefore with particular pleasure that the courtiers pounced on a truly astonishing bit of gossip from Germany, which Liselotte denied for all she was worth even before receiving Sophie's reply to her anxious enquiries. Could it be true, she asked, that George William had elevated Eleonore so far above her station that she was now a reigning Duchess? All France was talking about it, and it was thought especially amusing as this lady had allegedly once been spurned in marriage by the Prince de Tarent's chief valet, who had since joined Monsieur's household.

This last piece of intelligence was news to Sophie, but the rest was, alas, all too true. After the children's ballet, as George William hurried away to be reunited with Eleonore in Celle, he had casually remarked that he was now going to celebrate his marriage to her in a final, legal, ceremony. Ernst August hardly liked to believe his ears, although he should have known better in view of so many broken promises and Eleonore's unceasing labours for promotion and recognition.

She had scored some remarkable successes, even before this latest triumph. Her first informal marriage, which Sophie and Ernst August had witnessed, had been followed by a more binding morganatic one. She had been created a Countess of the Empire, as had her daughter Sophie Dorothea, and had been admitted to the Empress's own Order of Slaves of Female Virtue. But neither this honour, nor the girl's Imperial status, nor indeed her naturalisation by the King of France soon after her birth, had effectively made Sophie Dorothea any less illegitimate: she would still bring a bar sinister to the escutcheon of any family into which she married.

It was this fact which caused Duke Anton Ulrich of Brunswick Wolfenbüttel, a member of the senior though less important branch of the Brunswick-Lüneburg dynasty, to concern himself in Celle's private affairs. This Duke was a man of many talents. His novel, *The Roman Octavia*, which Liselotte said was as long as the Bible only not so well written, was appearing in instalments; his collection of works of art was so constantly augmented that he built gallery after gallery to house it. An ambitious man, he had long envied the grandeur of his cousins in the junior line. To share in their *gloire*, he was anxious to marry his eldest son to Sophie Dorothea, who had handsome expectations on her mother's death—only her birth would first have to be made respectable.

Together with Eleonore and the Celle Chancellor Schütz, whom Sophie detested as the greatest rogue and troublemaker in the world, Anton Ulrich had persuaded George William to apply to the Imperial Courts for his daughter's legitimisation. After vast sums of bribe-money— half of which even Anton Ulrich suspected to be lining Schütz's own pockets—had been sent to Vienna, the patent arrived, and now the only anomaly was that the legitimate Princess Sophie Dorothea of Celle owned parents who were, strictly speaking, not married.

Clearly, this had to be remedied. In spite of objections from Osnabrück, the church-bells of Celle pealed for Eleonore's marriage, and her name was

Ernst August of Brunswick-Lüneburg by David van der Plaes.

George William of Brunswick-Lüneburg, anon, 17th century.

added to the list of gracious sovereigns in the prayerbook. Eleonore had fitted herself for her new station by having an elaborate family tree drawn up in Paris, which linked her with the royal blood of Hugh Capet, first king of France. (Sophie said if to invent such illustrious relationships weren't so expensive—Eleonore was known to have spent thousands— she would be tempted to have one done for her chambermaid.) On the day the marriage was made public, Anton Ulrich announced his son's engagement to the Princess of Celle, and a few days afterwards came the announcement that Eleonore was pregnant again.

Typical of Eleonore, thought Sophie, to have kept her condition secret so that Anton Ulrich might think he was acquiring a sole heiress for his son. But her heart was far from bleeding for this Duke, who had un-accountably asked her to join him in propagating the fiction that Sophie Dorothea had been legitimate all along. Sophie told him that she was not in the habit of telling lies, and moreover the thing defied all reason: why go to all that trouble and expense if the first marriage contract could conceivably be made to stand up?

The fact that Eleonore was expecting a new baby was a great worry to Sophie and Ernst August, since it would be indisputably legitimate and might be male. George William brushed away all Sophie's gloomy warnings about warring cousins and the ruin of the whole country in the following generation. He blithely assured her that he was a man of his word, who would personally guarantee the claims of *le népotisme*. He agreed to more and more cast-iron safeguards which Ernst August worked out with his councillors, but which Schütz took good care never to have promulgated. Until they were, said Osnabrück, Eleonore's new title could not be recognised. (The original objection to addressing her as Mme de Celle no longer applied, for Christian Louis' widow had meanwhile remarried and become Electress of Brandenburg.) George William agreed to defer official recognition until all Ernst August's conditions had been met, but enraged Sophie, when she complained that the Empress had styled Eleonore 'duchess' in a letter, by mildly replying that he was in no position to countermand what he had not ordered in the first place. So weak, thought Sophie, and was only half-appeased when the Empress explained that a mistake had been made in her chancellery.

Three months after he had become Sophie Dorothea's fiancé the young Duke of Wolfenbüttel died on the battlefield, and Sophie reported to her

E

brother in Heidelberg a suggestion which had ostensibly come from the government of Celle and which Ernst August had passed on to her. If George Louis, her eldest son, were to marry Sophie Dorothea, the problem would be solved; succession, country and family would be secure. What did the Elector think? For herself, Sophie wished for nothing less than this marriage, and Ernst August appeared to agree with her. Would not the kinship be intolerable? She was envisaging a pleasant, modest daughter-in-law, perhaps one of John Frederick's growing nursery of daughters, not a girl who was ill-bred and already apparently well on the way to becoming a *coquette*.

Sophie Dorothea, a well-developed twelve-year-old, had inherited her mother's looks but none of Eleonore's deceptively modest airs: she lacked her mother's cool and calculating gaze—Sophie Dorothea's eyes were bold. On one of Sophie's last visits to Celle they had been demurely lowered over a lace-border that she was working on to a handkerchief for the visitor—but even then scandal had not been far away. Already her pocket was bulging with love-letters, of which one, duly discovered, was presented to the horrified George William. 'The Fräulein Sophie is now made to sleep in her parents' bedroom,' wrote Sophie to Charles Louis, for although Celle tried hard to hush up the affair, it soon became common knowledge. Sophie, who had never heard of quite so youthful an indiscretion, did not blame George William for doing what he could to conserve his daughter's virtue. (Indeed, the girl must have been under strict surveillance, for Count Königsmarck, who was in Celle as a boy—and was later to cause her ruin—spoke of the impossibility of approaching her.) But both Sophie and her brother laughed when George William actually announced the beginning of his daughter's monthly cycle, and felt that this must be an attempt to publicise her marriageable condition.

The proposed match between the Brunswick cousins was sporadically discussed by George William and Ernst August over the next few years, but Celle was also exploring other possibilities. Since Eleonore's legitimate baby, another girl, had followed the long line of her little sisters into what Sophie piously called a better world, and Sophie Dorothea's prospects remained undiminished, there was no lack of suitors. Anton Ulrich, having spent too much money on her legitimisation to give up easily, proposed his second son. But Eleonore thought she could do better, and boastfully announced that another cousin, Prince George of Denmark, brother of

Wilhelmine Ernestine, had offered for her daughter's hand. The Queen of Denmark had written that this was, of course, perfectly untrue. She could only marvel at the gullibility of those who believed it when they read of it in the Gazette, and Sophie suspected that Celle had supplied this news-item to attract further offers, 'like people who advertise articles for sale by making them sound more desirable than they are'.

George Louis hardly cared one way or the other. He viewed his seduc-tive little cousin of Celle without enthusiasm, but, having been brought up to put duty before inclination, would, said Sophie, 'marry a cripple if it were to benefit *la maison*'. He was, however, less cold-blooded than his mother thought: his virginity had long since gone to a chambermaid in Hanover. Although Sophie had at first refused to believe it, she had been assured by the Dukes that boys will be boys; later, when her sons enter-tained the Court with their comical account of an unfortunate maid-of-honour's wedding night, having witnessed every cut and thrust from behind the curtains until their giggles had given them away, she laughed as hard as anyone. But when, at her own Court, it came to the expanding belly of Anne, under-governess to her daughter Sophie Charlotte, Sophie was not amused. 'No, it was not Ahasuerus's sceptre that touched the wretched Esther,' she wrote to her brother. Ernst August 'is no longer of an age to *encanailler* himself in this way'. Such *viande* was reserved for younger *gourmands* and, like George Louis, Esther-Anne had admitted all, 'wondering only how it was possible to get into trouble in a single night'. Since she also admitted to a fiancé in the wars the baby's paternity was doubtful, but George Louis was in deep disgrace. However, when the Elector pleaded on his nephew's behalf, Sophie replied, 'The Duke has already forgiven my son, and given him permission to sleep with anyone he likes, as long as no one ever comes to hear of it. You see, he means to make him into a discreet lover.' The bore was that her daughter now required a new, accomplished, virtuous governess with good French; could the Elector help?

Charles Louis, as always, shared in his sister's worries. But on this occasion her troubles paled into insignificance beside the events in his own life, since Louise von Degenfeld, for whom he had recently revived the ancient title of 'Raugravine', had died as uncomplainingly as she had lived, in March 1677. She left the inconsolable Elector with three daughters, the Raugravines Caroline, Louise and Amalie Elisabeth, called Ameliese, and six Raugraves, all of whose first names were Charles.

Charles Louis could hardly see his writing-paper for tears when he told Sophie of his bereavement, and the strange document in which he surveyed his life with Louise is dictated to his secretary, except for some small autograph additions.

In it he listed all the qualities that comforted him, not least her recognition 'that I was doing my utmost for her, and more than she was worth', and the fact that he had at once forgiven her when she had admitted any fault and said that she was sorry.

The column of 'what grieved me' lists her occasional dissatisfaction with her condition; coolness during the first years; some disobedience; jealousy without cause; babies who did not survive, including the fourteenth who died in the womb two days before the mother, and particularly the death of a two-year-old daughter, on account of which Charles Louis had almost murdered the nurse.

Under 'consolation after her death' comes 'that I did not spare care, trouble, physical and spiritual medicine', and the fact that Louise was now spared from seeing misfortune befall Charles Louis and her children in these hard times.

What would grieve him forever was that he had not known she was dying—she was only thirty-nine—and that when he had realised the seriousness of her condition he had not comforted her as much as he might have for fear of frightening her. Finally, that her death prevented her from perceiving his grief, and that she would never know all he planned to do for the children whom she had recommended into Sophie's protection when she died. She had dreaded what the future might hold for her innocent *pucelles*, although the electoral Prince Charles had faithfully sworn on her deathbed that he would look after his stepsisters. This promise had not materially contributed to the Raugravine's peace of mind, for Prince Charles was becoming very odd, and there was always his disappointing wife to be reckoned with.

Wilhelmine Ernestine had not lived up to Sophie's high hopes. The marriage had not taken, there were no babies, and she so prided herself on her piety that she had made it a point of honour to show Louise that she regarded her as a sinner. She had, Charles Louis was certain, hastened the Raugravine's death through her unyielding unkindness. She had always stared at Louise in such a blank, peculiar way—'like a cow at a new gate'—

had never called, never invited the children to the meals that she preferred to take in her private apartments, surrounded by her own household that largely consisted of religious advisers, and never even sent to ask after Louise in her final illness. It was no use Sophie's saying that it was only shyness: it was bigotry coupled with arrogance. Moreover, for all that her husband disliked her, she was having a disastrous effect on him.

Wilhelmine Ernestine was, perhaps, excessively devout—but Charles was rapidly developing religious mania. He not only spent unreasonable hours at his devotions, but also sank to his knees for extemporary prayers in the middle of other activities. It was quite impossible to conduct a conversation with him. As soon as the Elector touched on political or family affairs he would reply in monosyllables or excuse himself altogether, saying that he did not understand anything about such things.

Where had the Elector failed, to have produced so unsatisfactory a son, so sadly different from his spirited, attractive Raugraves? Liselotte, too, was proving a disappointment. What was the use of her friendship with the *très Chrétien*, if she could not turn it to advantage for the Palatinate? Charles Louis was still being dunned for enormous sums by France, who had lately sent over an army of officials to examine 'the wills of dead and long-forgotten Palatine great-aunts' with the object of reviving ancient territorial claims as part of France's Reunion policy. Their behaviour was intolerably impertinent. Something should be done, but Liselotte's sole object in life seemed to be to amuse the King, if only by a *pétard*, and although she had once broached the matter she had not pursued it when he said '*Je verrai*', which everyone knew meant 'no'. The situation appeared hopeless, and although the long war seemed finally to be coming to an end, the prospect for the Palatinate was dark.

In November 1677 the marriage between Louis XIV's most implacable enemy William of Orange, son of the late Princess Royal, and Princess Mary, eldest daughter of James Duke of York and Anne Hyde, drove a wedge between France and England. Charles II's neutrality, an important factor in Louis' design, could no longer be counted upon. 'Will the Prince bring us peace?' hopefully asked Sophie, but Charles Louis thought that even if it did 'its ligaments will be no stronger than the Princess's maidenhead, and as easily broken'. Delegates from all the warring nations travelled to Nijmegen to discuss terms by which hostilities might be ended.

Holland and Spain made peace with France in 1678, and the Empire followed suit in 1679. In accordance with Charles Louis' gloomy forecast, Louis XIV emerged stronger than before. Nevertheless, Sophie's letter to her brother, written when the news of the final signature on the instrument of peace reached her, was dated '*ce jour fameux, ce jour pompeux*', and in it she expressed the hope that there would be no more fighting as long as she lived.

Thoughtful politicians regarded the peace as no more than a truce, but there was of course much personal rejoicing all over Europe, and no one was more delighted than Liselotte, who could at last put a long-cherished plan into effect.

For the past few years she had unceasingly tried to arrange a meeting with her beloved aunt. Dutifully, she had written that her joy would be complete if she could also see papa, uncle and brother, but it was for *tante* that she pined. She had been particularly enraged by George William's unsuitable marraige, because it undermined all her efforts to convince Monsieur that the pure-blooded lineage of her German relations entitled them to grander treatment than that which he had in mind. She had never succeeded in obtaining his agreement to armchairs all round, and it would, she knew, be the greatest wrong to each and every German prince to expect Sophie to sit on a lowly tabouret while a mere Bourbon like Monsieur was enthroned in a *fauteuil*. So her plan had foundered. Nor had anything come of various projects for secret meetings. But now Sophie's visit—incognito—could at last become reality. It was timed to coincide with the marriage of Liselotte's stepdaughter to the King of Spain, which was to seal the peace between that monarch and Louis XIV, and Sophie would be able to see the Court at its elegant and festive best.

'I am no longer of an age to go and see the *faschions*,' wrote Sophie to Charles Louis, complaining of the dreadful expense involved in her journey. But she was to love what she saw. In her first letter from France she writes, 'Another historian might describe the journey, but I am quite overwhelmed by the here and now, and all that has gone before went clean out of my head'.

She was travelling as Mme d'Osnabrück, accompanied by a small party that included her daughter Sophie Charlotte—'my Infanta'—and Mme von Harling. The Abbey of Maubuisson was the travellers' official destination. Arriving there in the dust-covered clothes that she had worn throughout her long journey, Sophie found not only the Abbess, her sister Louise Hollandine, but also Monsieur, Liselotte and their daughter, the future Queen of Spain, to greet her. She descended from her coach in some confusion; neither 'our venerable Abbesse' nor Liselotte would, she was sure, notice her crumpled appearance, but Monsieur was a different matter, *la propreté* being one of his passions. There he stood, beaming welcome, in his great lion-wig, satin bows and high-heeled little shoes, looking much like a performing poodle, while Liselotte came bounding up and leapt at her like an over-excited sheep-dog puppy. Tears of joy were streaming down her cheeks, and Sophie thought she would cling to her for ever. But there was Mme von Harling to hug, and Sophie Charlotte to admire, so that Sophie had an opportunity to catch her breath and salute her sister, Monsieur and his daughter.

Monsieur lost no time in planning Sophie's timetable. Tomorrow she must inspect his daughter's trousseau and wedding presents. As long as she wore a black sash as a sign of her incognito, she could feel free to go any-where and need have no hesitation in entering the Palais Royal where everything was on display in the gallery. Monsieur truly loved finery, and it was sad that Liselotte did not share this interest. She never dressed up if she could possibly help it, and wore her riding habit from morning to night. 'It suits her better than other clothes,' wrote Sophie to Charles Louis, reporting that his daughter looked fat and happy, as well she might, being 'the most fortunate woman in the world,' and her Monsieur was 'the best prince in the world and looks exactly what he is', which may have been a reference to the perversion for which he was famous.

In Paris Monsieur modelled his daughter's trousseau for Sophie, and very kindly became her own fashion adviser. He took infinite trouble in choosing stuffs for her wedding *toilette*, advised on the cut of her sleeves and the shape of her coiffure, and even personally chose the *mouches* for her face and engaged a make-up artist. Sophie had long since dropped any nonsense of rising above such bagatelles. She took an intelligent interest in Mademoiselle's jewels, not informing Monsieur, as she did her brother, that 'the diamonds were fine, the emeralds, sapphires and rubies so-so, and the topazes, set with small diamonds, pretty but not very valuable'. The beauty of the pearls, however, made up for all that, and she was sincere in her admiration. Monsieur, with his talent for such things, took the trouble of redesigning all her own jewels in modern settings, and she repaid the compliment by exclaiming about his wedding-coat, newly studded with diamonds poinçons, and helping him to arrange a ribbon on his hat.

He had yet another jewelled treat in store for her, when he led her into the presence of the Queen of France. Squat, short-necked little Maria Teresa looked, Sophie thought, less hideous from nearby; but when Monsieur all but ignored the civilities, took hold of the candelabra to let the light play over the stones that adorned the Queen and invited Sophie to tour around her, this seemed to carry an incognito visit too far: the pleasure of seeing her Majesty, she said, prevented her from concentrating on anything else. The Queen smiled, exposing teeth as dark brown as the chocolate that her female dwarf was forever preparing for her. She modestly indicated her diamonds with her white little hand, saying, 'This is what you must look at—not that', vaguely motioning towards her face. But Sophie knew how to behave, and began singing the praises of the French Court. Although the Queen still clung to the traditions of her childhood, and had never lost her thick accent, Sophie said she was sure Her Majesty had found no difficulty in getting used to French customs. 'It was easy,' the Queen replied, 'I am so happy here.' Then she said, twice, 'The King loves me so much, I am so grateful to him.' Sophie, who, together with the rest of Europe, had taken a lively interest in all the royal mistresses and their successful royal pregnancies, from Mlle de la Vallière onwards, answered, 'as was *comme il faut*, that this was not surprising,' and listened politely when the Queen told her how many children she had borne.

The Dauphin, sole survivor of the royal babies, turned out to be fair, fat and dull. Of marriageable age, and single, he was the reason for Sophie Charlotte's journey. 'Figuelotte'—as her mother called her—was a vivacious, pretty eleven-year-old. At the age of eight, in a pastoral ballet before the Queen of Denmark, she had sung '*à présent je suis bergère, je puis être reine un jour*', and the assembled company, especially Mme von Harling, had all agreed that this might well be so. But while her mother and Liselotte were planning her royal future, she thought only of the guinea-pigs* and tortoises she had left at home, and did not in the least worry about the lack of effect that she had on the Dauphin.

---

* Sophie said of these pets that nothing could be more suitable for a Westphalian princess: everything connected with pigs contributed to the country's wealth.

Liselotte's stepdaughter, on the other hand, who was about to become Queen of Spain, was perfectly miserable at having failed to move his sluggish heart. When the King had informed her of the advantageous match he had arranged, he had found her cooler than he had expected. 'I could not have done more for my own daughter,' he said, to raise her enthusiasm. She replied with feeling, 'Sire, you might have for your niece.' But the Dauphin's total indifference to her forthcoming marriage helped her to accept her fate, and Figuelotte's company cheered her up. In fact she fell in love with Figuelotte completely, and told Sophie that she only wished to be a man so as to be able to marry her. Anything, it seemed to Sophie, would have pleased her better than to marry the ailing Spanish monarch with his dreadful protruding Habsburg lip. But when the bride, moodily fingering the charmingly worked medallion that held his unattractive portrait, observed that he looked like an ugly monkey, Sophie kindly said that it was clearly the painter who was at fault, not the subject. Privately she thought of the girl as a lamb to be sacrificed on the altar of peace between France and Spain. This was formally signed at the same time as the marriage contract, and directly afterwards the party moved on to the royal chapel. There Sophie noticed Mme de Montespan, the mother of four of the King's living children (who were being secretly brought up by the future Mme de Maintenon), fat and dressed *en négligée* instead of proper Court dress, with an embroidered coiffe and a black sash to indicate official non-presence.

Mlle de Fontanges, however, whose star was in the ascendant, was as advantageously dressed as might be expected of a lady who gave her name to a head-dress copied by all the world. Considering her advanced state of pregnancy, she could not have been comfortable in her stays, and had with unusual solicitude been placed near an exit in case she was overcome by the heat and the smell.* The King's eyes, Sophie noticed, rested on her rather than on the altar, and she, too, was casting loving glances in his direction. 'Assuredly, she loves him more than the King of Kings,' said Sophie, 'and it is hardly surprising, as he is the most charming of men.'

To Liselotte's joy, the King was much taken with Sophie and was particularly gracious to her. He was highly complimentary about the Dukes' exploits at Trèves, and she replied that she was glad these times were now in the past, having seen him confirm the peace of Nijmegen by

* Her baby, by the King, died soon after its birth, and so did she.

signing the Spanish marriage contract, which contained a clause promising
the end of French activity in the Spanish Netherlands. He reminded her of
a further clause stipulating that the peace would last only as long as it was
compatible with the well-being of France. She hoped that it would be so
for a long time to come, and he replied that he did not believe any German
Prince would ever make war on him again. She curtsied and the conversation was over, but not forgotten. The King was frequently to refer to
Liselotte's clever aunt, whom he remembered less for the wit of her
repartee than the adroitness of her address. 'Ah,' he was to say when,
years later, Benedicta made a *faux pas* in his presence, 'give me the *other*
Duchess of Hanover; now there was a truly intelligent woman.'

Following Sophie's royal interview there were plays, fireworks and
dances. Sophie congratulated herself on being suitably attired for the
magnificent Court ball, where cloth of gold studded with precious stones
reflected the light of several thousand candles. If some of the ladies seemed
modestly dressed, their husbands made up for it by the number of
diamonds that flashed on their coats.

Nothing could have astonished Sophie more than to see her niece take
the floor with her husband. When she observed that other husbands and
wives, and brothers and sisters, were dancing together, she thought that a
new golden era had dawned, until she realised that pride, not love, was the
reason: no one would be seen dead partnering anyone of inferior rank.
The King, she thought, looked embarrassed as he danced with his Queen,
who was not graceful at the best of times and was now encumbered by a
dress so heavy that she could scarcely waddle.

Sophie only just avoided sullying her lips on the hem of this garment,
which the Queen on retiring held out, helpfully, for her to kiss. Sophie
dealt with this predicament by bowing so deeply and lowering her head so
humbly that she might have been thought not to have noticed the ploy.

This was to cause amusement at St Cloud, Monsieur's country palace,
where Liselotte's six-year-old son the Duc de Chartres—later to become
the rakish Regent—expressed his fellow feeling. He, too, had devised a
method by which he avoided the royal hem, for which, he said, he never
felt the least appetite. 'You don't imagine that I kiss her dress,' he explained.
'Oh no, I only kiss my own hand.' Sophie was very taken with him and
with his younger sister, another Liselotte, and as much a tomboy as her
mother had been.

Knowing how much of the old Liselotte there still was in Madame, Sophie was surprised at her niece's patience as she drove with her to St Cloud at a pace that even Sophie considered excessively sedate. If her Dukes at home prided themselves on providing speedy transport for guests, and even supplied fresh horses at every convenient posting station, she did not see why the French royals did not do the same. Could Liselotte's coachman be persuaded to go faster? It appeared he could not. Since the contents of Monsieur's stable would in case of sudden death become the property of his *écuyer*, the coachmen did their best to spare the animals the least fatigue, lest the value of the legacy decreased.

Accidents, however, were commonplace, and even as Sophie drove up at St Cloud carriages and cherished horses came to grief in the forecourt. No bones were broken, but Monsieur sent for chamber-pots in case of shock. Another French habit, Sophie supposed, seeing that the French-women who had travelled with her gratefully availed themselves of the proffered comfort. German bladders, she was glad to say, were stronger.

St Cloud pleased her in every respect, owing to Monsieur's talent for interior decoration and his faultless taste in pictures and bibelots. The gilt, the looking-glasses and crystal chandeliers, the silver furniture and silken walls combined to make his house the grandest and most comfortable Sophie had ever seen. She told Charles Louis that Monsieur, conducting her over Liselotte's apartments, which were as admirable as his own, had paused, pointedly, before some of the most valuable items, and remarked on the splendour in which he housed his wife, of whose *dot* there had so far been no sign. Sophie marvelled at Liselotte's *bonheur*. She herself always counted comfortable lodgings and good service among the greatest blessings in life. Her room at St Cloud led straight out into the garden. The layout and the renowned water-display pleased her even better than those at Versailles, 'where the fountains could play only at a day's notice after the water pressure had been especially raised,' and where 'money rather than nature had produced the greatest marvels'.

Sophie returned to Paris when the new Queen of Spain left for Madrid among the traditional *hurlement*. Sophie herself could not help crying, and only the dull Dauphin remained dry-eyed. What an unfeeling son-in-law he would have made.

Figuelotte accompanied her mother to Maubuisson for a final stay, where she had a lovely time riding on one donkey with two other little girls over the gardens and orchards, while Sophie enjoyed her sister's company. Louise Hollandine ran a trim convent. (The story of the Abbess who swore by the heads of her bastards, spat on her chessboard and threw her men on the floor, and was so eccentric as to raise a chamberpot to her face, saying, 'this mask stinks and has no eyes'—often told about Louise Hollandine—belongs to another, earlier Abbess of Maubuisson.) Any time Sophie's sister could spare from her duties she spent in painting and walking in her beautiful gardens. It was a simple, wholesome life,* and one to which Sophie now thought she might easily adjust, especially after the whirl of Paris, 'had God not given me other responsibilities'.

Sophie's homeward journey was filled with disappointment. The King's parting gift of pearls—flat—and diamonds—flawed—had been too wretched to please (Monsieur was so ashamed of them that he had them exchanged for worthier gems). Charles Louis was too ill to keep a rendez-vous with his sister in Weinheim; she had longed to see him and his *pucelles*, but they did not appear either. At Osnabrück Ernst August was still wheezing and coughing, and preparing to go to Italy, where he had great hopes of the climate. The worst news of all came from Herford, where her sister Elizabeth, described as dropsical, seemed to be beyond human help.

After Ernst August had left for Venice together with John Frederick, Sophie set off for Herford with deep reluctance. It was, she knew, her duty to go; Elizabeth was asking for her. She dreaded her visit. Let others mortify the flesh as the preachers advised; she always avoided it if she possibly could. She did not care to think of death, and hated to hear it spoken of, since 'to speak of the devil was to conjure him up'. 'Like David,' she told Charles Louis, 'I prefer to serve the Lord in joy.'

Not that the devil entered into the picture where Elizabeth was con-cerned. She had become wise with age and grown almost humble. She had done a great deal of good in the neighbourhood, although her championship of obscure religious orders, like the *Labadistes*, a Protestant sect whom she housed, caused raised eyebrows. But visiting Quakers,

---

* The days when Louise Hollandine had given elegant parties as well as keeping a stable of thoroughbreds were over, since the French authorities had frowned on such worldliness. The nuns of Maubuisson now had to provide their own entertainment and were fortunate in having a dancing-mistress in Liselotte, whose version of the energetic coranto led to broken bones among the older sisters but did not deter them from regarding her as a saint.

from William Penn to Robert Barclay, sang her praises. Her ladies loved her, and everyone admired her frugal, well-ordered existence, her clear intellect, her learning and her philosophy, which Sophie, too, had reason to admire.

Now a skeleton except for her monstrously swollen abdomen, she had already ordered her coffin and made arrangements for her funeral. She had seen to such details as ordering her table silver to be packed up as soon as the breath left her body, and sent to her benefactor the Elector of Brandenburg. Her household was instructed to eat off her English pewter before dispersing, and meanwhile Elizabeth made jokes about dying, and talked of her painful swellings—Sophie was made to touch them to see how hard and horrible they were—in terms of pregnancy after sixty virginal years. Charles Louis dreaded what the *médisants* would make of that, and wished she wouldn't.

Together with the other surviving Winter children, he did what he could to help her. He sent his own physician from Heidelberg, together with crates of bottled spa-water. These, he said, had cured him of a similar disease, but should they fail he warmly recommended the efficacious *eaux de Tonbridge*.

Rupert, now Constable of Windsor Castle, sent drops and a promise of superior ones which he would make with his own hands in the laboratory that he had fitted out in the Round Tower. (These were not his great invention, Prince Rupert's Drops, slender, long-tailed glass drops which shatter when even the tips of the tails are broken, but medicine which he hoped would ease his sister's agony.)

Sophie arranged for music to alleviate Elizabeth's suffering and help her to bear her ladies' grief while Elizabeth occupied herself with codicils to her will. Sophie was to have some of her jewels, including the two pearl bracelets, each with four table-diamonds, which had been a gift from the Queen of Bohemia, and all the family portraits except for Edward's, which she left to his daughter Benedicta. 'They'll only end up with the servants otherwise,' wrote Sophie to Charles Louis regarding these pictures —mostly by Honthorst and Louise Hollandine—and explained that the rest of Elizabeth's estate would have to go to the Elector of Brandenburg, who had enabled her to settle in Herford in the first place. There would be small legacies to her ladies and her friends, but as there were hardly any debts Sophie assured Charles Louis that he would have much less trouble with Elizabeth's will than with the Queen of Bohemia's, which still infuriated him whenever he thought about it. Charles Louis quite understood that Brandenburg had to be the principal heir—which was just as well, as that Elector sent troops to Herford with orders to seize Elizabeth's estate as soon as she was dead. Charles Louis asked only for a small painting by one of the Limbourgs—famous for their magical, minutely observed scenes for the Duc de Berry's *Book of Hours*—and a little profile of himself by Honthorst. For the rest he was content to have nothing, always provided that nobody would ever claim anything from him.

As the weeks passed, Elizabeth's bones threatened to pierce her skin. Her face became entirely dominated by the nose that had always been one of her mortifications, but she was still quite lucid and seemed to draw strength from the conversation of Helmont. This old family friend and philosopher, who had lately become a Quaker, sat by Elizabeth's bed in his brown coat, with his hat upon his head, and called her 'thou'. He was working on his theory of metempsychosis at the time and, to Sophie's mystification, Elizabeth was comforted by the thought of the previous and future transference of her soul. What earthly good was it, wondered Sophie, to have been Caesar or Alexander in some previous life, if one had no recollection of it? Or what harm if, in a future existence, one's soul inhabited the body of an animal? For herself, she could only think of her loved ones and herself in their familiar shapes—but she agreed it was a blessing that Helmont was able to help Elizabeth.

While death was hovering in Herford, a messenger arrived to tell Sophie that John Frederick had been found dead in his bed by his valet in Augsburg, where he was awaiting his health certificate before continuing to Venice. '*La fin couronne l'oeuvre,*' she wrote on the outside of the letter that she had been about to post off to Heidelberg, and announced the news. By the next mail she had been able to take stock of her reaction. Why should she have turned ashen and been overcome by consternation, briefly, when the death of the Duke, '*gros et gras* and in apparently perfect health', gave her every reason to thank God for securing the future of her children? She was able to reassure her brother that it had not been from grief, but from the realisation that 'what has happened to my poor niece might also have happened to me'. The fate of her family, unprovided for and dependent on George William's goodwill, was too terrible to contemplate. As it was, she had every reason for being delighted.

The news brought Sophie's visit to Herford to an end. Elizabeth, half-way over the threshold of death, shared her sister's pleasure in the un-expected turn of events and said goodbye forever, begging her to carry her legacy away with her to save packing and posting later.

Ernst August's first words, when he arrived home a few days later than Sophie, were, 'I'm glad it's not me that's dead'. The excitement of his new dignity had such a tonic effect on Sophie's spirits that they were not markedly dampened when, a few weeks later, Elizabeth's life was peace-fully extinguished. (The leaden platter which she had caused to be placed on her stomach to mitigate the effect of a possible explosion had happily turned out to be an unnecessary precaution.)

All the Winter children agreed that Elizabeth's death was a blessed release. Charles Louis cancelled the French comedians whom he had engaged for the Carnival, but not the Italian musicians, because their celestial harmonies might at any moment be required to aid his own passage into the next world, 'in imitation of John Frederick who, God forgive him, was too fond of his ease in this one, thus precipitating his death'.

Congratulating his sister on her good fortune in his New Year's letter of 1680, Charles Louis fondly wished that each New Year might bring her a new duchy. 'God looks after his own while they sleep,' he wrote. 'While Ernst August goes to Venice for diversion, he has the pleasure of succeed-ing to a large and beautiful country. It is to be hoped that this will make up for missing a game of *berlan* or a performance at the opera.'

Sophie was happy to report that John Frederick's affairs were in splendid order. All that Ernst August had to do was to take possession: there were no useless persons on the payroll, and John Frederick had employed none but very honest men. Otto Grote, head of the Council, Bodewils, Lieutenant General of the Militia, and the Abbé Molano, for the clergy, all came to pay their respects as soon as they heard of their old master's death, and all were assured that they would remain in office. The greatest acquisition of all, not least from Sophie's personal point of view, was John Frederick's librarian.

Gottfried Wilhelm von Leibniz, whom the late Duke used to refer to as 'my walking dictionary', was a universal genius. At the age of twenty-one he had turned down a professorship, and had worked on his mathematical, historical, political, religious and philosophical theories in the service of various princes. His love of Court life as opposed to that of academic institutions prevented him from ever writing his *magnum opus*, and his embroidered coats and coffee-coloured coach painted with flowers, mostly roses, were ludicrously showy for a sage. But he was, in the words of Liselotte, 'that rare being, a learned man who knew how to behave and did not stink', and Sophie found great pleasure in his company and conversation.

She did not always read his books, in which he took trouble to present complicated arguments with simplicity 'so that they might be popularly read', but both she and Figuelotte, who when she was grown up would have had no trouble in understanding him had he expressed himself only in symbols and formulae, provided him with the intellectual stimuli that he needed.

No bachelor, it was said of him, ever valued women more highly. He laid the greatest store of all by princesses, because they had more leisure than their princes for taking an interest in the affairs of the mind, and were ideally placed to persuade their husbands that flourishing arts and sciences, directed by Leibniz, were an essential part of their *gloire*.

None of Sophie's gentlemen was ever fully to appreciate 'M le Philosophe'. Ernst August, who made him his historiographer, was pleased enough with his services, but George Louis, on inheriting him from his father almost twenty years later, still awaited the finished family history, and bad-temperedly complained at the slowness of progress. *Théodicée*—dedicated to Figuelotte—and the Differential Calculus were all very well, but what he wanted was the History of the Guelphs. But Sophie remained for Leibniz 'the oasis in the intellectual desert of Hanover', and it is through her friendship with him that she became known as 'the learned Electress'.

CHAPTER FIVE

Duchess of Hanover
(1680–1693)

LEIBNIZ CELEBRATED SOPHIE'S elevation in a very long poem. In questionable verse, but in the good French that he habitually wrote—even when urging his literary compatriots to rescue their language from becoming a mere local dialect—he said that the entire land was awaiting the *sentences divines* of the new Duchess of Hanover. Heroes, he said, needed heroines to appreciate them; with her help, Ernst August would be a noble successor to 'the demi-god' John Frederick, as would be, in time, *les jeunes aiglons*, the boys.

After her initial excitement, Sophie appraised her new status coolly. 'All beginnings,' she said, 'are *incommodes*.' There were a thousand *douleurs* for each *plaisir*. Ernst August was overwhelmed by business which, although his health was still worrying, he handled as to the manner born. From his new position of strength he recognised George William's marriage, though less from magnanimity than because of a strong suggestion from William of Orange. He now called Eleonore 'Duchess', but this title caused Sophie's pen to falter for some time to come. She referred to her sister-in-law as the sweet Duchess, the gentle, charming, delightful Duchess, and sometimes the Duchess Eleonore, but not for a long time to come as the Duchess of Celle.

All coolness between the two brothers melted away, particularly since the question of their children's marriage seemed to have been shelved. 'Who needs a bride now,' said Sophie delightedly, 'especially that one?'

Her views on her children's upbringing underwent a change. Formerly she had thought it downright cruel to send them abroad: they might acquire an appetite for elegance and culture that could never be gratified in their land of ham and sausage, where the state of the porkers was the only topic of conversation. Now the outlook was grander, and George Louis was sent to France on an educational trip. He had firm instructions to pay his court to all that was noble, and especially the ladies: it was hoped that polite society would render him less boorish at home.

The rest of the family moved to Hanover in March 1680. After the comforts of Osnabrück, Sophie had difficulty in settling into her 'princely *palatio*' on the Leine, so cold that fires were needed in every room in spite of the warm spring weather. But '*pour quelque chose malheur est bon*': the smoke which filled the rooms enabled her to shed without trouble the tears that decency demanded for John Frederick's demise.

However, the discomfort of the rooms, crowded with visitors come to offer their condolences, and the stairs, 'too narrow for two chickens to pass each other—one has to wait for a quarter of an hour for the jammed traffic to clear', were fit only for her husband's mediaeval ancestors. John Frederick had principally concentrated on improving the facilities for worship and on collecting art treasures for his chapel, which had an altar-piece by Lucas Cranach. He had done all too little about the amenities of the '*palais du bois*', where Sophie fancied that she saw spectres of bygone dukes, their hunting nets spread over the table in the dark panelled hall, passing the wooden goblet of *Broihahn*—the local beer, still brewed—content as long as they had a stout pair of boots and a dinner of salt cod.

The vision appalled her. For the time being she lodged her sons in the apartments vacated by the departing Catholic clergy, and a great pro-gramme of clearing began. John Frederick's library, housed in apartments hung with tapestries and paintings—his collection included Poussin's Apollo—was the first to go. To Leibniz's grief the books were bundled up and stored in a neighbouring house that happened to be vacant, and the rooms were remodelled on baroque lines. The rest of the palace was slow to lose its old dark Renaissance character, and Sophie, bitterly regretting her *boiseries* and medallioned ceilings, longed for Osnabrück, which had been filled with light and air. She sometimes wished, as did Ernst August, that John Frederick were still alive. But these were fleeting sentiments, and the new Duke of Hanover's gratitude for his predecessor's departure was expressed in the pomp of the funeral arrangements.

'If he could see all that was being done for him,' said Sophie of the ceremonies, 'he would think them splendid even in Paradise.' Although everyone worked as fast as possible, it took more than a month to prepare the catafalque, but all was ready when the widowed Benedicta returned from France, where she had gone for a visit during what was to have been her husband's long Italian holiday.

John Frederick's two funeral services took place in May. After the Protestant one, Ernst August delivered his brother's body in solemn procession to the Capuchins so that, led by five Catholic bishops, they might '*assaisonner* him after their fashion', before committing him to the golden vault under the choir which he himself had built for the purpose during his reign. It was all very magnificent, and Sophie sent a book of engravings illustrating the ritual to Heidelberg 'to amuse the young Raugraves when they have been good'. After the interment she gave a dinner to the 'five mitres who assisted the Capuchins in their final performance'—she called it *la comédie*—and turned her mind to other things.

Benedicta, 'our little dowager', was the only person sincerely to mourn the Duke. She wept from morning to night—so odd, thought Charles Louis, for a Frenchwoman. Ernst August treated her kindly, allowing her to take away all her furniture, although he need not have done so, and promising to look after her girls.

Charles Louis wondered whether Sophie could not find her a new husband, 'one with a stomach less inconvenient than that of the precedessor? It would be less expensive in the long run and could in no way affect the succession.' Sophie regretted only that Benedicta was Charles Louis' niece. She would make him an ideal wife, but alas, neither Imperial nor Papal dispensation for such a match could be hoped for.

She urged her brother to look for a bride elsewhere. Not that Charles Louis actually wanted to marry: he had grave doubts whether his strength, which still kept him on his feet and, haemorrhoids permitting, in the saddle, was equal to the conjugal bed. But it was true, the Palatinate needed heirs, and these Prince Charles was unwilling or unable—probably both, thought the Elector—to provide. This hypochondriac Prince had now developed a positive phobia for his wife, and convinced himself that physical contact would lead to nameless diseases. Nothing, Charles Louis explained to Sophie, would persuade him otherwise; and her helpful suggestions of trickery were useless; women might, perhaps, make babies in their sleep, but Charles Louis had never heard of a man accomplishing this feat without being wide awake and aware of what he was about. It had to be faced, his son's *cul* was as useless as his head, and if the Protestant succession was to be secured he himself would have to take the appropriate steps.

But what was to be done about Charlotte? She was steadfastly refusing the formal divorce for which he had consistently asked her from the moment Louise had died. Meanwhile, his treatment of her had become the scandal of Europe: for years he had refused to pay out a penny for her maintenance, claiming that since it had been she who had broken the marriage contract there was no reason why he, as the injured party, should adhere to it.

It was a point on which even Sophie was unsympathetic and critical of her brother. She said that Mme Colonna, Ernst August's old friend, who had run away from her husband and was leading a life of scandal, had behaved much worse than Charlotte without being left to starve by her husband. Besides, Charlotte was no longer a coquette but a byword in piety. 'At her age, she'd hardly have the opportunity to be anything else,' said Charles Louis: virtue did not enter into it. As far as he was concerned the subject was closed. He sent back an Imperial demand for arrears of maintenance, saying he knew no such person as the Electress Palatine to whom it referred.

Sophie told him that Liselotte was beginning to receive offers of help on her mother's behalf from virtual strangers, since it was known that she had no fortune. He reluctantly sent part of his daughter's *dot*—not yet settled in spite of Sophie's earlier hints—in order not to appear a complete miser, but not a penny to Charlotte. Outraged, he enquired why Liselotte should sympathise with Charlotte, who had been lacking in maternal feeling even during pregnancy, and had threatened to give birth to 'vipers and adders' instead of his beloved children, whom she had then abandoned, so that he had been both father and mother? Far from criticising him, even by implication, she ought to stand up for him and ease his lot. Charlotte, having taken to religion, should in any case be as anxious as he was for Protestant Palatine heirs, because without them the Papist Neuburg branch of the family would inherit the country and catholicise it again at once.

There was, however, another possibility. Might brother Rupert, always so fond of propagating the gospel by the sword, be persuaded to propagate it by other means and return to marry and settle down? Sophie was given the task of sounding him out, and began by sending him a boat-load of Hanoverian deer for Windsor Great Park. They travelled amazingly well, with only three casualties among them, and greatly contributed to the sport of Charles II's Court. But Rupert remembered his oath: he had finished with the Palatinate for ever. Besides, he had no wish to leave his morganatic wife, the actress Margaret Hughes, his daughter Ruperta or his laboratories, where he was experimenting with mezzotints* and perfecting a type of brass called Prince's metal after him.

Charles Louis was not surprised. He had not really believed that any-thing would come of the plan, and was convinced that his luck, such as it was, had run out. Sophie's heart bled. She wished that she might cheer her brother, as in the old days, when she would *bouffonner* to make him laugh and sing to make him forget his sorrows, but her voice was no longer true, and his misery too great. She wondered how Liselotte could bring herself even to look at her idol Louis XIV when he was harassing the life out of her father by allowing his men in the Palatinate to behave so insufferably. In accordance with Louis XIV's reunion policy any former connection with France, however slight, was enough for his troops to occupy places in the Palatine—five villages on one day, the town of Germersheim on another, the province of Selz next. Louvois, the French Minister of War, went so far as to issue orders causing Palatine peasants, forced to abjure the Elector under pain of being driven from their farms, to build French fortifications on Palatine soil. The Elector's protests were being ignored as usual. Sophie herself complained to the French envoy to Hanover on her brother's account, but was told that the King could not be aware of all that Louvois was doing, and in any case no longer paid attention to Charles Louis' protests because he was such an incessant moaner.

Short of providing him with an army to drive out the French, said Charles Louis, there was little that Sophie could do for him, unless she could send him two of John Frederick's *castrati*? They might help him fleetingly to forget that the *Très Chrétien*—more the Grand Turc, really—intended to govern all Europe according to his own arbitrary ideas, and treated princes like himself as his *porteurs des sabots*, expecting them to scratch at his door humbly to petition for what was theirs by right.

Sophie duly despatched the singers, with grave misgivings as to their quality. Nothing from Hanover not entirely made of Pumpernickel was

---

* The Prince had introduced into England what Evelyn calls 'this new way of graving'.

likely to be much good. They proved acceptable, but Sophie began to take good care never to read her brother's letters last thing at night—they were too upsetting. She had trouble enough in sleeping as it was. Her head was once more becoming stupid from lack of exercise, and the *sale maison*, where progress was slow, added to her depression.

So that she should be able to get her nose into the fresh air without the business of setting out in coaches, Ernst August promised to pull down about forty ramshackle houses that faced her apartment and throw a bridge across to an island in the Leine. But it would take so long and be so expensive, especially since the Duke meant to rebuild all the houses elsewhere, that she felt she was likely to be dead before this plan was accomplished.

She was therefore very glad to receive an invitation from the Queen of Denmark to Nyköpping. At least there would be some air and exercise. Before she set off on this trip—during which she impressed everyone, and not least herself, by killing a rabbit with the first shot she had ever fired from any gun—Charles Louis wished her joy, a long life and good health. He mentioned that he had sent his son Prince Charles to England, to urge Charles II to support him against the French, and his son the Raugrave Carllutz to France, to see if anything could be done at that Court. He added that he hoped for little or nothing from any quarter, but was arming himself in patience because 'at my age one cannot wear a heavier cuirass'. He would leave no stone unturned, he said, 'for the sake of the Empire, for which I am sacrificing my life'.

On Sophie's return to Hanover she found a letter from the Palatinate written in a strange hand. It had been dictated while her brother 'was trying to season his body as best he could before the good earth took charge of it'. His spirit, he said, was uplifted by watching the flight of birds, and he was picturing the rapture of his soul once it had left his body, 'as Seneca says in his letter to Lucille—*si non è vero è ben trovato*'. Apologising that he had not written himself, he hoped that she would nevertheless believe that he died entirely hers. His customary signature was faintly traced by his own hand. The next communication from the Palatinate informed the Duchess of Hanover that her brother was dead.

Nine days before his death, Charles Louis and his Court had been returning from one of the regular visits to Friedrichsburg. In the village of Edingen, half-an-hour away, the Elector had suffered what must have been a slight stroke. He was taken back to Friedrichsburg, where he complained of a fever and pains in his head. Two days later he was sitting up and dining on chicken-wings, while twenty grains of English powder, three heated English stones wrapped in napkins and a pile of carpets on his bed made him sweat. To ease his cough, his chest was plastered in paper permeated with butter blended with oranges, and the soles of his feet were poulticed with yeast dough to draw down the vapours.

The doctors came and went. Over the next few days they bled and purged him in turn, and when one ordered more coverings, another asked to have them removed. They prescribed, variously, poached eggs, more chicken, English porridge with raisins, water-panades with and without lemon, broths of marjoram, sorrel and chicory, and rinses of vinegar and cherry-water. On the sixth day Charles Louis was suffering from dizziness and convulsions and temporarily lost his powers of speech. When he regained them, he insisted that fresh air would benefit him more than the medical faculty, and against his doctor's advice set off in a litter for Heidelberg, leaving early in the morning to avoid the heat of the day.

Arriving once more at Edingen, he asked to be placed under a tree in a garden close to the spot where he had first been taken ill. 'How good it smells,' he said, taking a deep breath of the scented air, and fainted. He may have been vaguely aware of the application of invigorating ointment to his limbs, of spoonfuls of capon-broth held against his lips, and of torn carcasses of young doves, still warm, pressed over his heart, but he never fully regained consciousness.

His daughter Caroline cradled his head while the doctors and apothecaries argued whether to bleed or to purge. Before they could reach an agreement they realised that the Elector was passing beyond their competence.

The Court turned to God. Medical attendants, servants, Raugraves, courtiers, guard-officers and troopers, all persons high and low, knelt on the grass. The two Court preachers led the service, and by the end of the second prayer, when the last Amen, Amen, Lord Jesus, Amen, had been intoned, Charles Louis died as though in his sleep, with no alteration in expression or gesture.

His body was embalmed in Friedrichsburg. His heart, carefully encased and strewn with herbs and flowers, travelled to Heidelberg and was laid to rest in the family vault.

Since the new Elector was in England—he learned of his father's death while receiving an honorary doctorate at Oxford—the Regency Council passed its first resolution: to send a courier into France to purchase the mourning requisites. Thus the Prince, who in his lifetime had never ordered a new suit of clothes while the old one could still be patched up—and then had it cut down for one of Louise's boys, saving the lapels for his own future use—the man who had even cobbled his own shoes, came to lie in state on a canopied bier in his library bereft of the codices, but hung with several hundred yards of black Lyonnais velvet of the very finest quality.

Charles Louis' death was the first great sorrow of Sophie's life. At first she could not believe it, just as she had never really believed in his illness. 'For some time past he had almost constantly spoken of death,' she told the Raugravine Caroline, 'sometimes *en sérieux*, sometimes *en raillant*—who would have believed that it could happen in earnest, and so suddenly?' She begged her niece for details. 'It will be some comfort to know exactly how it happened, and whether, at the end, he said a word for me.'

When the account arrived it was no consolation but pure torture. Would, Sophie wanted to know, a final bleeding have saved him? Had the body been opened? She expected that internally all had been in order—small comfort, this, but she could think of nothing else night or day. Only repeated assurances that everything humanly possible had been done, and that Charles Louis had not felt his death, finally made her accept it, and she sadly wrote, 'God has given him peace; in this world he had nothing but *fâcheries*'.

The extent of her loss was immeasurable. She missed his letters, which had been the joy of her life, she missed the shared jokes and the memories of the past, and she missed most of all the point which his existence had given to her own. No event in her life had assumed its final form before she had discussed it with him in her letters: everything had acquired an extra edge when she had told him about it. Triumphs and trivialities, political news, a new cheese, scandal, a pattern for a nightcap or a bed-canopy of muslin for keeping the flies out, everything Sophie heard of, thought and experienced would wing its way to the Palatinate. There was no one, now, with whom to share such things, and hardly any point in living.

She sat miserably in her hated house, unable to concentrate on either her needlework or her correspondence, although there were mountains of letters to answer and the Degenfeld children to attend to.

Incredibly, for such a methodical man, Charles Louis had neglected to make adequate provision for his daughters. Sophie tackled their half-brother, the new Elector Charles, on the subject, and was able to inform her nieces Caroline, Louise and Ameliese that there was cause for confidence: he had promised her that he would do his duty by them. Sophie could only pray that Charlotte would not change his mind for him. The dowager Electress was apparently so afflicted by Charles Louis' death, wrote Sophie hopefully to the girls, that she was closeted in darkened rooms, too sad to emerge, and 'could not conceivably display animosity towards those whom the Elector had loved so well.' Her attitude would soon be known: Charlotte was planning to speed to the Palatinate, at her son's urgent invitation, as soon as her mourning wardrobe was ready; and should it be required Sophie put her own purse, 'though far from fat', at her nieces' disposal.

She did not allow herself to wallow in grief, and dutifully played her part during the ceremonies which accompanied Ernst August's succession to Hanover. On 12th October she watched the country's nobility, clergy and officials kneel before her husband and two eldest boys to swear their allegiance. George Louis, home from France, where Liselotte had disconcerted him by her stormy welcome, and again on his leave-taking by her torrent of grief at having herself to stay behind 'with the people who killed the Elector', acquitted himself well. So did Frederick August, nineteen, tall, serious and passionate, 'looking like Rupert *tout craché*'. By the tradition of *la maison*, only the two eldest boys were in line for succession. Maximilian, Sophie's third son, watched the ceremony in an armchair by her side. The younger princes had been left at home: Charles Philip, eleven, a thoughtful boy; Christian, nine, slow and good natured; and her youngest, Ernst August, a clever child of six, who had been her most convenient baby and happy so long as he was clutching his rag doll, called Hans Lump, which he covered with passionate kisses.

Sophie wondered what the future would hold for them all. Really, she thought, she had enough boys to supply all who lacked them: the King of England, the Elector Palatine, the Dauphin* and the Prince of Orange.

* Married to the Electoral Princess of Bavaria, who in due course produced the Dukes of Bourgogne, Anjou and Berry.

She asked Charles Philip whom, given the choice, he would most like to succeed, and he made her laugh by gravely replying that he required notice of such a question, but thought on the whole he would pick William of Orange—'his task being less arduous than that of a king'.

On 13th October, which happened to be Sophie's fiftieth birthday, the ducal carriages rode in procession down the Dammstrasse, which had been decked out in greenery from the pinewoods that surrounded the city. Their destination was the Gothic town hall, where the family sat down to a banquet served by the hands of the councillors, led by the mayor. This was the final official honour bestowed on the newly installed prince, and Ernst August could hardly wait for it to be over. He was all packed for Italy, where he was planning to make up for lost time.

He duly departed, leaving the palace in the hands of the workmen; true to his word, he had also begun his building programme outside the palace. At Herrenhausen, a *plaisance* about a mile and a half from Hanover which John Frederick had started improving during his lifetime, contractors were also busy.

Sophie remained at home, alone with the grief that she had successfully repressed while fulfilling her official duties, but which now so aggravated all the physical discomforts of middle age that she felt it could not be long before she followed Charles Louis and her sister Elizabeth, although she was 'far from ready to go the way of all flesh'.

A bulky parcel of her letters to her brother came, at last, from Heidelberg . . . 'not that there is anything in them of which I am ashamed,' she had explained to her niece Caroline, requesting their return immediately after Charles Louis' death, 'only I used to write so freely and so full of *raillerie* that I should not care for other people to read them and laugh at me.' To Sophie's annoyance, the letters arrived only after they had been minutely examined. Meaning to have a final look before burning them, as she thought them hardly worth keeping, she fortunately became so engrossed in re-reading them that she conceived the idea of using them as the basis for a volume of memoirs.

She wrote not for publication, not to present herself as a romantic heroine as some ladies had lately been doing (among them Mme Colonna, whose book had created a sensation), but simply as a therapeutic exercise, to raise her spirits and take her mind off her misery, for there was nothing like a large project 'to preserve health and life, to which I cling'. When she had finished writing, three months later, she was well on the way to recovery, 'although I should have told my story better had my spirit been less troubled'.

It was the garden of Herrenhausen that completed the cure. In the spring of 1681 Sophie was once again supervising the creation of terraces and *tapis verts*, grottoes and cascades, and a great outdoor theatre with bowers for dressing rooms and an auditorium with tiered, grass-covered seats. Charbonnier *père*, and later *fils*, were responsible for the layout, but it is with Sophie that the creation of the Herrenhausen gardens is most closely associated. She came to love them more than any other place on earth, and it was during their construction that she stopped brooding on the past. Like any true gardener, she began looking forward to the delights of the future: pleasant walks in the dappled shade of the saplings that were now being planted, and hedges alive with the song of nightingales. Since a way of establishing fully grown trees had recently been found, parts of the gardens took shape under her very eyes, but, as earlier at Osnabrück, she found herself discussing progress 'as though it was a matter of thirty days instead of thirty years'.

In March 1681 George Louis returned from a visit to London. He had crossed the Channel three months earlier at the instigation of his uncle Rupert, who had been receiving overtures from the Court of Whitehall regarding the possible marriage of the Hanoverian prince to the Princess Anne, younger daughter of the Duke of York. Rupert presented him to Charles II, who talked of Sophie in an obliging way, and gave him express permission to salute Anne with a kiss. In writing home, George Louis did not dwell on the pasty Princess, and England had occasion to note that his courtship lacked ardour. Nor was Anne greatly taken by her reserved cousin. Contemporaries, including Spanheim and Bishop Burnet, were to suggest that her life-long aversion to the Hanoverians and all their works was rooted in hurt feelings at not being more ardently courted. Some believed that there had been no proposal because of Anne Hyde, her commoner mother. But negotiations for the marriage continued for over a year after George Louis had returned to Hanover, and ceased only when his betrothal to his cousin Sophie Dorothea of Celle—of far less respectable birth than Anne—was finally announced.

This match had become vital to Ernst August's programme for the aggrandisement of *la maison*, for which he had been working with single-minded determination ever since his succession. Were Sophie Dorothea to marry outside the country, there was no telling what claims might be made on her behalf: and if Brunswick-Lüneburg was to be strong, Celle and Hanover must be united. Sophie swallowed her pride and realised that opposition was useless. Eleonore's daughter would, after all, have to be welcomed as a daughter-in-law. 'In future, Celle and Hanover must be regarded as one and the same thing,' Sophie wrote in July 1682 to the Abbé Ballati, a diplomatist in the service of Hanover who was travelling to France and Italy on church business.* She was confirming what she thought he might already have seen in the untrustworthy Gazette, and explained, 'It is highly advantageous for *la maison*, as long as one can overcome the scruples of the Germans, who desire their genealogies to be equally illustrious on both sides'.

She feared that Munich, also on the Abbé's itinerary, would be scandalised by the marriage—an annoying thought because the Abbé had instructions to offer Figuelotte's hand to the Duke of Bavaria's heir. But when this plan foundered it was for another reason—the prince, to Sophie's fury, did not consider Figuelotte pretty enough.

Prince Rupert, to whom Sophie had written that her son's betrothal was 'a bitter pill, but so well gilded that one must shut one's eyes and swallow it down', was rather put out. 'All I can say,' he replied, 'is "now thou art chosen, thou art well chosen",' and he wished the couple every blessing. He could not resist adding that the conditions under which his nephew would have married into England had been excellent and certain, and all moneys were to have been paid by the Duke of York himself. 'However,' he closed, 'I can never regret any pains that I have taken in your service.' It was the last service he was to render Sophie—he died even before the marriage was officially announced.

In September, when all details which would help to make the match equally respectable from every point of view had at last been settled, George Louis' formal proposal was conveyed to Celle and duly accepted.

---

* The reunion of the Church was a constant live issue. Sophie, with her undogmatic religious beliefs—which caused James Stuart to refer to her as one 'sitting lightly in her religion'—took an interest in and was often instrumental in introducing to one another exponents of opposing factions. In one of her joking letters to Leibniz she wrote, 'As Christianity came into the world through a woman, I should be proud if its unification were due to me.'

The bride's father shed tender tears of emotion, and his *chère moitié*, who heartily disliked her new son-in-law, kept her countenance as best she could.

Sophie Dorothea—sixteen, pretty, vain and shallow—took pleasure in being the centre of attention. Even if she did not greatly care for George Louis he was better than the dwarfish, penniless Prince of Nassau Siegen who had been all that was left of her long line of suitors. 'A very poor choice', Sophie had said of this sad specimen when Celle had informed Hanover, in the middle of negotiating Sophie Dorothea's Hanoverian marriage, that this affair was *bien avancé*. Why it had ever begun was a mystery to her. She did not mention that Celle's claim of other irons in the fire was an attempt to gain greater bargaining power in the haggling, since she herself was hopefully casting around for an alternative daughter-in-law. 'If my son were as much in love with her as I am,' she said of a Brandenburg Princess whom they had met just as the marriage to his cousin was about to be made public, 'he would be married to her already.'

But George Louis, although he now had an official mistress—Maria von Meisenbug, the sister of Mme von Platen, his father's friend—was hardly the man to be carried away by emotion, and in November, in a ceremony that Sophie described as simple although the full panoply of state was mustered, he dutifully acquired a hopelessly ill-suited wife, while Sophie Dorothea gained a husband described as dry, hard, dour and sour even by those who loved him.

The marriage, a disaster that was to end in a catastrophe, began much like any other. Leibniz sent another of his poems and Sophie Dorothea settled into the Leine palace, which had by now become *'très logeable'* even in the eyes of the French ambassador, who generally had a poor opinion of the ducal residences—'ill-built, without proportion or comfort'—and who regretted that the Duke's interest did not extend to architecture or furniture.

The Princess duly conceived, and George Louis went off to assist the Emperor against the Turks who were besieging Vienna, leaving his wife to while away the time before her looking-glass. Liselotte darkly observed that if this wasn't coquetry, it was at least next door to it, but was put to rights by Sophie, who said that for a pretty girl to admire herself was natural and not a crime.

On the first anniversary of her wedding Sophie Dorothea gave birth to a son, George August. According to custom, the confinement was attended by members of the family and officers of state. Only Eleonore had sent her excuses. She could not, she said, bear to witness suffering. In Sophie's opinion women should be made of sterner stuff, and bring up their daughters more reasonably, too.

For all that she spoke well of her daughter-in-law to Liselotte, for all of Sophie Dorothea's prompt and obliging production of a son, for all her assurances of respect and obedience, Sophie was beginning to be maddened by the girl. Affectation always had this effect on her, but she kept her feelings well under control. There is no evidence to support the allegations of unkindness and cruelty which Sophie Dorothea's partisans were later to level against her, but privately both Sophie and Mme von Harling came to detest her sly airs and pretty little ways, and dreaded her influence on Figuelotte.

The sooner 'my Infanta' was removed from her sister-in-law's company the better. It was in any case time to settle her future. Ballati, now in Paris for talks with the Bishop of Meaux, was instructed to offer Figuelotte to Louis XIV, whose Queen had been 'murdered by her doctors', as Liselotte wrote in June 1683. Madame was once again desired to do what she could. Once again she failed lamentably to turn things to her family's advantage, just as she had in the case of the Degenfeld girls, for whom she had been bidden to find either husbands or appointments. In Figuelotte's case she could not have succeeded if she had been as clever as the recently deceased Anna Gonzaga herself, for the King had secretly married Mme de Maintenon soon after burying his wife.

While Ballati was trying in vain to interest him in Figuelotte, Frederick, the Elector of Brandenburg's son, became a widower. Sophie sent her condolences and suggested that he might find consolation in Hanover. She remembered with satisfaction that Figuelotte had been extravagantly admired by her Brandenburg relations, whom she had met in Pyrmont. Her portrait, in fireworks, had been set up to celebrate her beauty; the inscription, also in fireworks, said that it failed to do justice to the brilliance of her eyes. The Great Elector, Sophie recalled, had exclaimed, 'That's what we need in Berlin instead of what my sister sent us'—a reference to his deceased daughter-in-law.

Hopefully, Sophie asked the Veronese painter who was working on one of her ceilings to climb down from his scaffold to paint Figuelotte, and said of the result that it was always a good thing for the original to have the edge over her portrait. The painting pleased in Berlin, the negotiations began, and as usual dragged on. France, with whom the Great Elector had been enjoying a close and profitable relationship, did not like to see two formidable German princes in close alliance. 'I fear that French *pistoles* are very powerful in Berlin,' wrote Sophie to the Raugravine Caroline, 'and may deflect the Elector from the course set by his noble nature.' Another worry was the Electress of Brandenburg, known to dominate her husband. This lady, the former Duchess of Celle and once Sophie's own childless sister-in-law, had presented her second husband with five sons, for whom she claimed territories that Hanover expected to go to Figuelotte's prospective husband.

While the ministers on both sides were arguing, Figuelotte's French marriage continued to be discussed in Hanover. The Princess herself, going on for sixteen but deliberately not yet confirmed in case her faith narrowed her chances on the marriage market, said that she would accept whatever providence had in store for her. As realistic as her mother, she replied to a friend who pointed out the constraint endured by the Queens of France that she would live in constraint wherever she went, and with Louis XIV '*il en vaudrait plus la peine*'. Meanwhile, she conducted herself wonderfully well during an interview with an envoy from Brandenburg, sent to Hanover to explore her sentiments. He departed highly satisfied with her answers, 'which', Sophie informed Ballati, 'doesn't commit her to anything.'

By June 1684 Ballati heard that matters had so far advanced that another official visit was expected from Berlin. 'We'll soon have company for which my daughter must dress up,' wrote Sophie, sending a list drawn up by Figuelotte: one *manteau*, two gowns complete with underskirts—urgent, urgent. Accessories, too—gloves, fans and *fontanges* (these head-dresses, lace or ribbon on tall wire-structures, were by now nodding on every well-dressed head). And since Sophie felt that the regular Hanoverian agent in Paris was not to be trusted with so particular an assignment, she hoped the Abbé would see to everything in person.

Accordingly, Ballati took time off from conferring on the unification of the Christian religions, and went shopping. 'I've never had anything from France better chosen or cheaper,' wrote Sophie when the consignment arrived, leaving comments on quality and workmanship to Ernst

August and Mme von Harling, 'who have a better eye for such things'. Everything was much admired, and her only disappointment was to discover, 'on looking through the packages again to find something destined for me, there was only the *Mercure Galant* and the *Procès de Bussy*—you've forgotten me?'

In the summer of 1684 Otto von Grote, greatest of Ernst August's ministers, signed a defence treaty between France, Brunswick and Brandenburg, and the Elector asked for Figuelotte's hand on his son's behalf. 'I hope it's good for *la maison*,' said Sophie, and, in view of the bridegroom's impatience, toyed with the idea of asking her daughter-in-law 'for her state-bed and coach, because she's never used either, and new ones would only be ready six months after our wedding'.

Ernst August considered Sophie Dorothea's coach too ordinary for a *carrosse de parade*. He wanted to have it covered inside and out with *broderie*. 'If time's too short, it'll have to be gold brocade,' wrote Sophie to Ballati, attaching a list of Figuelotte's further requirements, which was shortly to be followed by Hanoverian tailors. Should Ballati, heaven forbid, be obliged to leave Paris to follow the Court on its circuit of palaces, the tailors would just have to do their best, but the ladies of Hanover would be happier to know that their commissions were in the hands of such an expert as he. Figuelotte, for instance, was worried about her skirt of *aurore et argent*—would it go with a gown of gold and silver? And was the black velvet she had ordered to set off her jewels *à la mode*?

Sophie did not care whether it was in fashion or not. Velvet made people look fat, and Figuelotte was too fat already, although otherwise in splendid looks, with jet-black hair and bright blue eyes fringed with long black lashes. So would Ballati please find an alternative for such an unbecoming material (a battle that Sophie was to lose, for when no black velvet gown arrived from Paris, Figuelotte had one made up in Hanover).

Sophie's own requirements were simple. 'I've given my tailor my commissions, they're not very great for I always wear black; but I shall need a brocade *manteau* of some dark colour for the official entry—maybe like the Princess of East Friesland's in black and gold?—and perhaps another one, embroidered, with a matching skirt. You choose, because I don't know if embroidery is still in fashion. I shall like whatever you do, provided it's not too gay.'

By September Sophie feared that Ballati must be trembling whenever

George Louis of Hanover as a young man, by Godfrey Kneller.

Eleonore d'Olbreuse and her daughter Sophie Dorothea, both anon, 17th century.

her letters arrived, 'all with new commissions so that we're making you look after the affairs of state right down to bagatelles like clothes'. And as though four new suits for Ernst August and four further dresses and five more *manteaux* for Figuelotte weren't enough, would he please 'obtain a doll, dressed and coiffed like a little girl of quality aged four', with which Figuelotte 'would be able to delight her stepdaughter of that age'?

Mme la Poupeé arrived, to be much admired, shortly before M von Grumkow, Chancellor of Brandenburg, came with tender messages from Berlin. Figuelotte received her Prince's compliments from Grumkow's little son, who delivered them prettily, saying he had been chosen to be the first messenger of love. Among her presents were huge diamond earrings from which trembled pearls, a bracelet with lovers' knots that made her blush, and her future husband's portrait, set in diamonds which failed to blind her to its unprepossessing aspect. The miniature—head only—did not show that Frederick's shoulders were uneven owing to a spinal injury in childhood, which might have been fatal if it had not been dealt with by the miracle-man now at Clèves, though even he had not been able to untwist Frederick's body. When the Prince appeared in Hanover, tiny and covered with jewels—he was inordinately fond of splendour and pomp—the Court called him 'the manikin'. Sophie maintained that once one had become accustomed to his figure, and concentrated on his face, he was almost handsome, and in an assessment that was more hopeful than realistic said that Figuelotte, luckily, 'did not care for externals'.

With the Prince arrived a tremendous crowd of people, all brilliantly dressed. 'Berlin itself could not be more magnificent,' wrote Sophie to Ballati, 'only our own new clothes are missing.' Maddeningly, the latest consignment of Paris modes had not arrived. Ballati would be glad to hear, however, that 'Figuelotte looked like the Virgin Mary on her name-day in the wedding present jewels, and was receiving more offerings every day'.

During the wedding in October there was some consternation when Frederick's ring, made in the shape of two clasped hands, which had belonged to his previous wife, fell in fragments to the floor. It was taken as an ill omen, but 'the newly-weds seem content, and the presents are magnificent'.

F

A week after the wedding, when the ballets, plays, operas and fireworks —'prepared as best we could in the short space of time' said Sophie, and '*fort, fort mal*' said the French ambassador—were over, Frederick took his enormous train out of the country and returned with only a few people for a private stay at Herrenhausen with his bride. George Louis, recovering from another attack of smallpox, through which he had been nursed by Mme von Harling, was also there to keep the couple company. His red complexion had embarrassed him too much to join in the celebrations, and Mme von Harling's devotion to him had consoled her for missing some of the fun. She now busied herself with alterations to Sophie's clothes. Figuelotte's all fitted, but Sophie's tailors had let her down; all her waists needed to be taken in, and the *Point d'Espagne* trimmings had not been sewn on to her own black velvet, embroidered and in the height of fashion after all. Everything had to be done as fast as possible, since the Elector was anxious for celebrations to begin in Berlin, fearing that his gout would prevent him from enjoying them if there was too much delay.

Early in November 1684 Sophie and George Louis—their spouses were both ill—took Figuelotte to Berlin. Mother and daughter wore their richest *toilettes*, which had been saved for the ceremonial entrance, and the state-coach looked resplendent in the new *broderie*. The problem of the state-bed had been solved: a new one would have cost the earth, even without the dais on which Ernst August insisted, so Sophie Dorothea's had been refurbished and packed off to Berlin together with its matching set of chairs. It, too, had been considered too plain at first, but it looked quite presentable and, after all, 'taste there is not as *fin* as elsewhere'.

All sensible people who had been in favour of the match, especially Danckelmann, Brandenburg's powerful premier minister, who had supported it from the start, received the party from Hanover with every mark of delight. There were, however, some sour faces. Without specifying their owners, Sophie noted that several ladies greeted her daughter coolly, 'their *coiffes* pulled down over their noses'. This at least saved her from bestowing kisses upon them, a fashion deplored in Hanover but laid much store by in Berlin. All the unkissed ladies duly took offence, and Sophie could only hope that Figuelotte would soon cure them of 'taking every fart for a thunderclap, and get them used to the ways of Hanover where intrigues are unknown'.

Figuelotte took good care to steer clear of all intriguers at that difficult, scheming Court, and concentrated on being a good wife. Her husband was enchanted with her and could be seen, nightly, marching into her bedroom, carrying his own pillow in front of him as though to suffocate her.

In Hanover, where Figuelotte's departure had left a huge vacuum in Sophie's life, an unpleasant surprise was awaiting her. On the second day of Christmas 1684, Ernst August informed his family that he had arranged to depart from the ancient tradition of his House. Formerly, the two eldest boys had both stood to inherit, just as the two senior Dukes of his own generation had done. Now, since the *gloire* of Brunswick-Lüneburg required a strong, united government, he was introducing a system of primogeniture. He had already made a will to the effect that George Louis alone would succeed both George William and himself, and not share the sovereignty with Frederick August, his next brother. Imperial approval had recently arrived, and the new scheme was now only awaiting confirmation by all his younger sons, whom he also requested to swear allegiance to their eldest brother.

It was no surprise to Sophie that Frederick August, his expectations suddenly shattered, refused to do any such thing. Even if she could recognise the political advantage of the plan, not least that it was a large step towards the Electorate for which Ernst August was still angling, she was appalled that her husband could be so heartless. Her sympathies were visibly with 'poor Gustchen'. In so far as she shared her husband's ambitions for the House, it was to see her children decently established in the world, and now this very ambition seemed to be depriving her second son of his heritage. As Prince Rupert—whom he resembled in character as well as in looks—had done before him, Frederick August appealed to his relations for help in regaining his birthright. He found a willing supporter in Anton Ulrich of Brunswick Wolfenbüttel, so jealous of the rise of the Hanoverian branch that he was not averse to putting spokes into Ernst August's wheels.

Frederick August went off to stay at Wolfenbüttel, and there, with the help of Duke Anton Ulrich's secretary, drew up a document presenting a well-argued case against his father's design, which convinced Sophie and enraged her husband. 'Does the egg,' he demanded, 'consider itself wiser than the chicken?' Was his son trying to rule him? If Frederick August persisted in his obstinacy, and continued to defy him on the advice of people whose object was to alienate him from his father, he would have occasion to repent at leisure. Sophie wrote to her son that if he agreed to the will without causing too much inconvenience and quarrelling he might be installed in a duchy of his own, and enjoy an easier life and greater revenues than many ruling princes. 'Your father's intentions are good. Take care not to offend him. I will do what I can, but I have no power over him, and he argues that to make the House strong will benefit all its members.'

Trying her best to be a loyal wife as well as a loving mother, she did what she could to keep the differences between father and son hushed up. People who asked where Frederick August had disappeared to were told that he was ill. 'The real reason could be to your disadvantage,' she wrote, begging him to be sensible, and observing that history was filled with praise for men who sacrificed personal advantage for the sake of their Houses. Moreover, 'to accept reverses of fortune with so little moderation is not the mark of a great soul.' She, too, had been obliged to do several things that were highly disagreeable, like 'accepting a d'Olbreuse who had for so long been your uncle's concubine', a thing that still rankled because 'it went against honour, for a king's daughter such as I'.

Even though Sophie had recourse to her *autorité maternelle* in commanding her son to submit, he refused to moderate his passionate opposition. He left Wolfenbüttel for Vienna, in order to lead a detachment of Imperial troops against the Infidels. However, it was not long before he wrote to his mother, 'I am *au bout de mon latin*. My purse is empty, my regiment on bread and water, and I dream of a miracle in the desert.' There was nothing for it but to ask his father for his allowance, and a word from Sophie on his behalf would help.

Ernst August's refusal was prompt and definite, and he refused to hear another word on the subject of his rebellious son. 'Poor Gustchen is quite disowned,' sadly noted Sophie. 'His father won't even allow him his keep.'

Frederick August was to become what she most dreaded for any of her sons—just as the Winter Queen had dreaded it a generation earlier—a poor soldier of fortune. He described his life as resembling that of Lazarus, 'while my brothers enjoy all the pleasures due to princes to which I, too, am entitled.' He sometimes joked about his fate. 'I have,' he said, 'a baker, a brewer, a doctor, a tailor, and a *bouffon* to make me laugh. All that is missing is the money to activate this apparatus.' But usually his letters to his mother were sad, and Sophie told Anton Ulrich, 'I smile by day and cry all night, loving all my children equally, because I have carried each one under my heart.'

Inevitably the affair created a breach between Ernst August and Sophie, and he found comfort with Mme von Platen, politically more astute than Sophie and full of encouragement for his ambitious plans. Consequently it was she who accompanied him on that year's visit to Venice, in a stitch-by-stitch copy of Sophie's travelling sables, while Sophie refused his half-hearted invitation as she had in the past refused many warmer ones. This time she made a point of telling her niece Caroline that Ernst August had left it to her whether to go with him or not, but 'not being as fond as all that of Italy' she had decided to stay at home. Besides, she hoped in due course to travel to Berlin to be present at Figuelotte's confinement. She could only pray that 'they will be polite enough to ask me', a courtesy so far neglected—hardly surprisingly, since Figuelotte was barely nine weeks pregnant. But it was none too early for Sophie to begin thinking of the christening, and to plan the baby's layette with the same energy as she had expended on her daughter's trousseau.

'It's the best *divertissement* for me, now the Duke is gone. He took Charles with him; Max is with his regiment, fighting for the Venetians; Gustchen is going into Upper Hungary; my eldest marches against the Turks with eleven thousand men, and only my two youngest are at home,' Sophie wrote to Louise and Ameliese. She would dearly have liked to include her nieces in her household, but Ernst August feared eternal squabbles about precedence between them and Mme von Platen. 'If it depended on me, I should long ago have asked you to come, but the Duke does not want me to have *Gräfliche Fräuleins* at Court,' wrote Sophie to her nieces, 'and I am not so fortunate as to be able to do as I please.'

The Raugravines were still in Heidelberg, where their half-brother Charles had not lived up to his promises and the dowager Electress was difficult and ill-tempered as usual. When Charlotte died in the following year, Sophie said that the maids who wrapped her into her shroud must have had a unique experience. 'It'll be the first time anyone has dressed the Electress without being beaten.' Only Caroline had escaped, by marrying Meinhard von Schomberg, who belonged to a distinguished military family.

In the years that had passed since Charles Louis' death, his life's work had gone to wrack and ruin. All the old faithfuls had been dismissed, the precariously balanced budget had been thrown to the winds by the new favourites, and bit by bit parts of the Palatinate were sold off to France. Even these measures failed to keep the economy afloat. Charlotte's accumulated debts alone were a burden greater than the exchequer could bear, not to mention the continuous masques and ballets with which the new régime and its parasites hoped to divert their gloomy Elector.

Even more ruinous than these expensive pleasures was Charles' mania for playing soldiers. At the old castle of Eichelsheim on the Rhine, entrenchments had been dug by peasants who would have been better employed tending their fields. He rechristened it Negroponte (the contemporary name for Euboea, the scene of many battles with the Turks), and besieged it for months on end. His opposing armies, composed of students, courtiers, citizens and militia men, were dressed up as Turks and Imperials. Trench-fever, dysentery and the other miseries of the war that was being fought in earnest in the eastern part of the Empire caused many casualties, and Charles himself had become a victim of the heat and the unhealthy conditions to which he had exposed himself in the previous summer. The two distinguished Swiss physicians who were called in to him in the spring of 1685 diagnosed consumption, but they came too late to save him. Deliriously shouting commands to an imaginary army which was apparently struggling in vain against a foreign invader, he died in May, and with him died the Protestant Palatine line.

'By rights,' wrote Sophie to Mme von Harling, 'the succession goes to the Duke of Neuburg, but I hear France is claiming it for Madame's son, the Duc de Chartres, under the pretext that her renunciation was valid only for her own person, not for his.' The Duke of Neuburg in fact succeeded, while France sent agents to claim the country for Liselotte, in lieu of her dowry that had never been paid in full.

But in the autumn of 1685 all was still quiet in Heidelberg, as Sophie packed the layette she had lovingly assembled to go to Figuelotte's confinement. She felt sure that the *Point de Venise* lace, the little vests, untrimmed so that the baby's arms would not get sore from being tightly swaddled in the padded cocoon that was still being used for carrying babies about in Brandenburg, and the crested, quilted cot-blanket of white satin that Ernst August had sent from Venice would far outshine any gifts

A Hanover le 26 Juin / 6 Juliet 1682

Vous me faites grand tort ma chere
Madame d'auoir oublie que ie suis de
race Angloise, et qu'on ne me sauroit
faire de feulies trop petit, quant on
autres les peut flatter, ceux que vous
m'auer enuoie sont les plus ioly du
monde ie les montre come vn miracle
icy car on n'en peut pas faire de
mesme, ie vous en suis infiniment
obligee et ne seres pas contente, iusquaue
que vous m'ayes donne lieu de vous
tesmoigner par les seruices combien
ie cheris tous ce qui est aime de
mon cher frere. Sophie
Je suis impatiente d'auoir les nouv

First page of Sophie's letter to Margaret Hughes

from the other side of the family. She longed to take a Hanoverian mid-wife along, but realised that this would be construed as an insult to local talent. Berlin was in any case apt to think that Figuelotte had remained unduly Hanoverian and tied to her mother's apron-strings.

Sophie Dorothea, distressingly truculent of late, changed her tune and became all charm when she saw the travelling preparations. 'That is because she wants to come with me to Berlin,' wrote Sophie to Louise, whom she hoped to take with her, 'but I close my ears to her pleas. However, I shall willingly allow her to go to her mother, whose company she prefers to anyone else's in any case.'

To Sophie's and her own regret, Louise had to refuse Sophie's invitation because she was needed to look after the ailing Ameliese. 'If one can't fly falcons,' said Sophie, 'one's got to make do with owls,' and took with her instead Frances Baird, known as Lady Bellamont, the first of Rupert's two morganatic wives.

Reserving her intolerance of irregular attachments exclusively for Eleonore, Sophie accepted Frances and her successor Margaret Hughes as a matter of course, and was specially charming to both. Margaret, on sending shoes from London, 'the prettiest in the world, only too small', received only the mildest reminder that Sophie was 'a member of the English race', whose English feet needed room to stretch; while faulty gloves even from Sophie's beloved Louise were greeted with scorn— 'never been near England, all more left hands than right, only one wear-able pair'. And when Frances was left unprovided for at Rupert's death, Sophie made her one of her pensioners and a member of her household.

When Sophie's party arrived in Berlin Figuelotte was in good health and spirits, having taken her mother's advice and subjected herself to regular precautionary applications of leeches to the nose. Her Court was very civilised indeed. It teemed with French Huguenots, who were part of the mass immigration welcomed by the Great Elector after Louis XIV had shocked the world by revoking the Edict of Nantes. Any educated refugee had automatic entrée, and the atmosphere was so delightful that several of them wondered whether their hostess could actually speak German.

In due course Figuelotte gave birth to a prince so beautiful that Sophie wanted to carry him off with her directly after the christening. Her offer to have him brought up by Mme von Harling was, however, refused, and she returned empty-handed to an almost childless palace.

Her two little boys had gone to France, to be made a fuss of by Liselotte, and Sophie occupied herself with making a good Christian of a little Moslem boy, a present from her eldest son. George Louis was given to sending exotic creatures home from the wars—once it had been a sick camel. On the day of the three Kings, Sophie stood sponsor at the christening of Ernst August Mustapha Ali. Her husband and her eldest son, both formally invited to be godfathers, sent stand-ins to the Schlosskirche, and the ceremony was followed by cutting the traditional Epiphany cake. It would have been merrier if the lady who found the hidden bean, and so became queen for the day, had not just suffered a bereavement; as it was, she could hardly swallow her cake for her tears.

Sophie Dorothea's little boy, cared for by Mme von Harling, partly made up for the absence of Sophie's own children. Luckily, her secret dislike of her son's marriage did not extend to its product. Sophie Dorothea herself was mercifully absent, having been invited to Venice by Ernst August. Sophie had been all in favour of her going there, but, regrettably, the scandal-prone Princess had already become the subject of disagreeable stories. These were retailed to Sophie by Liselotte, who had them from the rakish Marquis de Lassay; he boasted of enjoying the Princess's friendship, and had in fact been forced to leave Venice in a hurry and under a cloud. He told of parties in the Princess's ante-chamber, of guests begged to lower their voices so as not to wake Mme von Platen—Sophie Dorothea's chaperone in Italy—'because she was sleeping with the Duke next door', and of spiteful remarks about Sophie.

Liselotte readily believed the worst. According to an earlier bit of gossip, Sophie Dorothea had rolled her eyes at Carllutz, Liselotte's half-brother, so that, rather than risk a scandal, he had left Hanover and gone to the wars. To Liselotte, Sophie Dorothea was capable of anything. Sophie questioned the reliability of Lassay's tales, and suggested to Liselotte that notorious adventurers rarely make reliable reporters. She realised that a young princess could hardly help acquiring a buzz of admirers in Venice of all places, especially as her husband was known to be inattentive.

For a girl who loved above all to feel her own devastating effect on the opposite sex, a husband like George Louis must have been a great disappointment. Nor, when he came to join the Hanoverian party after the Turkish campaign, did he seem affected by the Venetian atmosphere. He stayed only long enough to make his wife, whom he had not seen for four

months, pregnant, and departed to Naples, while she accompanied Ernst
August on his usual rounds.

In the spring of 1687 Sophie Dorothea gave birth to a daughter. In July
Figuelotte, whose first son had died soon after his birth, prematurely produced a second boy, and lost him at once. (It was not until 1688 that the
more durable Prince Frederick William arrived, 'giving every sign of
intending to survive'.) The poor dead baby had been born while Figuelotte
and Frederick were in Magdeburg on their way to Hanover, on something
very like a flight from the Electress of Brandenburg, whom both considered
the very pattern of a wicked stepmother. All the Great Elector's sons by
his first wife shared this view, and when one of them had dropped dead
after eating an orange in her apartments, Figuelotte and her husband
suspected poison and left the country at once. There was no telling, Sophie
jokingly agreed, where that *poudre de la succession*, clearing the way for the
Electress's own sons, might next turn up, and it was better to be safe than
sorry. The Elector, furious with Sophie for mischief-making and with the
young couple for their hysterical departure, ordered them to return
without delay. Sophie had only a single day with Figuelotte, much of
which was spent at the opera.

Meanwhile all hope of making her husband less harsh towards Frederick
August had gone, as had the prospect of persuading her son to submit to
his father. 'It is necessary to accommodate oneself to the ways of the world,'
she had told him, 'it will not accommodate itself to us and one cannot have
all that one wants.' She patched up her estrangement from her Duke. Her
private feelings can only be guessed at, but she did her best to be a dutiful,
loving wife. She filled his pipe—he had taken up smoking, unwisely in
view of his troublesome chest—and accustomed herself to the smell of
tobacco in order to spend as much time as possible in his company. Together
they revisited the silver-mines, and together received an unwelcome reminder of being close to sixty: 'I thought all would pass off as pleasantly
as it had twenty-four years ago, but we emerged stiff and tired and felt as
though we had been caned. We could hardly walk for the next three days.'

Joint concern for their sons in the wars might have drawn them closer
together, but Sophie could not help fretting about Frederick August, and
was still hoping against hope for a reconciliation. So far he was well, as
were the others; all were performing wonders against the Turks. The only

family casualty as yet was poor Carllutz, who had died at Negroponte. He was sadly mourned; even in Hanover 'the populace wept for our good Raugrave in the streets'.

Imperial successes at the Turkish front meant that the Princes of the Empire would shortly be able to turn their attention towards France. William of Orange was urging the German Princes into the League of Augsburg that was to give the ensuing war its name. Meanwhile, Louis XIV continued to buy support, or, failing support, neutrality, from his neighbours. His tactics had for years been working well with Charles II of England, and continued to work with James II, who succeeded his brother in 1685.

'Things will go badly for the people of our faith,' Sophie had supposed at the time. In fact, James' Catholicism did not lead to anything like the dreadful persecution of the Protestants in France; nevertheless, there were signs that the country was not taking kindly to Papist policies. When James became the father of a son by his second wife in June 1688, and the baby was immediately christened in the Catholic faith, thus to all intents perpetuating his régime for another generation, the English decided to save the Protestant religion. They deposed the King and called on his elder daughter Mary and her husband William of Orange to rule in his stead.

The acceptance of this invitation meant that the English throne would in future be occupied not by a 'client' of Louis XIV's, but by a bitter antagonist who would do his utmost to bring England into the war on the opposing side. Louis, counting on a lengthy civil war across the Channel, lost no time in taking action. In September he published a manifesto listing his grievances against his neighbours, and high among them was the non-recognition of his Palatine claims. This was a point on which he took immediate action: almost before the ink on the document was dry, a French army appeared in the Palatinate.

In November William embarked for England as the Protector of the Anglican religion and to mount the throne reluctantly vacated by his father-in-law, who was also his uncle. James wrote to Sophie that he hoped adverse winds would give him time to prepare 'a fitting welcome for the prince', but his optimism was unfounded. William, his banners emblazoned with the legend 'For religion and liberty', entered London in 1688.

Sophie's loyalties were divided: both princes were her friends, as was

William's wife Mary of Orange. James, Sophie knew, returned her affection, but she could, of course, sympathise with the English Protestants, whose grievances William had published in a manifesto before setting out. However, Sophie deplored the passage dealing with their reasons for believing the Prince of Wales to be a changeling, and quite agreed with James, who wrote that those who believed him capable of such deception seemed to judge him by their own standards, not his.

Early reports from England had suggested to her that James was holding his own, and she was not sorry to hear it. Eleonore wondered who Sophie's informant might have been; a good Catholic, no doubt, and one who had coloured his reports accordingly. 'I am not in the habit of examining the creed of my informants,' Sophie wrote back. She was pleased that all was well with the Protestant cause, and sorry only for James' misfortune. If Eleonore insisted on regarding William as 'a second Joshua, called by God to defend His people', might he not have begun by defending the Protestants in France, rather than those in England, where persecuted Huguenots were given generous asylum? Nor could Sophie consider it a godly affair to descend upon England with an army. And nothing could be less Christian than to slander a perfectly respectable baby by calling it a fraud. There was nothing to suggest that William had received any special revelations from above, like Joshua, to whom Eleonore had likened him. She only hoped he would not begin emulating him by hanging kings. 'It is plain to see, Madame, that there are no relations of yours among them, since you wish them such a dreadful fate.'

In due course James was allowed, indeed urged, to escape to France. He was received with royal honours at St Germain, and William and Mary ascended the English throne to safeguard the balance of power in Europe. Sophie, writing to congratulate William, made a point of expressing her grief for King James, 'who has always honoured me with his friendship. I should be afraid that Your Majesty would think me insincere if I dissimulated my feelings. I am sure that my frankness will give you a better opinion of me, and that you will more readily believe all my wishes for your good fortune. Since it has pleased God to make you the defender of our faith, I hope that he will soon free your hands to assist us poor mortals, who are so close to the roaring beast that is trying to devour us all.'

Brunswick-Lüneburg troops were guarding the middle Rhine. However, *la maison* was not yet whole-heartedly committed to the League of

Augsburg, and William told Sophie that he was hoping for stout allies in her family, adding that she had good reason to take a deep interest in the well-being of England, since to all appearances one of her sons would succeed to the throne.

By the Declaration of Rights, to be passed in 1689, Catholics were debarred from the English throne. Since neither William and Mary nor Princess Anne, now married to Prince George of Denmark,* had produced living children, King William had nominated Sophie and her issue for the succession—a suggestion that Parliament had not adopted. Who was to say, asked the Commons, that Mary or Anne would remain childless, particularly as the Princess of Denmark was expecting another baby at the time? So Sophie's name did not appear in the Bill, and she wrote to William expressing the hope that 'all who do not support Your Majesty's plan enjoy the benefit of second sight, to account for the confident expectation of heirs from the royal persons named'.

In July Anne gave birth for the seventh time. Sophie wondered whether the new baby would follow 'the other six, who all inherited the Kingdom of Heaven in order to bring me closer to the crown, or whether it was put into the world to inherit England'. It appeared that the latter was the case. Prince William, Duke of Gloucester, was sturdier than his predecessors, and his arrival put a temporary stop to discussions of Sophie's '*royauté*'.

Hanover did not, of course, lose sight of interesting English possibilities, and Ernst August had reason to congratulate himself on his auspicious marriage at a time when such developments could not have been guessed at. In the meantime, he had been energetically pursuing his plan to become 'the first gentleman of Europe'. Under his management, his country had become a power to be reckoned with. His army was large and well-equipped, and the ninth Electorate was becoming a distinct possibility. The Emperor would not bestow it willingly, of course, but he relied on Hanoverian troops to help him against the Turks who were encroaching on his eastern possessions, and would shortly have need of them in the west against France. So Grote, who had triumphed on the occasion of the alliance with Brandenburg that had culminated in Figuelotte's wedding, and who was now negotiating in Vienna, had been able to argue his master's case from a position of ever-increasing strength. It hardly signified any longer that Ernst August's Imperial fellow-princes in the Empire would be

* The Prince of whose alleged attentions to her daughter Eleonore had previously boasted.

loud in their objections unless commensurate favours were bestowed upon
themselves; even the Protestant ones had withheld their support. But with
the death of the Great Elector of Brandenburg, in May 1688, the voice of
the loudest objector had been stilled, and the situation had changed.

When the great man had breathed his last, after ennobling all his doctors
and begging Figuelotte's pardon for lacking the strength to raise his nightcap to her on her deathbed visit, Sophie had put her Court into deepest
mourning—'the least we can do in return for his *complaisance* in dying'.
Liselotte, writing from France, hardly know whether to send condolences
or congratulations. She thought that Sophie could hardly be heartbroken
at knowing Figuelotte to be Electress, and safe forever from her step-
mother-in-law's plots. This was the second occasion on which Sophie was
required to send words of comfort to this lady on the loss of a husband.
Recalling her former sister-in-law's scanty tears at the funeral of the
drunken Christian Louis, Sophie told her daughter 'last time she had
to work hard at producing a semblance of grief; this time she will feel
it more'. The dowager Electress's power was at an end, and among the
other changes that occurred in Brandenburg was the new Elector's
attitude to Ernst August's ambitions.

The bestowal of the ninth Electorate looked certain; it was only a matter
of time and bribe-money. In anticipation of the great day, Leibniz had for
months been ferreting about in the untidy archives of Modena—where,
incidentally, he discovered the common origin of the Houses of Guelph
and d'Este—to 'produce an impartial, exact account of the Guelphs'
history' worthy of the family's future, beginning with Henry the Lion,
the great Guelph prince of the twelfth century, and his wife Mathilda,
daughter of Henry II of England.

Leibniz's discoveries were put to immediate use. A painter was despatched to copy portraits of newly discovered ancestors, and when the
cartoons for the tapestry that Ernst August commissioned did not meet
with Sophie's approval—too many unheroic hunting scenes reminded her
of the *Broihahn*-drinkers—she turned to Leibniz for suggestions of more
suitable subjects. Congratulating the philosopher on his 'efforts to make us
all immortal', she was confident that 'the present generation will be
adding a worthy chapter to our story'.

The Duke and his eldest son were stoutly defending the Rhine. 'You
see, the French have not yet reduced us to ashes,' she wrote to Leibniz,

informing him that her husband was building 'the most beautiful opera-house that was ever seen' next to the Leine palace. Since this edifice, built of wood from the local forests, but to be described as a '*vraie maison d'or*' by an admiring visitor, arose on the site where John Frederick's books, turned out yet again, had found temporary lodgings, his pleasure must have been tempered with concern. Nor would he have been wholehearted in his admiration of the first opera that was performed in the new building. Complaining to Sophie of uphill work in view of the inefficiency of Modenese historians, past and present—'all the names and dates muddled' —and assuring her of his determination to reject all suspect information, he ended by observing that 'truth is usually more glorious than fiction'.

Enrico Leone, the first performance of which opened the 1689 Carnival, bore, however, only the most tenuous relationship to Henry the Lion as presented by Leibniz. The creators of this opera—Agostino Steffani, diplomatist and composer, later to become a bishop, who wore his appurtenances with positively theatrical flair, and Hortensio Mauro, Ernst August's Italian secretary, whom Sophie called '*notre Apollon*' for producing the libretto—treated their audiences to more than five hours of Henry's legendary adventures. The Court—and later the citizens of Hanover, free of charge—were transported to strange and wonderful places. There were no less than ten elaborate changes of Tommaso's magical scenery. A ship was wrecked in the storm-tossed Mediterranean; a ghost appeared in a puff of smoke; a griffon swooped from the tree-tops to snatch Henry to its eyrie; devils, Jews, fauns, nymphs, heroes and Amazons danced: and after a realistic battle-scene came the finale, in which Henry's triumphal chariot was drawn by four live horses through a replica of the Lüneburger Tor.

It was Ernst August's firm intention to make the Hanoverian Carnival the grandest and most colourful of the north. 'Subjects used to entertain their rulers, but now rulers are entertaining their subjects,' an onlooker remarked in the hearing of Hortensio Mauro as the Court, in fancy dress, drove through the streets in open carriages dressed like floats, accompanied by musicians on horseback. Anyone with the price of a mask and a domino, on sale at the town-hall entrance, could at certain hours walk freely through the public rooms of the palace, where musicians played, and cold collations, constantly replenished, were laid out on long tables. It was all exceedingly grand, and designed to impress foreign visitors.

Between Carnivals, Ernst August would issue regular economy-edicts. 'At the risk of displeasure from up high'—the Duke's, not the Lord's—kitchens, bakehouse, patisserie and cellars were instructed to cease all extravagance in day-to-day management. Except on his own and his son's table, no expensive French wines were to be served, only ordinary German ones. The steward was to see that it was wholesome and drinkable, and should there be jokes or sarcastic remarks these were to be reported and punished at once. The silver was to be counted both before and after meals. Only members of the family were occasionally allowed to have meals served in their apartments. All others were to present themselves at the hall as soon as the trumpeter on the tower sounded the dinner hour, and the footmen at the door were to make sure that only those officially entitled to eat gained entry. Should persons of quality try to sneak in, they were politely to be turned away; common folk might be chased off with sticks, or arrested and taken to the guardroom, except on Wednesdays, when by tradition the poor collected rations in the forecourt. Dogs were banned except for family pets; others, if found wandering about or barking during church services, would be clubbed to death or taken to the hangman. Moreover, the practice of throwing them scraps from the kitchens would cease, and all bones would be sold to the glue-makers.

Leibniz composed a humble petition signed, over paw-prints, 'Lelaps', 'Mopse' and 'Amarille' for the Hanoverian gamedogs, mastiffs and lapdogs. With quotations from Homer and the scriptures, they reminded the Duke of the role which dogs had played in the history of the world, and requested the reversal of his decision. Otherwise, they would be forced to withdraw their services and the woods would be overrun by wolves, villages would be unguarded and their mistresses' laps left to lovers.

In 1690 Carnival visitors again arrived to make merry, but all turned out contrary. News reached the Court of the death of Prince Charles Philip, Sophie's fourth boy, at the Battle of Pristina, and the festivities were cancelled. The Raugrave Charles Edward lost his life on the same occasion, but Sophie so grieved for her son, 'whose merits made him agreeable to all the world, and especially to his mother and father', that she was scarcely able to mourn her nephew. Conflicting rumours followed the first positive report of the young man's death. Few officers had lived to return alive from Albania, and Ernst August, finding no one who knew for certain what happened, sent Captain Klenck to the location. Sophie did not flatter herself with false hopes, but her blood almost stopped running when the Captain reported that her son had been found by the Turks, surrounded by his dead officers and pages. 'They said he was a brave Pasha who asked for no quarter, killed many of them with his own hands, and had four horses killed under him. It makes him all the more to be regretted,' she wrote to the Raugravines, who responded with sorrowful letters, glad only that Sophie's life had been saved by judicious bleeding.

Louise and Ameliese were still leading a twilight existence in the Palatinate, as guests of the new Catholic Elector. 'You must be pleased that King William has Ireland,' Sophie wrote to Louise in July 1690 after the battle of the Boyne. 'What a comfort that Meinhard reaped such glory and apparently made his fortune. It pleases me for Caroline. I expect she'll be going to England now, and perhaps you will go to join her? The late Elector always wanted to establish you there.'

Caroline's husband, created Duke of Leinster for his services, had distinguished himself in this battle, in which William III defeated James II, who had been sent to Ireland by Louis XIV. Caroline and her husband settled in London, as Sophie had predicted, but the Raugravines remained where they were, while Sophie travelled to Carlsbad with her son Maximilian to regain health and spirits. Her melancholy, however, only increased when, as he was shooting swallows, his gun exploded in his hand and took off two of his fingers. In December Frederick August was killed in Transylvania. The death of her second son, following closely on Charles Philip's, which Sophie still found hard to accept, was almost too much for her. She seemed to have run out of tears. She envied Louise for still being able to cry when yet another Raugrave died—in a duel, not in battle—in April. She herself could neither weep nor sleep.

Liselotte, subject to nightmares ever since the destruction of Heidelberg and Mannheim by the French in the previous year, which Sophie could not bear to think of either, wrote full of sympathy that she knew well what it was to be unable to go to sleep from grief, and to start up from having dozed off with one's misery stark before one's eyes.

Frederick August's death revived all Sophie's resentment of Ernst August's harsh treatment of her son. Although she had tried her best to remain loyal to her husband, she had always thought that there was justice in the Prince's case. Nor did she change her opinion when, at

Anton Ulrich's instigation, these claims were now revived by Max, supported by two Hanoverian officers called Moltke—the one Master of the Hunt, the other an Equerry—and assisted by Anton Ulrich's secretary Blume.

At the end of November 1692, Figuelotte told her father that Max was planning a *coup d'état*, and that Blume had called on her husband's premier minister, Danckelmann, for support. On 5th December Max, the Moltkes and Blume were placed under arrest and confessed all, and more than Sophie had ever known.

She begged M von der Bussche, her son's tutor—in writing, 'since it is at present a crime to speak to me'—to explain to the Duke that he was mistaken when he accused her 'of wishing to plunge the country into a bath of blood and fire'. Until the arrests were made, she had not known that there had been talk of mounting an army against him. She had not revealed what little she knew of Max's plan in order 'to save him from being in the condition in which he now finds himself'. No loving mother could do less. The Duke was wrong to accuse her of crimes against his person, and she wished that he would realise it. Thinking of Clara von Platen—'I wish they would not mention my name in the same breath as that woman's'—she added sadly that 'there are, of course, people in the world who would do their utmost to prevent the Duke from returning to me. They won't leave anything undone to rob me of his friendship.' Even George Louis now believed that she had sided with his younger brothers because she loved them better than himself.

Max was released on George William's intercession and, after renewing his oath of loyalty, returned to his father's good graces. But he was to spend little time in Hanover, and lived at his uncle's Court in Celle until he eventually moved to Vienna, where he made periodic attempts to regain his inheritance and finally became a Catholic.

Blume was released after seven months, when Equerry Moltke was also set free and banished from the country. Huntsman Moltke was found guilty of high treason and condemned to death. On Easter Sunday 1693, his jailer found his cell empty but for a note '*Kyrie Eleyson*, Moltk' is gone'. On Easter Monday, however, the street urchins were singing 'Christ has risen and Moltk's been caught' under the prison window where Moltke was lying behind newly mended bars, awaiting his execution—by the sword, as befitted a gentleman.

These troubles cast a shadow over the joy occasioned by the success that Grote had at last achieved in Vienna. In December 1692, dressed in the outmoded Spanish barrel cape and puffed trousers that were still worn at the Imperial Court, he had driven to the Hofburg in a coach drawn by six dappled greys to collect the ninth Electorate for his master.

He had knelt three times before Leopold, who was almost swamped by his Imperial regalia as he sat on his throne with the habitual immobility that made people wonder if he were indeed alive. (An impertinent courtier had once walked all around the motionless figure, 'to see if it breathed'.) After addresses and oaths of allegiance on Ernst August's behalf, while the sword of state, unsheathed, was held high, Grote received what came to be called the most expensive bonnet in the history of the world.

Twelve of the famous creamy-grey or Isabel-coloured Hanoverian horses, bred only in the ducal stud, with golden trappings, which Grote had presented to Leopold before the ceremony, were the least of it. In return for the Electorate, Ernst August undertook to furnish armies for Hungary, battalions for the war in Flanders, money for the Turkish war, and an auxiliary army of 2,000 men whenever the Emperor might need it. He also promised to help the Emperor to maintain his rights in the Spanish succession in case of the King of Spain's childless demise, and a further fortune had gone into the pockets of all the Electoral ministers, whose masters were still implacably refusing to welcome a ninth, and were not to do so for another ten years.

When the bonnet arrived in Hanover in March 1693, Ernst August ordered a Gala Court in the Rittersaal, where the fields in the coffered ceiling were newly painted with the arms of ancient Guelphs as unearthed by Leibniz, and the familiar family portraits on the walls were interspersed with copies of Guelph countenances in a decorative scheme worked out by the philosopher himself. Ernst August and Sophie sat under a canopy in ermine mantles. They were flanked by George Louis and Sophie Dorothea, by whose side stood George August, aged nine, and the five-year-old Sophie Dorothea. All who were not in state-robes had new clothes, and the official mistresses made an especially rich and ostentatious picture. Mme von Platen, hung with jewels and in a regrettably colourful costume, was set off by a semi-circle of maids of honour, as though she herself was a princess.

Melusina von der Schulenburg, who had taken over the office of mistress of George Louis from Mme von Platen's sister, stood behind Sophie as *dame d'honneur*. In front of the assembly, on a table covered in red velvet, rested the bonnet and the diploma. The party rose while M von Platen read out this document, and remained standing as Ernst August placed the bonnet on his head, saying, 'by the grace of God we clothe ourselves in this symbol of temporal power'. Sophie's maids of honour placed a tiara on her carefully arranged, thinning hair.* Special services were held in the churches all over the country, and special envoys were simultaneously despatched to other Courts to inform them of the new honour. Liselotte heard that her uncle had spent a whole million thalers on his promotion, and wondered why he should have wished to alter his condition at all, since it brought nothing but disharmony to the family, a sentiment which Sophie was secretly inclined to share.

The Carnival of 1693, the first Electoral one, was attended by more visitors than ever. Figuelotte came with her husband, and the Raugravines appeared in the retinue of the Princess of Eisenach. Princes prevented from joining the festivities begged friends to write detailed reports. One such report was ordered by the Queen of Sweden from the hand of Aurora, Countess von Königsmarck.

As admired for her beauty as she was criticised for gallantry, Aurora, owing to her rudeness to Mme von Platen during an earlier visit, was almost *persona non grata* in Hanover, in spite of being a member of a family that had for years been friendly with the Courts of Brunswick-Lüneburg. The old Countess had been a guest at Celle during the late 1670's, when her youngest son, Philip Christopher, had been prevented from so much as talking to Sophie Dorothea (he had since been able to make up for lost time, having held a commission in the Hanoverian army for over three years); an elder son had lost his life in Ernst August's service; an eminently respectable daughter was with the Queen of Denmark, Ernst August's sister; and no one liked to believe that a further Königsmarck son had murdered Thomas Thynne of Longleat, a crime of which he had been acquitted after establishing a doubtful alibi.

On the whole, white sheep outnumbered the black in the Königsmarck flock, and *la belle Aurore* just managed to scrape into Hanover and to send

* 'Lots of combs but little hair' her impossible Prussian grandson said later, much to her amusement.

a very full account to Sweden after all. She assured the Queen that the new Elector's majesty was quite unimpaired by the modest peasant-costume which he wore on the first night of the Carnival. Sophie's Scaramouche costume, on the other hand, may have been amusing but was highly unbecoming. Aurora's view was apparently shared by Sophie's ladies, because they had improved their harlequin motley by adding belts and hats spangled with diamonds. As she described Sophie Dorothea and Figuelotte, Aurora became breathless: '*Beauté tyrannique et beauté charmante . . .* who was to say which was the more enchanting?'

Her brother Philip was well qualified to supply the answer. As Aurora knew well, he had conceived a passion for Sophie Dorothea—she herself had helped him to obtain the Princess's portrait by pretending that she wanted it for herself. She also knew for a fact what most of the Court could only suspect: Count Königsmarck had for the last two years given up his philandering habits, for 'all women were distasteful compared with the *aimable brune*'. He no longer slept with Ernst August's mistress Mme von Platen, through whose good offices he had hoped to achieve speedy promotion, but instead slept with George Louis' wife whenever—all too rarely—there was a safe opportunity.

The Carnival season proved to be a godsend for meetings, and masks and dominoes were helpful. But the Electoral family had to make count-less official appearances, and Königsmarck, the most jealous of lovers, suffered agonies. While the Italian Company went about its business on the stage at the opera, and Aurora admired the spectacle of the ladies 'in boxes, richly decorated with gilded sculptures', against a background 'hung in cloth of gold striped in fire-red velvet, lit with thousands of white candles that made their jewels sparkle', he moodily wondered what his *adorable Léonisse* might be whispering behind her fan. On Shrove Tuesday in the final fancy dress processions he had the pleasure of spending a whole evening close to her. Cast as the *Grand Vezier* in Sophie Dorothea's con-tingent of Turks, with a horse's tail carried ceremoniously before him, he entered the ballroom in her wake together with a party of infidels. Aurora was one of the wives of the Prophet, there were quantities of slaves in chains, and Ameliese von Degenfeld was a sultana in the quadrille that brought the six weeks' celebrations to a close.

Figuelotte had chosen a classical theme for her party in this event. Preceded by musicians, she led Orpheus, Muses, Bacchus, satyrs, nymphs,

Bacchantes and Silenus's ass into the ballroom in procession. The donkey, frightened by a trumpet, kicked his hindlegs about him and had to be led away. Peace was restored when Orpheus—a German prince—sang the story of Eurydice, accompanied by the Muse of Music—an Italian nobleman—on the clavichord, and the first Electoral Carnival ended at four o'clock on Ash Wednesday morning.

CHAPTER SIX

Electress of Hanover
(1693–1705)

In the spring of 1693 Hanoverian troops were sent not only westward but also to the northern border, where the King of Denmark, wrote Sophie, 'seemed to be copying Louis XIV'. Eleven thousand Danish troops were massed by the River Elbe opposite Ratzeburg, and 'if they cross the river, we'll shoot'. During the engagement that followed, Königsmarck distinguished himself through bravery and foresight. Sophie, who had always liked him, sent him a favour for his standard, although George Louis said that he would have thought his old Mama well past such coquetry.

Sophie Dorothea complained to Königsmarck of Sophie's constant desire for her company. She was bidden to join outing after tedious outing, during which Sophie mentioned him so often that 'if she were younger I should be jealous'. Königsmarck, who had felt Mme von Harling's gaze rest strangely upon him when before his departure he had built card-houses with the Princess's children, begged her not to give herself away. 'Trust no one,' he wrote, 'particularly not *la Romaine*', his code-name for Sophie. One could never tell what lay in the backs of people's minds. It was likely that the Electress had found that the Princess would leave off day-dreaming at the mention of his name, and this alone might arouse suspicion.

He was quite certain that the love-affair was no longer a secret, although neither he nor the Princess could tell exactly what was known and by whom. Sophie had once again spoken to Sophie Dorothea on the subject of suitable behaviour—did she know more than she would reveal? And Figuelotte had sharply responded to her sister-in-law's joking reference to her love for music by saying, 'It is fortunate, Madame, that my passions are so easily satisfied'—did she know the truth?

Königsmarck himself had outgrown his earlier rashness. At one time he had thought nothing of dipping Sophie Dorothea's grubby chemise ribbon into his wine and drinking a toast to his *Léonisse* with his brother officers. Now he tried to behave with the utmost circumspection, and urged his beloved to do the same.

But Mme von Platen called on her and dropped worrying hints, and it was more than likely that 'the great *Dondon*' knew exactly what was going on. She had, after all, a two-fold reason for keeping herself informed; she was as interested in the family affairs of her faithful elderly lover as in the private ones of her young unfaithful one. To allay what he hoped were only suspicions Königsmarck, back from the wars, once more attended her orgies and even returned to her bed. But since he moodily ignored the half-naked girls hired to entertain the officers, and remained sadly unenthusiastic during his private meetings with 'the old Tartar's mare', she remained as suspicious as before.

It stood to reason that in a small town, where to go down the Leinestrasse by day was to bow to a hundred Court ladies peering from their windows, a cloaked figure whistling strains from 'La folie d'Espagne' under Sophie Dorothea's window at night whenever Königsmarck's regiment was in town could not go unnoticed forever. And when Königsmarck's and Sophie Dorothea's carefully coded letters, sometimes written in invisible ink supplied by his secretary Hildebrandt, began to disappear out of the Count's hat, where the Princess's *confidante* Knesebeck posted them, and later went astray between the front and the palace, it was likely that all would soon be discovered.

Not only did Mme von Platen have her spies everywhere but clear, independent warnings were beginning to be issued to Königsmarck by Bodewils, his general, and by the younger Princes themselves. The lovers discussed their chances of flight, first in general terms—'I would willingly beg our bread from all four corners of the earth'—and then as an actual possibility.

But how could he ask an Electoral Princess to run away with him, asked Königsmarck, in a rage of frustration when George Louis' arrival in Hanover was announced, earlier than expected, at the end of 1693? Had she become too grand for him? Were George Louis' embraces more exciting now that he was an electoral Prince? Did his own suffer by comparison? How could his *déesse* bear to '*monter à cheval*' with that brute? He could hardly bear to think of it. Königsmarck only hoped that she would remember, if not actually recite, the poem that began '*Hélas, mon prince, comme vos amours sont minces*'. And what would happen if she became pregnant by her husband? It would be the end of all their plans.

But perhaps she had changed her mind? Found someone else? Max, perhaps? Königsmarck knew that Max was lodged in the apartment adjoining hers, and wrote furious reams of jealous fantasy. Did Max see her with her hair loose about her shoulders and her incomparable bosom? No connecting door? Max might have drilled a hole through which to observe her in her shift or even out of it. And who could blame her, he said, for preferring a lover whose discovery would not bring her lifelong imprisonment?

Königsmarck and Sophie Dorothea had long enjoyed frightening each other to death by imagining the possible consequences of their liaison. Königsmarck, who liked to call himself 'a poor butterfly burnt by the flame', had even dreamt of his own execution, with Grote and Bodewils as judge and hangman, and woken up screaming and streaming with sweat. They knew they were playing with fire, and it kept them at sizzling point. The idea of running away was sufficiently dramatic to appeal to them both. They laid their plans, childish and inadequate. Königsmarck would apply to his sister Aurora's new lover, the Elector of Saxony, for employment, and Sophie Dorothea would ask her parents for an allowance and use her husband's affair with the Schulenburg as the pretext for wishing a separation.

George William refused to hear of any such thing, and both he and Eleonore made pious speeches about the necessity of living well with one's husband. Eleonore, who had never liked George Louis, made secret attempts to raise money for her daughter, but did not collect enough for practical purposes. So nothing had been settled when Königsmarck returned from Dresden with—Sophie noted—a black eye, acquired during a mock battle with his prospective employer, who had pelted him with hard-boiled eggs.

It is unlikely that the Princess followed his despairing advice to confide in her parents. 'Say that you'll do something desperate, then they'll either have to accept me or get rid of me altogether,' he had suggested. Now committed to the Elector of Saxony, he was in Hanover only to tidy up his affairs and to take his official congé from the Elector. George Louis, on the point of leaving for Berlin, dismissed him ungraciously and hoped that the Count would settle his gambling debts before he departed.

Just before he was due to leave, on the evening of 15th July 1694, Königsmarck said that he was tired and was going to bed. His secretary was not surprised to see him leave the house about midnight, wearing his assignation cloak. But when he had not returned on the following morning, or during the next four days, Hildebrandt notified first Aurora and then the authorities of his master's disappearance. A search for the Count proved fruitless and his rooms were sealed—normal procedure when officers were missing—but not before various papers had, ominously, been carried away.

Sophie Dorothea's anguished enquiries about her friend, for whom she had waited in vain all through the night of the 15th, kindled much gossip, which blazed up when she and Knesebeck were placed under arrest a few days later and taken away from Hanover.

The Court denied any connection between the Count's disappearance and the Princess's sudden departure. 'On the Holzmarkt, they're saying that the witches of Dresden have spirited him away,' wrote Sophie to Louise a few days later, alluding to a recent witchcraft scare in Saxony, adding that she had lately been rather chagrined but would not make a journal of her troubles, and only say that to restore the young man, as the Elector of Saxony was by now demanding, was beyond her dear Duke's power.

By August, when there had still been no sign of Königsmarck, the affair had become a *cause célèbre*. Hanoverian envoys had strict instructions not to discuss it at the Courts to which they were accredited, where little else was talked about. Sophie quite saw that Königsmarck's friends 'must regard his disappearance as strange, especially since all the world knows what time of day it is', but to enquiries about her daughter-in-law she replied that the Electoral Princess had conceived an aversion for her husband, and that the two fathers had decided to let her live apart. 'My son is enjoying himself with his sister in Berlin and does not know what has happened here,' she wrote soon after the events of 15th July. 'We have now stopped thinking of this unpleasant affair.'

Aurora von Königsmarck dismissed it less lightly, and asked the

Brandenburg envoy in Dresden for his opinion on all the conflicting unofficial reports that were pouring in from Hanover and Celle. Four assailants, hired by a lady whom he had spurned, were supposed to have pounced upon her brother? A mysterious prisoner was allegedly being served daily with three-course meals at the Leine palace (a miserable menu, since palace repasts comprised ten courses in two or three removes)? Rooms were being prepared in an old fortress in the Harz—did not all this suggest that her brother was alive and kept in custody?

The envoy behaved with exemplary discretion. He had told Aurora, he reported to Hanover, that 'in his opinion Count Königsmarck was either alive or dead', and had advised her that in either case it would be wiser to stop her enquiries at once. If Königsmarck were alive, probing might hasten his death in view of Ernst August's declared ignorance of his fate; and if he were dead no purpose would be served.

So Aurora confined herself to making venomous remarks about Mme von Platen, who became quite ill because no one had ever dared to speak of her in such a way. Sophie and Figuelotte said that one must really marvel at Aurora's power of invention, and Liselotte quite agreed; in spite of Aurora's revelations, it was most unlikely that Mme von Platen had pursued Königsmarck on her own account—she probably wanted him for her daughter, who eventually became Mme von Kielmansegg and was later known as Lady Darlington. As for Sophie Dorothea, Liselotte only hoped no one was thinking of sending her to France, where she would shame them all. She spoke from the heart, for misalliances were her greatest aversion. 'Mouse-droppings in the pepper' was how she described girls of unequal birth who married into noble families, and she declared that they brought with them nothing but disaster. To her undying fury, her own son had been married to a daughter of Louis XIV and Mme de Montespan —not only a 'mouse-dropping' but 'the product of double adultery'.

Königsmarck was never seen again, alive or dead, and his disappearance remained a mystery for years. He is now believed to have been assassinated by officers of the Palace and his body dumped into the Leine, where a few years later dead cattle and other noxious substances so polluted the water that the palace bakehouse in due course got a new well.

At the secret divorce hearing in December the wretched Sophie Dorothea incriminated herself by pleading innocence and repentance in the same breath. She had to tread carefully, as she had no means of knowing which part of her correspondence was in the Court's possession—the letters that Königsmarck carried against his heart together with her portrait, the ones that he kept in the secret drawer which was a feature of his and every other desk, or those that she and Knesebeck had laboriously stitched into the lining of her curtains. She insisted, however, that there had been no criminal intimacy, and said that it was her husband's indifference to her that had caused her ruin. Appearances, she realised, were against her, but if her plea of innocence would do nothing else, it would contribute to her *satisfaction intérieure*.

This was indeed all the comfort she was to have for the rest of her life, which, with a short exception, she was to spend at the timbered *Schloss* of Ahlden. Except for Eleonore, who occasionally visited her—grieving for the rest of the time as for a lost child—Sophie Dorothea never again saw a single member of her family, including her children, until she died in 1726.

Knesebeck was found guilty of alienating the Princess from her husband and sentenced to life imprisonment, but she successfully defended herself against the charge of attempting to murder George Louis by insisting that she always used the nitric acid which was found in her possession for the care of her complexion. After three years she escaped from prison to Wolfenbüttel, and wrote the memoirs on which Anton Ulrich was to base Volume V of his literally endless novel. This was published in 1707. 'Under which name is Count Königsmarck hiding?' asked Liselotte, who did not at first reading recognise any of the characters. Once Sophie had identified them all for her, she supposed that Anton Ulrich would have made his heroine—Sophie Dorothea, disguised as the Roman Octavia herself—innocent to save the honour of the family.

There were countless spin-offs from this novel, from the romance by an anonymous woman-writer which Liselotte threw into the fire in disgust to innumerable German, French and English historical novelettes of the nineteenth and twentieth centuries. All these served to establish the legend of Sophie Dorothea as an angel of virtue wronged, and Sophie as the cruel, dominating mother-in-law who drove her to her doom. The myth persisted even after part of Sophie Dorothea's correspondence, marked '*Lettres d'amour de ma grandmère*', in Frederick the Great's hand, had been discovered in Sweden. These not only irrefutably disproved Victorian notions of the Princess's innocence but also showed her to have been a tease, caught up in a banal affair that got out of hand not so much through ennobling passion as through mismanagement. Sir Adolphus Ward, Sophie's distinguished English biographer, was among the first to prick the romantic bubble surrounding her daughter-in-law. He said that while it was only natural to regret Sophie Dorothea's very sad fate, it was almost impossible to feel any sympathy for the girl herself.

Certainly Sophie felt none. 'It's an ill wind . . .' she wrote to Louise, expressing some pleasure that the Provost of Ahlden's salary had been increased since he was in charge of the Princess, which he found most useful as he had seven children to bring up. And Eleonore's sadness was taken as yet another mark of her inferior character: anyone else, said Liselotte, would pretend that nothing had happened, since it was through her own fault that the Princess had been so hopelessly brought up. Had she enjoyed Mme von Harling's ministrations, all would have been very different.

Mme von Harling's nannihood was famous. Even very loosely connected princes had applied to Sophie to accept their children into her care and she had unfailingly done wonders with their manners and deportment. Young ladies had arrived behaving like bumpkins and looking like 'things they put into the cherry trees to scare the birds away', but with her help, and that of 'the gallows'—a structure to prevent slouching—the dancing master and Sophie's tailor, they had departed as presentable persons who married well and continued to write loving letters which they signed with humble respects and eternal gratitude.

But even a paragon like Mme von Harling knew defeat when Figuelotte's five-year-old son Frederick William was sent from Brandenburg for an extended stay. He was Sophie's favourite grandson, but his visit turned out to be an unmitigated disaster.

The catalogue of Frederick William's misdeeds grew daily: hair pulled out by the fistful; valets and play-fellows kicked downstairs; a new brocade dressing-gown, braided and not to his liking, flung on to the nursery fire; and the life tormented out of his Hanoverian cousin George August. At the mention of punishment the miscreant would scrabble on to a high window-ledge, threatening to dash himself and any rescuer to the courtyard below. Plainly, he was too difficult to handle, and when he almost choked to death on a buckle the visit was cut short.

Sophie continued to dote on him, sure that he would improve in time, and Liselotte agreed: no one exposed to Mme von Harling's regime could fail to draw some benefit. After the boy had been taken away his grateful father, planning to reward Mme von Harling's noble, civilising attempts, had her walls measured for a set of tapestries from Berlin. Her satisfaction at being relieved of her fiendish charge quite over-shadowed the fact that her wall hangings never materialised; Sophie was sure that the Brandenburg minister Danckelmann had pocketed the tapestry money, just as he had the board-wages for the boy's own large, helpless nursery staff.

After the official divorce hearing at the end of December, which left George Louis but not his wife free to remarry, life in the Leine palace resumed its normal course. Sophie went on an unending round of comfort visits, for there was hardly a family of her acquaintance that had not lost a son, father, cousin or brother in the wars. She returned home to face another sad spectacle, for Ernst August's health was seriously failing, and Mme von Harling's many ailments caused her the torture of the damned.

Shortly after the new year had been played in with the customary early morning violins and cymbals, news came from England that Queen Mary, still childless, was dead. The new mourning wardrobe that Louise had earlier chosen for Sophie in Frankfurt arrived just in time. Sophie, out of touch with fashion, did not know what to do about the sleeves, which barely covered her elbows. 'Do you wear them with lace undersleeves, or what?' In the end she had them let down, and Court mourning inhibited the dancing at the 1695 Carnival.

The opera, however, presented two new pieces, and Figuelotte, in Hanover on one of her regular visits, liked them so much that she had them performed over and over again. She had not yet tired of them when she travelled on to join her husband in Clèves, where the Princes of the Empire were meeting to discuss the next season's campaigns. Ernst August was too unwell to attend, having suffered a nearly fatal 'access' in Wiesbaden. He recovered, but not completely and not for long.

Sophie was once more spending most of her time in his company, and as his health deteriorated further she became the only person whom he could bear to have about him. Liselotte said this showed that he was sorry for making her unhappy in the past. As always, Liselotte longed to be with *tante*. The quiet life in Hanover sounded to her preferable to the relentless round of fêtes in France, where she was becoming a greater misfit every day. She longed to walk down the gravelled paths of Herrenhausen, where Quirini was constructing the largest greenhouse ever seen (the diversity and beauty of its lemons, oranges and pineapples later impressed Lady Mary Wortley Montagu), and desperately envied all princesses who had the freedom to travel. Lucky Figuelotte, much better off than if she had married into France, since she was able to see her relations. Lucky, lucky Benedicta, who had been away from France for two years and was now, in fact, in Hanover for the marriage between her daughter and the Prince of Modena, a match that Leibniz had personally initiated on the strength of the d'Este connection which he had earlier discovered.

The Modena wedding, in November, was the last occasion of magnificence that the Elector was able to enjoy. Even the strain of travelling from Herrenhausen to Hanover, to see a Pastorale that Figuelotte had arranged, was so great that all the pleasure was spoilt. He was also gradually losing the sight of one eye, and neither his own doctors nor the many recipes and remedies that poured in from all over Europe were of any avail.

Sophie did not spare her usual comments on the entire medical profession, but Leibniz told her that the patients themselves were to blame. They either asked for miracles (Sophie herself put great store by a quack who manufactured Aurum Potabile as a panacea for all ills) or despised them altogether (she did that, too). Neither course was designed to further the progress of science. What he suggested was a pooling of knowledge in a Society of Medicine as part of a society of all the sciences. (Berlin, he privately thought, was a more likely place for such a body than Hanover, and later on he sent Figuelotte a fossilised mammoth tooth found near Brunswick, accompanied by a learned dissertation to stimulate her interest in science and whet her appetite for more.)

Ernst August was still able to take notice of the Peace of Rijswick in 1697, and to regret that it did nothing to curb the power of France. But he was far too ill to entertain the gigantic young Tsar, who was expected to pass through Hanover on his way to study naval engineering in Holland.

News of Peter's progress through the Western world, of which he meant to make Russia a part, enthralled the Courts of the Empire. Sophie's Brandenburg son-in-law, first to welcome the Tsar on German soil, wrote from Königsberg that no detail of the administration was too small to be noted by his visitor. The penal system, especially, had fascinated the Tsar, who had been so anxious to see a man broken on the wheel that he had offered one of his own servants for demonstration purposes when no suitable Prussian candidate had been available. He had become very bad-tempered when this offer had been declined, and no less put out when his host refused to put to death a footman who had startled the company by dropping a silver platter on to the marble floor.

None of these stories affected in the least Peter's reputation of being a *fort honnête homme*, and Sophie was most curious to see him and his bearded courtiers in their long exotic robes, and the fur hats trimmed with plumes and aigrettes that covered their shaved heads. Unfortunately, Frederick's gala treatment had rather overwhelmed the Tsar. He preferred simplicity, but he agreed, finally, to take a meal with the Hanoverian *Herrschaften* provided there was no fuss. On 25th July Sophie led the family party, including Figuelotte, to Coppenbruck near Hanover, where cooks, stewards, pages, waiters and musicians from Hanover were making their preparations. Quantities of poultry and several hundredweight of fish had been sent from Hanover. The meat course marched to the feast on the hoof, followed by kitchen-waggons carrying the ingredients necessary for its preparation, including mountains of the best butter and a minute quantity of nuts.

At the appointed hour in the afternoon members of the Electoral family, with their ladies and ten specially selected gentlemen, stepped out on to the ramparts to see the arriving Russian cortège stop dead some distance away. Peter sent word that there were too many people, more than he had stipulated, more than he could face. He would therefore proceed to the town hall and camp down informally. Since that was where the kitchens had been arranged, it was most awkward. In the end Sophie's Hofmarschall cleared the ramparts, and she took her Court into hiding within the house. Still Peter refused to stir, but finally promised to join the party, on foot, after dark. He further asked that the Hofmarschall should receive him alone, and climb up the stairs in front of him to shield him from the gaze of the assembled company.

Sophie and Figuelotte managed the occasion with great tact, and almost an hour passed before they had gradually approached the Tsar. Peter at first covered his face with his hands when they addressed him, but in time agreed to sit between them, and they entertained him in turn. Figuelotte wrote to Berlin that her Mama, with her accustomed liveliness, asked questions on every subject, and that Peter's replies were invariably *à propos*. She was surprised, she said, that he did not tire of

Sophie and Figuelotte by Louise Hollandine, *ca* 1679.

Liselotte and her son Philippe by Caspar Netscher, *ca* 1679.

conversing, a pleasure in which, she understood, the Russians did not much indulge.

Sophie found the young man 'a mixture of good and bad, like everyone else'. His habit of pulling faces—he had a tic—she thought beyond his powers to control. His table manners were decidedly odd, but as his education had been neglected he was not to blame.

Peter relaxed amazingly in the course of the evening. Calling for wine, he handed out glasses with his own hands, wrenching one from the grasp of a page about to serve Quirini. 'This was a *politesse* which we had not expected,' said Figuelotte, who later saw Fernando, leader of the orchestra, similarly complimented.

The Tsar loved Fernando's melodies—Leibniz was later asked to send him the music—but said he could not dance. Sophie led off with Count Menschikoff to demonstrate how simple the steps were. Still he would not take the floor. It emerged that he had lost his gloves, but after both ladies had felt his calloused hands and exclaimed at his cleverness in knowing to perfection fourteen trades, in the exercise of which he had acquired them, he took them both around the room, marvelling at the hardness of German rib-cages, since whalebone was unknown in Russia. Of all the ladies, the Russians most admired Mme von Platen, because, Sophie explained to Liselotte, of her colourful appearance: thick paint was all the rage in Muscovy. The party became even merrier when Peter and his suite performed Russian and Polish dances, and before it broke up the Tsar sent for a broom and swept his favourite dwarf, whom he had alternately fondled and cuffed all night, out of the room.

When he departed, he took little Sophie Dorothea by the ears and planted a moustachio'd kiss on her face, disarranging her *fontange*. He let go of her to prevent his interpreter from drawing his sword on her brother, who was standing by the door and was thought to be barring the way. He, too, received an enormous kiss. Figuelotte was presented with a crested silver snuff-box which the Tsar had made himself, and, although it was almost dawn when he left, Sophie was sorry to see him go and said she would not have missed the excitement for the world.

Her own presents turned out to be rather a disappointment: four sable skins which were found to be infested with moth, and three pieces of very fine damask, unfortunately too small for anything but chair-covers. Her Hofmarschall fared better, but Sophie magnanimously said that he fully

G

deserved his superb sable cloak for managing everything so neatly, and for drinking the gentlemen of the Tsar's suite under the table and decanting them into their carriages on the following noon.

For the rest of 1697 Sophie did not leave her husband's side. In spite of her dread of disease and the thought of death she sat with him, took all her meals in his rooms and, except during her walks in the afternoons, saw no living soul. At first Ernst August could still move about a little, laboriously, on slippered feet, but soon he could no longer walk even the length of his bedchamber. He still managed to swallow the broths, jellies and minces that made up his diet, no longer served on silver-gilt, because of the danger of verdigris, but on china. By December he could no longer speak. Sophie sometimes imagined that she could see an improvement in his condition. She did her best to amuse and interest him, and to keep him informed of what was happening in the world. Just after Christmas she read out a letter from Figuelotte reporting the dismissal of Frederick's avaricious minister Danckelmann—no friend of hers or the House of Hanover— and thought she detected approval and pleasure in his eyes.

Early in January 1698 Ernst August died. His body was carried from Herrenhausen to Hanover and lay in state, bonnet and ducal crown on velvet cushions to the right and left of the head, sword by the right hand, bishop's staff by the left, and all his standards spaced out around the *lit de parade*.

Strangely, says the historian Nöldeke, no affectionate anecdote survives him. In spite of his enormous luck and his energetic statesmanship he did not capture his country's imagination, and the following generation tended to remember him only for marrying Sophie, which, they said, was the best thing he did in his life.

Sophie did not appear in person to hear the Elector's will, which was read immediately after the interment in March. Her representative, the surviving Princes (except for Max who was plotting from Vienna), George William and government officials were informed that Ernst August had left his widow, besides her apanage, the estate of Herrenhausen including the surrounding villages, and an extra 2,000 thaler a year to maintain the fountains and water artifices. In May Sophie arranged with George Louis, the new Elector, that all revenues and bills would go to him, while she would have the free use of Herrenhausen for her lifetime.

Widowhood did not materially alter her style of living. Since her son had not remarried after his divorce, and showed no sign of wishing to do so, there was no young Electress, and Sophie continued in her official position. Her household remained unchanged except for the addition of Ernst August's old secretary, who understood accounts, and who helped her to supply the younger Princes with regular amounts from her private purse, 'because campaigning is expensive and I cannot let them starve'.

Even Mme von Harling was still about. She had for some time seemed even closer to death than the late Elector, but had miraculously survived him. Just to see her old friend creep about the palace, groping her way from chair to chair, made Sophie hold herself a little straighter and walk a little faster, as usual outpacing even her more mobile ladies. Since it was clear that the duties of Mistress of the Household were beyond Mme von Harling, Sophie again tried to introduce the Raugravines into her ménage, but the problems of precedence remained insurmountable. Instead of the 'old Pantocrate' there were now two official mistresses basking in Electoral glory. One of them, Mme von Kielmansegg, was actually George Louis' half-sister, but was widely assumed to be his mistress as well. Neither she nor Mme von der Schulenburg would dream of yielding the *pas*, and Sophie refused to see her nieces slighted. They sent anxious enquiries about the state of her health, and she put their minds at rest by replying that 'one does not die of grief'. Mme von Platen's pitiful condition, however, hardly bore this out. At palatial Linden, the scene of so many in-decorous parties at which she had loved to see her guests dance on her tables, she suffered a complete physical and mental breakdown. She no longer drove about accompanied by scarlet liveried footmen in her carriage that resembled the state coach, she was no longer seen in her dreadful mustard yellow *manteau*, her make-up melting drop by leaden drop; indeed, she was no longer seen at all, and within two years she was dead.

Frederick wrote from Brandenburg that he wished his dearest Mama would come for a long visit. The delightful walks that could now be taken at Lützenburg, where the gardens had been laid out even before the build-ing of Figuelotte's palace had begun in 1689, were quite lovely, and were sure to dissipate melancholy thoughts. He was also looking forward to telling her all about Danckelmann, who, after being most politely dis-missed, had been most ungraciously arrested and put to trial.

Eberhardt von Danckelmann had been accused of every crime under the sun because Brandenburg was found to be on the verge of bankruptcy, whereas the Elector's profitable deals in men and arms should have made it rich. Nothing, however, was proved against the minister, not even misappropriation of funds. This surprised Sophie, but although she wrote to Figuelotte of Mme von Harling's untapestried walls, she begged her not to mention them to Frederick, 'in case he thought that she was still expecting hangings, when she is very comfortable as she is'. In spite of Danckelmann's apparent honesty, all his property was confiscated and he himself exiled, convinced that Figuelotte's intriguing was the cause of his ruin.

Figuelotte always stoutly maintained that she never meddled in affairs of state, but she made no secret of her delight at Danckelmann's fall. He had tried his best to set her husband against her, for fear that Frederick, as weak as he was obstinate, should come under her pro-Hanoverian influence. He had insinuated that she was intent on promoting Brunswick-Lüneburg at the expense of Brandenburg, and had even persuaded Frederick not to appoint her chosen candidate as the Electoral Prince's governor. He had produced a man of his own choice, who was bringing up Frederick William 'like a fool'. It was a good thing Danckelmann was gone.

When people accused Figuelotte of ingratitude to the minister and reminded her that he had personally removed the obstacles to her marriage, she said she owed him no thanks. The point was not to be married, but to be happily married. Now that this *filou* was gone, she looked forward to enjoying a second marriage. Emerging from Lützenburg, where she had increasingly withdrawn into her private circle of intellectuals, her books and her music, she hoped it would be happier than the first.

Frederick wrote to his *herzallerliebsten* Mama, who had been unable to accept his invitation, that now the concord between Berlin and Hanover would once again be as perfect as had been desired at the time of his marriage to Figuelotte. Sophie said to the Princess of Eisenach, 'they love each other more than ever now', and to Figuelotte, 'now they will see that you can do more than play the clavichord'.

'It is only fitting,' wrote Leibniz in a confidential memorandum addressed to both Electresses but discussed with Sophie beforehand, 'that the mother should assist the daughter with good advice on how to repair the damage done by Danckelmann and his government.' To this end, he said, the utmost delicacy was needed. Too great an appearance of intimacy between the ladies might undermine Frederick's renewed confidence in

Figuelotte, and revive the rumours that she meant to govern him, just when he was regaining his personal authority. Since letters were never quite safe because of censorship, what was needed was a man of intelligence, a *personne de confiance*, who had occasion to travel between the two Courts, and could receive and pass on information with such circumspection 'that all was done discreetly without causing suspicion or, God forbid, offence'. In all modesty, he could think of no one better fitted for this delicate charge than himself. Sophie was already honouring him with her confidence. Figuelotte would, he hoped, shortly be doing the same. He knew his way about affairs of state, and was often asked to write appraisals of political developments since he was thought to *approfondir* all he turned his mind to.

And since he was well known to have distinguished himself in the sciences, and was extravagantly applauded abroad if not at home, was he not the man to supervise the arts and sciences in Berlin? It would give him a plausible reason for regular visits and furnish him with excellent opportunities to insinuate ideas into Frederick's mind—to the common good and in the interest of the two illustrious ladies. This plan 'to the glory of Germany' should be pursued with speed and vigour. He humbly begged Figuelotte to send her mother a *petit mot* requesting his visit which Sophie might show to the Elector George Louis, and to acquaint the Elector Frederick with his scientific qualifications.

Leibniz's official letter, written for Frederick's eyes, to which this memorandum was attached, was a masterpiece of diplomacy. Among congratulations on the recent turn of events, and on the Berlin Academy of Arts that had been opened in the previous year, he expressed the certainty that the Observatory, now under construction, would be as fine as that in Paris (welcome praise, since Frederick tried hard to emulate Louis XIV's *gloire*). Astrology, observed Leibniz, was of course only one among many sciences, all equally beautiful and worthy of support. He could go into greater detail, but for the time being would confine himself to observing that God appeared to have chosen Figuelotte as His divine instrument in preserving the balance of power, the safety of the Protestant faith and the well-being of the Empire, since all three depended on a close alliance between her native and her adoptive countries.

Leibniz's official invitation to Brandenburg came in 1699, and in the following year he became the first president of the Berlin Academy of

Sciences. In this capacity he was to draw up proposals for a great variety of schemes, including a plan for founding a local silk industry—he appended full horticultural instructions for the raising of mulberry trees. His political influence, however, remained negligible, and Danckelmann's vacant place as Frederick's mentor was almost immediately filled by Count Kolbe von Wartenberg, whose power was to be, if anything, even greater than that of his predecessor, and whose wife became the Pantocrate of Brandenburg. But Figuelotte was glad of Leibniz's presence. She sometimes complained that he tended to be superficial in the philosophical arguments that were her special joy, but he was a constant guest in Lützenburg, where he advised on architecture, decoration and garden layout, never once agreeing with Quirini, whom Sophie had lent to her daughter. The new theatre was ready to be opened with a great fancy dress fête in celebration of Frederick's birthday. Leibniz was horrified to learn that he was expected to take an active part, dressed as 'an astronomer with a telescope'. This was not his style at all, and he was rescued in the nick of time, able after all to observe the proceedings from the sidelines through his '*petites lunettes*', and to send a full account to Hanover.

George Louis was grumpy about his historiographer's long absence. Where was the history of the Guelphs? 'The mice will have eaten your library if you don't return soon,' wrote Sophie, and Leibniz prepared to take his leave from the *padronanza* in Brandenburg. Before he embarked on his homeward journey he wrote on 21st August 1700, 'Here is a great piece of news of interest to *Votre Altesse Electorale*: the death of the Duke of Gloucester. Now it is time more than ever to think of the English succession.'

He himself had not let the matter rest since it had first been broached, and was conducting a regular correspondence on British affairs with several English political figures. Sophie had not allowed the question of her succession to trouble her sleep. It was a pleasant thought, but nebulous, and for all she knew England had forgotten 'everything Palatine and my existence with it'.

But now that Princess Anne's only surviving son was dead and no one but that Princess herself believed that she would yet produce an heir, and since William had no intention of remarrying, Englishmen had good reason to remember the Electress of Hanover.

George Stepney, English diplomat, in William III's confidence and one of Leibniz's correspondents, wrote her a long letter in September. He surveyed the situation, which he called *la plus délicate*, but which he felt a private person like himself might touch upon even without waiting for Parliament to make its feelings known. He drew up a list of all the persons who might, by blood, have a superior claim to her own. There was, first, James II's son, now eleven, still the guest of Louis XIV and hopelessly under the influence of France; there was his younger sister; there were the Savoys, one of whose sons, through their kinship with the Stuarts, could be put forward. Then there was Benedicta, who could claim seniority since her father had been born prior to Sophie. But all were Papists, and none could 'inherit, possess or enjoy the crown' according to the Declaration of Rights. As William had pointed out at the time of his accession, this act, while not explicitly naming Sophie, clearly implied that she and her descendants would inherit the crown.

Would Sophie, asked Stepney, be kind enough to give him an idea of her attitude by a single word from the pen of Leibniz or some other person? As for himself, he would gladly give twenty years of his life to prove his fidelity to her. He enclosed a book by Sir Peter Fraiser on the means by which she might press her claim.

While Leibniz penned a memorandum of twenty-eight long points, Sophie wrote to Stepney what was to become known as her 'Jacobite letter'. She had read the book, she said, and wondered whether its arguments were as valid as his letter was kind. His kindness was in fact too great. She only wished her life might be long enough to be of some service to him, without robbing his own of a single minute. If she were thirty years younger, forty instead of seventy, her opinion of her blood and her religion would be good enough for her to believe that England was thinking of her. But as there was little likelihood that she would survive two people who, though less fit, were much younger than she was, she feared that her children, after her death, would be regarded as mere foreigners. Moreover, George Louis was far more accustomed to acting the sovereign than 'the poor Prince of Wales', as she called James II's son, who was still malleable, too young to have been affected by the King of France's example, and who would, moreover, be so pleased to recover what his father had thoughtlessly lost that anything at all might be done with him. (Liselotte had written that on being presented with a toy chapel, large enough for a child to pray in, he had kicked it to pieces, saying on being

reproved, 'Why should I not hate what made me lose my kingdom?')
However, 'I am neither so philosophical nor so foolish as not to like
hearing a crown spoken of, and not to reflect on all that you say.'

She posted the letter from Aix, where she was acting as chaperone for
Figuelotte, who was taking the waters. In October the two ladies travelled
to Holland for a rendezvous with William III to discuss the Elector of
Brandenburg's prospective assumption of the title 'King in Prussia', and to
talk also about the English succession. Although the only kingdom to
which Sophie felt she could reasonably look forward was the Kingdom of
Heaven, she wished to neglect nothing that she could do for her House.
Her eldest son, of course, 'was very happy as he was, and did not ask for
a crown', but there were 'others of whom they might like to take their
choice'.

In Brussels the Electresses called on Maximilian Emanuel of Bavaria,
who had been appointed Stadholder of the Spanish Netherlands by his
cousin, the King of Spain. Figuelotte was interested to see that he had
acquired a virago of a wife, and took pleasure in observing that he would
have done better with her. She told him that they would have been ideally
suited, 'since you enjoy all the pleasures that I do not hate, and I'm never
jealous or angry'. She came away with his promise to recognise her husband as King in Prussia, even if Vienna should make difficulties, provided
that the maritime powers agreed first.

After fruitless attempts, in Rotterdam, to winkle Leibniz's philosopher-
friend Bayle out of his bed—migraine, he said—the Electresses reached the
palace of Het Loo. Both admired the house for its *propreté* and the gardens
for their beautiful lawns, which were regularly ironed smooth by a giant
roller pulled by a horse wearing what Figuelotte called 'special boots' so as
not to leave hoofprints.

During the long business talks with William, who looked far from well
but entertained them gallantly, all the parties gained their objectives. For
the promise of supporting Holland against France, Sophie could count on
her official nomination to the English succession, and might hope for an
establishment and annuity such as traditionally went to the heiress to the
crown. Figuelotte's Frederick could count on William's royal recognition
on becoming King in Prussia, so that all the Western states except for
France had now been won round.

In January 1701 Figuelotte, wearing a golden dress with the seams picked out in diamonds under a purple robe embroidered with golden crowns and eagles, acted what she called 'the player-Queen opposite my Aesop'. She looked so pretty that people congratulated the crown on the Queen as well as the Queen on the crown, which her own husband had placed upon her brow after he had performed the same office for himself. Except for a moment's aberration during the long coronation service when she drew out her *tabatière* to take snuff—to receive scowls from Frederick and a note saying, 'Madame, remember where and who you are'—she conducted herself with all the regality that her husband could desire.

Sophie, in Hanover, was kept occupied by the advent of her own '*royauté*', of which, she complained, she had all the bother without any hope for the benefit. News of the Act of Settlement, discussed by Parliament when it opened in February 1701, reached her through Louise. Her niece was always well up in English affairs owing to frequent visits to her Schomberg nieces in London after Caroline's death, and Sophie wrote, 'You seem to be much better informed than we are here'.

In June, when the Act was passed, Cresset, the English envoy to Hanover, brought her the official notification at last. In her handwritten letter of thanks to King William, Sophie wished that he might live a thousand times longer than she. 'Although it is now the fashion for Electors to become Kings, we await that event without impatience here, and pray with all our hearts "God save the King".' Many of her English friends were expressing the hope soon to see her among them, since an heir in London was worth several across the water. 'But how would it look,' she asked her man of British affairs in The Hague, 'for a person of my age to walk behind two people, young enough to be my children, who would not find my presence agreeable, particularly the Princess Anne? Otherwise I should be delighted to be with the people among whom I was raised at my mother the late Queen's Court. Perhaps they would applaud me as a novelty at first, but they would soon tire of an old woman.' In order to demonstrate the security of the Protestant succession, her friends in England thought it desirable to make her descendants known to the country, and a family tree was drawn up. It did not cross Sophie's mind that the genealogist might, in an excess of zeal, have done some deliberate topiary work, providing an extra brother for George August and suppressing Maximilian, whose Catholic leanings were becoming common knowledge. 'He has given the Elector one son too many, and me one too few,' she wrote crossly to Louise. 'I should like to see him better informed.'

English politics altogether mystified her, and she found it impossible to keep track of her supporters and opponents. Large shipments of French gold were apparently arriving in England. Did that mean that Louis XIV was buying support for an English Catholic regime? Were all the opponents of the Hanoverian succession in his pay? And would Schütz please explain the difference between Whigs and Tories? She thanked him for his prompt reply, but would he explain an enigma: how was it that the very first two Milords to cast their votes in her favour were now detested by the Whigs, who claimed to be such great friends of hers? Mercifully, she took Leibniz's advice and decided to ignore all party labels. There were pro-Hanoverians and Jacobites in each party, and both Whig and Tory adherents would find a welcome at her Court as long as they were friends of *la maison*.

She learned with pleasure that her first official visitor was to be Lord Macclesfield, who had been appointed by William to present her with the Act of Settlement in August. His father had been well known to her at The Hague, where he had tried to further her marriage to Charles II. Once again she wished that she were younger, 'so that the son's efforts to make me Queen might succeed better than the father's'. But even if she should not live to see the day, she wanted 'at least to give *en reine*'. Would Schütz please tell her what would be expected? Jewels? Medals? And to what value? Gifts to envoys played an important part in seventeenth century diplomatic intercourse, and any man who did not return home laden with magnificence might be suspected to have failed in his mission.

While Schütz was pondering over this question Sophie, with the help of Leibniz, ordered her Mathilda-medal as a felicitous reminder of the ancient connection between England and the Guelphs. She passed Mathilda's profile without comment, but her own absolutely disgusted her. Why had the artist continued the line descending from the side of her nose down to her jaw, around dewlap and jowl, right up to her chin? Quite different from the portrait she had asked him to follow, and moreover against nature and good sense. Would Leibniz please see that it was altered at once?*

---

* Vanity was, however, no longer one of Sophie's failings. She thanked Louise for a pocket-mirror by saying that she would think of her niece whenever she had occasion to contemplate her wrinkles, and when a relation asked for her portrait in 1707 she 'had it painted in profile ... so she'll have only one half of my horrible face'.

The philosopher was as unsuccessful in directing Sophie's engraver as he was when his own *taille-douce*, demanded by Berlin, made him look like a drunkard. But there he at least managed to get the incorrect 't' removed from his name; here, he failed entirely. The final version of the Mathilda medal, largely uncorrected, formed part of the bounty that Sophie bestowed on Lord Macclesfield's enormous entourage. The ambassador himself received a ewer and basin of solid gold—costing exactly half Sophie's annual income—and a more flattering miniature portrait set in diamonds.

The English visitors were royally treated. A correspondent approvingly wrote that each morning Sophie's own servants waited on every room with silver coffee or teapots, that burgundy, champagne and Rhenish wines were as common as beer, and that the English servants 'did not have to make do with their masters' broken meats, but received daily board-wages of half-a-crown in good silver'.

Whenever Lord Macclesfield stirred from the entirely refurbished house where he lodged at the Court's expense the sentries by his gate beat their drums, and footmen froze to attention wherever he passed.

After a few days of informal chats, entertainments and elaborate dinners, he rode to the palace in a full carriage procession for the ceremonial audience. Sophie, standing under a canopy with her ladies ranged by her right, received him in her presence chamber. Lord Macclesfield approached her, bowing, knelt to kiss hands, and presented her with the red leather *étui*, scrolled in gold, which contained what she was always to call '*mon parchemin*'. She made a little speech and he retreated, bowing. As soon as she decently could, she drew out the document and showed her ladies the sheets of vellum that were held together by a silver cord, from which was suspended a seal with William, enthroned, on one side, and St George and the dragon on the other. That evening the Clarenceaux Herald at Arms invested the Elector with the Garter, and in the morning Lord Macclesfield departed, leaving behind various members of his suite, and Sophie arranged English lessons for the younger members of her family.

In September 1701 news came that James II had died in St Germain and that Louis XIV had proclaimed his son James III of England. How that was supposed to rhyme with Louis' recognition of William III, as stipulated by the peace treaty of Rijswick, Sophie could only wonder.

Leibniz said that the French King desired to make satellites of them all. Louis XIV had already placed his grandson Philip on the Spanish throne and occupied the Spanish Netherlands in his name, having accepted the entire Spanish empire on Philip's behalf as a legacy from the late King of Spain. The partition treaty by which the Emperor's younger son, the Archduke Charles, would share the Spanish dominions with his Bourbon cousin had been brushed aside. The balance of power had gone by the board, and now it was clearly the turn of England. To have 'one of his creatures' on the English throne would give the House of Bourbon undisputed supremacy in Europe. But French interference in English affairs was unacceptable even to Englishmen opposed to the Hanoverian succession, and, on the day after James III had been proclaimed at St Germain, England joined the alliance formed by Messieurs les Etats and the Emperor. The secure Protestant succession in England was now as crucial an issue in maintaining the balance of power in Europe as the succession in Spain, and Herrenhausen became what Liselotte called 'a little England'.

Englishmen flocked 'like the swallows in springtime' to kiss hands and were rewarded with generous Hanoverian hospitality. At the Carnival of 1702 they were treated to the spectacle of their future King reclining on a Roman bed, as were his sister the Queen in Prussia, his youngest brother the Duke Ernst August and numerous courtiers, while the last surviving Raugrave, Charles Maurice, surrounded by empty bottles, represented 'the modern Trimalchion'. His wife Fortunata was played by Figuelotte's friend Mlle von Poellnitz. Together they regaled their guests with fare a long way removed from the preserved cabbage that was still thought to be the principal diet at Court. On this occasion carved chickens revealed eggs which contained not baby chicks but roast ortolans, and children in tiny togas sprang from pies, while birds flew out of others, and were recaptured by Trimalchion's *chasseurs*.

Trimalchion's slaves imitated the sound of Jupiter's thunder whenever he drank, and when he strode about reciting choice items from his *bibliothèque burlesque*—Charles Maurice seems to have collected erotica— they carried behind him a pot so large that Leibniz said he could have drowned in it, to save him the trouble of leaving the room when nature called. (He did, however, frequently disappear into the next apartment *sans cérémonie*.) The Goddess of Discord threw an apple into the proceedings, and Trimalchion threw a glass at Fortunata in the ensuing quarrel, but missed, and all ended most amiably.

Reports of this feast so shocked the King in Prussia that it was a long time before he forgave his wife for taking part in it. Sophie, who attended as a spectator, was less prudish, and only regretted that Charles Maurice, who could make George Louis laugh when even the witty Ernst August failed, was a drunkard in real life. (Indeed, within a few months of Trimalchion this last surviving Raugrave had drunk himself to death on the Italian wines that he preferred to all others, in spite of her and Figuelotte's warnings.)

George Louis regarded his mother's English visitors with lack-lustre eyes, but Sophie looked after them charmingly and they in turn appear to have adored her. Young Lord Monthermen would not even take his prescribed medicines before being assured that she desired it—he died all the same—and John Toland, who had come over with the Macclesfield embassy and was showing no signs of departing, was loud in her praises.

This Irish free-thinker, a Protestant convert, had already expressed his enthusiastic support of Hanover in his book *Anglia Liberata*, and was therefore considered to be to Sophie's taste. She regarded him as entertaining, though she did not particularly admire his intellect, and thought his earlier work, *Christianity, Not Mysterious*, which had been extremely disliked in high church circles, unimpressive—'After all, one thinks what one likes without the permission of authors'.

From the account of his visit, which he later published, it is clear that he was more than satisfied with Hanover, and in particular with his hostess. He described her as unbelievably youthful for her age, and admired her cheerful, agreeably unwrinkled countenance—'not one tooth missing'. He was amazed that she embroidered, read and wrote without spectacles—'I often saw her do letters of a small character in the dusk of the evening'.

Since the anti-Jacobites wished to establish the heir apparent as firmly as possible in England, they took understandable pleasure in the fact that Sophie was no tottering old lady, but in such excellent trim that a visit to England might again be discussed. Before any such arrangements were made William III died, and Anne ascended the throne in March 1702.

Keenly feeling the loss of the King who had always been her friend, Sophie supposed that 'we must console ourselves as best we can with the

Queen we've got'. But she felt apprehensive about the future, since Anne was known to favour 'all those who had opposed the late King'. However, formal letters assured Sophie and George Louis of Anne's friendship and affection, and she had declared on her ascension that she intended following the design that William had outlined. Marlborough was sent to Holland to reassure Messieurs les Etats that everything possible would be done 'to curb the exorbitant power of France', and Sophie and her friends were impressed by the Queen's statesmanship.

The first, and in the event the only, visible sign of the Queen's *bonté* and *amitié* was her command that Sophie's name should be included in the English prayer-book. Liselotte thought that the short prayer needed long *Bratwürste*. Since Sophie was heiress apparent, 'it is only right that they should send you the money that goes with it'. But though this point had probably been discussed with William at Het Loo, there was no sign of a grant, nor of any invitation to England. Liselotte was relieved that her aunt would not be exposed to the dangers of crossing the water, or the noxious London air. For her part, Sophie was resigned to the fact that 'the English Court does not desire my presence. Milady Marlborough herself is so fond of being the second lady in the land, because she rules everything.'

When congregations in England began praying for the Princess Sophie, the object of their supplication merely wished that she were as young as she had been when she had last been so styled—'it would be more use to me.' When an English friend sent her a dozen copies of the prayer-book itself she thanked him politely, saying that her entourage included nothing like that number of people able to join her in English prayers. However, she had no intention of creating an English Court without a commensurate allowance from Parliament, and unless this was sent there would be no Anglican chaplains or Anglican services in Hanover.

By May 1702, when the War of the Spanish Succession had begun in earnest and Marlborough had started to sweep from the Rhine to the Danube, Sophie set out on a visit to Figuelotte in Berlin, her first since Frederick had become King. 'Oh, the etiquette!' wrote Figuelotte to Poellnitz as Sophie's carriage rolled up in the forecourt. She would have preferred to behave as though nothing had changed, but Frederick insisted that all formalities due to royalty be observed, and kept an eagle eye on mother and daughter, neither of whom liked to pass through doors before the other.

In due course he went campaigning, and the ladies and their attendants moved out to Lützenburg, where life was *sans façon* and the garden 'a paradise only without apples'. Toland, who had arrived earlier at Figuelotte's invitation, saw little of Sophie, for Schütz had warned her to avoid him: Queen Anne's friends, the church Tories, would not like to hear of her keeping such company, and it might hurt the cause.

Sophie complained that no one would explain to which of Toland's crimes such exception was taken, and observed that she would not have thought him important enough to attract such powerful, well-born enemies. As for his books, 'so many more absurd ones come out of England. Clearly, he lacks judgement, but it had been the *esprit* of his conversation that had made him so agreeable.' However, she took care not to talk to him and not to be seen alone in his company. It was the only concession to English sensitivity that she ever made—for the rest, she remained faithful to her friends whether they were well-regarded in England or not.

Her visit to Figuelotte gave her immense pleasure. She loved the Court theatricals and the operatic performances conducted by Figuelotte herself, and never ceased to be grateful 'still to have so much pleasure in my old age, and my health as well'. After an incognito visit to Frankfurt to see Benedicta's daughter in the dignity of Queen of the Romans she did describe herself as dead—'*mausetot*'—but that was after eight hours' travelling, and 'a woman of my age can't complain'.

By August she felt that in all decency she could stay no longer. She only awaited Frederick's return to thank him for his extended hospitality, and departed at the end of the month, sad to leave her daughter, sad to leave her loutish grandson Frederick William, now fourteen, and not improved with age. Both his parents were in despair about him. He took no interest in his mother's intellectual pursuits, or in the amassed treasures that were his father's joy. He loved only his soldiers, whom he drilled and paraded like a sergeant major. All the Court ladies, terrified of his barrack-room manners, avoided him as best they could, and when he was prised out of the company of the stable boys that he preferred, he could be seen dragging his fellow princes by the hair.

Sophie forgave all his faults, for she 'liked a boy to be a little *vif*'. She assured Figuelotte that the boy's maniacal violence and *dureté de cœur* would, like his puppy fat—he was almost spherical—melt away in time. His appearance, she had earlier decided, was 'like they paint *Cupido*, especially when his hair is done'. She always maintained a special loving relationship with her grandson, and when she boarded her coach for Hanover he cried to see her go.

Sophie's next visit to Lützenburg was saddened by the news of her son Christian's death after a battle with the Bavarians, the allies of France. Trying to take on an enemy detachment with an inferior force, he had been driven into the Danube and drowned, together with his groom and his trumpeter; only his horse swam to safety.

Of Sophie's six beautiful sons, there were now only three left in the world. The eldest and the youngest were inseparable, and neither of them cared for Sophie as Liselotte felt they should. In her opinion, 'Ernst Augustchen would do better to wait on you, than to follow the Elector around like a little dog'. As for Max, he positively refused to come to Hanover even for a visit. Sophie blamed the Jesuit priest who, she said, had her son in his clutches and feared that he might lose his hold if he allowed him out of his sight. She tried to draw him by withholding his allowance unless he collected it in person, but even this failed to bring '*M argent court*' to her side. She was sad, with so many sons dead, that one of those left should elect to live '*comme s'il était mort pour moi*'. All she was ever to see of him was his portrait, which arrived a few years later, the picture of a stranger, looking so unlike her son that it needed, she said, 'attestation', for no one would have known it was Max.

But her good Calvinist upbringing helped her to accept what providence sent to try her. Figuelotte feared that Christian's death would make her ill, but her health was not affected as she wept over his day-book, which was returned with his things. She was further grieved by the loss of Mme von Harling, who had for so long prayed for death that when it came at last it truly was a merciful release.

The Court of Berlin did its utmost to cheer her up, and with her customary stoicism Sophie turned her mind from the dead towards the living. She was very much taken with an addition to the house-party in Lützenburg—young Caroline of Ansbach, a ward of the Prussian King, almost as clever as Figuelotte, as musical, as obliging, though not nearly as pretty.

This agreeable Princess had received a proposal of marriage from the

Archduke Charles, the Emperor's youngest son, who was beginning to be referred to as the King of Spain. It was a splendid opportunity for an orphan with no great fortune, and it only remained for her to enter the Catholic Church. It was a necessary step, but one which the Princess's conscience did not allow her to take lightly, if at all. Her reluctance pleased Sophie, who wrote home hoping that 'she would delight us all in Hanover'.

The Elector Palatine, brother of the Empress, sent a Jesuit priest to speed up Caroline's conversion. Compared with this Pater Orban, said Sophie, the Lutheran pastors and their counter-arguments were very unimpressive, but she noted that when Caroline and the Pater debated an issue across the Bible that lay opened between them, Princess and priest scored in turn, depending on which of them had most thoroughly studied the passage under discussion. Sometimes Caroline seemed on the point of giving in, then changed her mind only to reverse her opinion again, and meanwhile she was bombarded by beseeching letters from the Elector Palatine, who included loving epistles from his nephew, the prospective groom. Frederick I weighed in by telling his ward of the glory she would bring to his house through an Imperial connection. Sophie said nothing. Figuelotte, whom Caroline asked for advice, said that she must make her decision unaided. In the end Caroline's scruples won the day. Leibniz helped her to compose her letter of refusal to Pater Orban, and undertook to assemble a set of mathematical instruments in finest gold to console the priest for his failure to capture her soul. But the strain was too much for the Princess. She retired to Ansbach, fell ill, recovered, and then suffered a relapse so serious and so long-lasting that Leibniz cancelled the order for her present.

In spite of the European upheavals Berlin began once more to pick trivial quarrels with Hanover soon after Sophie had again said goodbye. No longer did Frederick I write to his dearest Mama, when he wrote at all it was frostily, to Her Serene Electoral Highness. 'How our enemies will laugh,' she commented to Leibniz, and in view of the obvious need for German solidarity in the face of the enemy beyond the Rhine such parochial squabbles seemed to him to be the last straw. 'The German nation appears to have a death-wish,' he wrote, 'and will be entirely to blame for a disastrous outcome of the war.'

The philosopher was to feel the effects of the cool relations on his own person. Having nearly burned his boats in Hanover through constant attendance in Brandenburg, he was now very strangely looked at in Berlin.

None of his ambitious plans for his Academy seemed to receive Frederick's royal sanction, and even his fellow-sages refused to co-operate with their president. It was not surprising that Berlin—'people who are such intriguers naturally assume that everyone is like them'— came to suspect that his long and apparently pointless visits must have some dark and private reason, and he became slowly aware that he was being regarded as a Hanoverian spy. In vain did Sophie write that Hanover had no need of such underhand creatures. In vain did Leibniz insist that Berlin and Hanover belonged together—in the words of the late Ernst August—'like *Braunkohl und Speck*'.

It was time for him to depart. Unluckily his recurrent effluxion of the leg, which he had often used as an excuse for staying in Berlin when George Louis would have preferred him to work on the Guelphs in Hanover—'My son says it is your head for which you are valued, not your feet,' wrote Sophie—was now preventing him from hastening his departure. Sophie suggested the ointment that had once cured her sister Elizabeth's leg; a herbal mixture that had helped on another occasion; or figs caramellised in *eau de vie*, with which she had cured a recent cold without the aid of the doctors. She was sorry that his leg was taking so long to heal, but hardly surprised, as she had heard that he regularly drank coffee. Did he not know that coffee was a killer which caused anything from consumption to brain tumours? Her old friend had much better stick to chocolate, as she did. Nothing could be more wholesome and delicious than a good lump, carefully grated and flavoured with cinnamon or lemon and dissolved in hot water, which she took every morning.

Leibniz was still in Berlin when Marlborough called there after having paid his respects to Sophie in Hanover. She had been most agreeably impressed by him, and returned the compliment of his gift—a portrait of Queen Anne, not a Kneller original but a copy by an assistant, less good and less expensive—with a priceless set of tapestries and a pair of silver sconces to go with them. (While Sophie was no true connoisseur she was not so blind as not to be able to tell the difference between a copy and the real thing, and was well aware of relative values. She had, for instance, urged Louise not to send George Louis the original of the late Charles Maurice's portrait. 'A copy will do admirably. He knows nothing about painting.')

In her eyes Marlborough, avaricious or not, could do no wrong. When the gossips said that he was making the rounds of the Courts in order to amass presents, she stoutly defended him; and when the battle of Blenheim had been fought and won, she again stressed the glorious purpose of his German tour. But it was after this victory, which put the Allies in a superior position and allowed the Empire to breathe again, that Milord Marlborough temporarily ran foul of the Electress. No mention appeared in the Gazette of Hanoverian bravery and Hanoverian losses; no letter from the Commander-in-Chief arrived in Hanover. Sophie, burning to have this wrong put right by publishing a separate Hanoverian gazette at her own expense, pointedly referred to this omission in her letter of cool congratulation, and from then on Marlborough praised the Elector's troops at every opportunity.

Figuelotte, forbidden to visit her mother while the quarrel between Prussia and Brunswick-Lüneburg was flaring, was allowed to go to Hanover early in 1705. The differences between the two countries were on the way to being settled, and the Prussian Prime Minister's wife, Mme von Wartenberg, was anxious to visit Hanover at Carnival time. It had been some time since Frederick had appointed her as his *maîtresse en titre*. *En titre* was, in the minds of most, the operative term, but Mme von Wartenberg was amassing as great a collection of jewels as had Mme von Platen for her more considerable services to Ernst August. She was an ambitious lady, and meant to be an intimate not only of the King but also of the Queen. So it was maddening that Figuelotte could barely bring herself to be polite and hardly ever asked her to Lützenburg, and even worse that, when she did accompany the King to his wife's palace, would resolutely address her in French, which she did not understand. Figuelotte was disgusted that her husband's mistress should be a member of her party now, but Sophie, preferring to see her daughter in unpleasant company to not seeing her at all, had extended a warmly worded invitation.

She was disappointed to learn that a small indisposition had kept the Queen in Magdeburg. By the time Figuelotte had again taken to the road, Sophie herself had been struck down by one of her horrible colds. She failed to cure it with her vaunted household remedies, and was sent to bed by the doctors.

Thus she did not attend the Carnival ball given in Figuelotte's honour, at which Figuelotte danced as usual in spite of suffering, still, from a swelling in the throat. Nor did she go to her daughter when, on the following day, Figuelotte's fever had returned. Reassuring messages passed from bedside to bedside. The Electress was on the mend. The Queen was slightly improved. On the morning of 1st February Sophie wrote to her son-in-law that her daughter had been bled to ease her breathing, and was now out of danger; in the evening Figuelotte died as philosophically as she had lived. She met her end with the greatest calm in the world. When the Hanoverian Court preacher came to pray by her bedside, she thanked him 'for offering his services at a time when I am no longer able to reward them' and sent him away with assurances that she was on good terms with her maker. She comforted her weeping ladies by saying that at last she would understand the mysteries of being and not being, and be able to explore the origin of matter that Leibniz had never satisfactorily explained. As for the King, by dying 'I am giving him fresh opportunities for showing his magnificence at my funeral'.

Sophie was in such consternation that even her daughter's steadfastness could not comfort her. That she had not seen her dearest child alive was to be an everlasting sorrow. Her heart was too full even to write to her son-in-law at any length, and for the first time in her life she wished that death had taken her instead.

'I have lost what I loved most in the world,' she wrote to the widower ten days later, when the first dry-eyed horror of her bereavement had passed and she had found her tears. 'It seems that God does not want our hearts to be set on temporal matters. His will be done.' A month later she still wept—'all my philosophy is of no use to me now.'

CHAPTER SEVEN

Heiress to Great Britain
(1705–1714)

Such a blow at so advanced an age might have crushed a spirit less resilient than Sophie's. But old, indisposed and bereaved of all that was most agreeable to her in the world, she refused to succumb to her grief. Nevertheless, all who loved her again felt concern for her health. Leibniz hardly liked to post off his condolences for fear of re-opening wounds and endangering her life. Caroline, whose own slow recovery at Ansbach had received a set-back when, as she told Leibniz, 'the jealous heavens, by taking our adorable Queen, plunged me into mortal affliction', asked him to convey her sympathy to Sophie, whose life, she hoped, would be increased by the number of years that had been lopped off Figuelotte's. Liselotte, too, was distressed for her aunt. She was haunted by the thought that her wedding present to Figuelotte, a clavichord, had encouraged her in her unfortunate fondness for singing, thus perhaps causing the throat ailment that had killed her. She asked miserably why she herself was still alive, useless and unloved as she was, when Figuelotte, so necessary to Sophie's happiness, was no more. She was glad that Leibniz would be by Sophie's side by the time Prussia was ready to send for the body of the Queen. He would be able to help her over the worst moments—learned men were always such a comfort to her aunt.

The philosopher was himself stunned by the loss, irreparable from his point of view, as Caroline rightly pointed out. The news of Figuelotte's death, of Sophie's illness and of Caroline's relapse had come upon him like a bolt from the blue, at a single stroke transforming into objects of grief and apprehension the three ladies 'whose kindness was the source of the greatest satisfaction of his life'. It was with relief that he saw Sophie give 'admirable proofs of strength of character and excellence of temperament' by attending personally to her correspondence, though every day brought her touching reminders of Figuelotte: 'I, who never bought a single jewel for myself without thinking that it would eventually go to my daughter, have now inherited the first necklace I ever gave her—when she was a child of five. I do not know how she could bring herself to think of it.'

In May, when Figuelotte's dreadful funeral procession at last got under way, news came of the Emperor Leopold's death. 'Our loss has been too great for the Emperor's demise to cause us much grief,' wrote Sophie to Frederick. 'It can serve only as a reminder that no one is spared, and that we must all be prepared.' Her Prussian grandson disapproved, as she did, of enormous *pompes funèbres*. Why, he asked, should they hack the Emperor's body to pieces as though he had been a criminal, and entomb heart, body and entrails in three separate churches? 'It seems even more senseless than our custom of believing that the dead are honoured by colossal expenditure at their funerals. But the King wishes to demonstrate his love for the late Queen, and his grief at her departure.'

When Figuelotte had finally been laid to rest in June and the memorial service, for which Leibniz composed the eulogy, had been held, Sophie wrote to congratulate the widower: he would now be able to turn his mind towards the living, while for her, an old woman, all had turned to ashes. No, she would not be able to accept his kind invitation to Charlottenburg, as Lützenburg was henceforth to be called; it would break her heart.

Their loss had drawn the two chief mourners closer together, but a sour note reappeared in their correspondence when at the end of June Sophie's Hanoverian grandson, George August, went off to look for a bride. She assured Frederick that she had no idea where he was going, but within a month she informed him with every appearance of surprised delight 'that he will have the happiness of marrying the dear Princess of Ansbach of Your Majesty's House. Truly, one must regard it as predestination at work.'

'Predestination?' wrote Frederick. He would be grateful not to be taken for a fool. Why not admit that the plan had been forged during Sophie's last visit to his Court?

This peevish tone made Sophie indignant. She would have thought, she said, that His Majesty had a better opinion of her. As little as a year ago neither of the young people had entertained any such idea. George August had been left a free choice, and it was his own inclination that had led him to Ansbach. He had arrived incognito, and fallen so much in love that he had looked no further. Aware that the Prussian Crown Prince had also been attracted to Caroline, Sophie wrote to her son-in-law, 'She was clearly meant for one of my grandsons. But Your Majesty must have thought her too old for your son, or you would hardly have let her get away.' For her own part, although 'I have never made a secret of loving the Princess from the moment I set eyes on her, or of desiring her for one of my grandsons, I certainly never discussed the matter with her.' And, since Frederick agreed that Caroline was indeed too old for his son, 'Perhaps Your Majesty had an eye on her for yourself? It is perhaps a *dépit amoureux?*'

Frederick in turn was outraged. Did Sophie think he had already forgotten his incomparable Queen? He took his son off to Tangermünde for the shooting, and although it was not far from Hanover neither of them called on Sophie. She was hurt. She longed to see Frederick William, who, in turn, longed to go travelling. He asked his grandmother to put in a good word for him with the King. 'I hear that my dear Crown Prince is growing silent and melancholy,' she obligingly wrote to Frederick. 'What a pity he never sees anything new. He has so many relations ... there are so many princesses to choose from, so that Your Majesty may be made a grandfather soon—which is, after all, a matter of importance.' Afraid that the King might accuse her of meddling, she added a postscript guaranteed to pacify: a description of a rope of pearls, on sale in Hanover.

Frederick replied that he already had more jewels than he could count, but his son could perhaps acquire the pearls as soon as he had found a princess who matched them in beauty. As for being melancholy, the Prince had never been gayer, and Frederick would like to get his hands on the whores and knaves who said otherwise. And how was it that he was forever being urged to send his son abroad when the Hanoverian Prince never seemed to leave home, except for his *sortie* into Ansbach? Sophie admitted that this was a cause of concern to her—all young men needed to see the world and were much improved by having their horizons widened.

When the marriage between George August and Caroline was officially announced, Hanover prayed that Vienna would not lay at its door the Princess's rejection of the King of Spain—the Archduke Charles, whose childless elder brother Joseph had succeeded the Emperor Leopold.

Fortunately, congratulations poured in from that and every other Court. The King in Prussia chose in the end to be gracious, and all the Protestant world applauded Caroline for remaining true to her faith. Even Anton Ulrich, though recently converted to Catholicism, had been sufficiently moved by her story to propose making her the heroine of a future chapter of his novel.

No one was more delighted by the news of the engagement than Leibniz. He had anxiously followed Caroline's slow progress to health and strength, had gladly renewed his order for Pater Orban's mathematical instruments when her recovery was certain, and had been living in hopes of gaining in her a patroness 'worthy of succeeding the lamented Queen in the possession of *un meuble plus précieux que moi*'.

It was only fitting, said Liselotte, that the time of mourning should be followed by a time of joy. In the event the rejoicing had to be muted, because George William died a few weeks before the wedding. George Louis, who, said Sophie, felt such things, looked quite ill in spite of acquiring the Duchy of Celle—thus uniting all Brunswick-Lüneburg under a single sceptre according to his father's plan, which had caused so much unpleasantness and personal suffering in the past.

All was temporarily festive when, in September, Sophie handed Caroline out of her carriage in the forecourt of the Leine palace, just as she herself had been welcomed on her arrival nearly half a century earlier. The wedding was solemnised at the Schlosskirche, much as Sophie's had been, except that the groom went to sleep during the long sermon.* For the two days that followed the Court changed out of long mourning mantles into the new clothes they had ordered as a compliment to the bride. 'Our faces were wreathed in smiles when we looked at the young couple,' said Sophie, 'and dropped when we thought of the good Duke.'

Liselotte's hopes that Caroline's presence would help Sophie to bear Figuelotte's loss more easily were not fulfilled, as she was not often allowed to enjoy the Princess's company. George August preferred to keep his wife to himself, and concentrated on her to a degree that made Sophie fear she would shortly tire of him. Liselotte agreed. 'Good-natured behaviour, not constant kissing and slobbering, is what makes a good marriage,' she said, but luckily the young people's union was pleasantly cemented by their common dislike of the Elector.

---

* 'What good news for the bride,' wrote Liselotte, 'that he should be well rested.'

George Louis had never been an easy father. Sophie thought that it was his dour, sour nature that had prevented him from showing his tender love to either of his children—'one can't be perfect in everything'—but George August must have wondered if his father harboured any such feelings. The Elector certainly kept him down, and did not allow him to take an active part either in the war or in the affairs of state. Enforced idleness had made the Prince difficult to live with: he was sullen and silent in public, and imperious in his sudden, often inexplicable, enthusiasms and hatreds in private. Caroline provided an outlet for his emotions and shared all his frustrations, not least those caused by the Elector's discouraging attitude towards the Englishmen who made a point of seeking out his son with a view to paying their respects to the man who might one day become their ruler.

The Elector's disapproval of the English visitors at his mother's Court, coupled with Sophie's determination not to meddle in English party politics, caused her English supporters to complain of Hanoverian apathy with regard to the succession. Things were made worse when Ruperta Howe, who was Prince Rupert's natural daughter and the wife of Emanuel Scrope Howe, the new English Resident in Hanover, filled her letters to London with reports of Hanoverian indifference. In an attempt to put the record straight, Sophie wrote in November 1705 to Thomas Tenison, Archbishop of Canterbury, declaring herself willing to cross the Channel if her friends should wish it. Not, she wrote, that she contemplated moving her residence for her own satisfaction—'I live in quiet and contentment, and have no reason for desiring a change'. But old as she was, she was prepared to accept an invitation to England for the sake of the Protestant religion, the European public liberties and the English people. (Privately, she told Schütz that she would naturally require a suitable grant to set up Court in London, but in her letter to the Archbishop she did not touch on financial considerations.) Her only stipulation was that 'Parliament must find the means to make my coming agreeable to the Queen, whom I shall never cease to honour, and for whose favour I shall ever strive.' She ended by observing that since Mr Howe had again assured her of 'Her Majesty's kind intentions towards herself and the family', the Queen 'might judge this the proper moment to declare herself in our favour'.

Sophie had never quite believed in Anne's protestations of friendship; she had, however, no way of knowing how thoroughly Anne loathed the idea of a Hanoverian establishment in London. Such a thing, felt the Queen, would be tantamount to having her coffin placed before her very eyes, as well as leading to serious factions in the nation. So she was far from pleased when the contents of Sophie's letter became known, and the disagreeable proposal to invite the Electress was placed before both Houses of Parliament. 'I shall depend on your kindness and friendship,' she wrote to Marlborough, on his way to Hanover at the time, 'to set them right in notions of things here, and if they will be quiet, I may be so too.'

Marlborough's task was difficult, as Sophie and her entourage were by now perfectly bewildered: the proposal to invite her had come, not from the Whigs, but from the Tories, who hoped by this move to split their opponents' party. The Whigs, recognising the trap, had voted against the motion, an inconsistency that Sophie found difficult to swallow. Nor did she approve of the measures by which they sought to secure the Hanoverian succession without political risk to themselves—the Naturalisation Bill, by which Sophie and her entire family would become English subjects, and the Regency Act, designed to secure the government of England until the arrival of the Hanoverian heir in the event of Anne's death. Both seemed meaningless to Sophie: '*mon parchemin*' was surely more potent than either. The Queen's proposal to invest George August with the Garter and make him Duke of Cambridge seemed to her yet another substitute for useful action.

Marlborough, in whom both Sophie and her son had the greatest faith, smoothed things over by explaining and charming as usual. But even he could not clear up all the misunderstandings which had arisen between the Electress and her English supporters. She felt that her friends, the Whigs, were lacking in integrity. They, more amazingly, accused her of having become a tool of their political enemies, believing that she had written her letter on Tory advice. Whig observers in Hanover began to regard some of her friends and correspondents with suspicion. They felt particular concern at the presence of the Catholic Frances Bellamont, still a member of her household, 'posing,' they said, 'as Prince Rupert's widow'. (Such is the fate of abandoned morganatic wives.) Frances was, they thought, a rabid Jacobite, and a traitress to boot. Awful warnings about her machinations reached Hanover from the pen of Lord Stamford, together with the suggestion that she should be dismissed at once. Nonsense, said Sophie; Frances, as far as she knew, had done no wrong, and until—if ever—she did, Frances would stay. (True to her word, she kept Frances with her, and grieved when she died.)

Perhaps it was excusable for a man like Stamford, faced with the spectacle of Queen Anne ruled by her favourite—for Sarah Marlborough's thumb was still firmly and unkindly upon her—to think that all princesses allowed themselves to be governed by their ladies. Nothing was less true of Sophie. That she was immune to intriguers and intriguing could, in Leibniz's opinion, hardly be over-stressed. He had often written to England to this effect, and now took the opportunity of saying so again. Over the signature of Sir Rowland Gwynne, pro-Hanoverian Whig and regular visitor to the Electress's Court, Leibniz rephrased her letter to Tenison, with which he had originally lent a hand, and went on to criticise the Whigs for not urging an immediate invitation.

Sir Rowland's part in the operation was small, and would have been smaller still had Leibniz not abandonded the idea of writing in English. As it was, Sir Rowland saw to the document's translation as well as signing it, but it was Leibniz who had it printed in Holland and arranged for the pamphlets to be shipped to England among bales of cloth from an Amsterdam merchant. He enjoyed nothing so much as pulling strings behind the scenes, and it is unlikely that anyone besides Sir Rowland knew of his part in the affair.

Sophie certainly had no idea, and informed him that a letter from Sir Rowland was circulating in London and had been brought up to the Speaker's table in the House, to be duly condemned as 'scandalous, libellous, false and malicious, tending to create a misunderstanding between Her Majesty and the Princess Sophie'. The Electress regretted the fuss but saw little wrong with the letter itself, and Leibniz, not surprisingly, shared her opinion.

Howe, shocked at their reaction, flattered himself with opening their eyes 'to the ill designs of it', and hoped that Sir Rowland would promptly be sent packing. But even after Parliament passed a resolution that 'the printers should be found for the purpose of severe punishment' he noted that 'no manner of discountenance was shown to Sir Rowland', and felt aggrieved at Hanoverian ways. The Queen, pleased with her loyal Parliament, expressed her delight at maintaining a good understanding with Sophie, and at the same time sent her a very cross letter by Marlborough. Prudently, he did not deliver it, but instead persuaded Sophie to assure the Queen that she had not been personally involved in any part of the incident.

Sir Rowland disappeared for what Howe hoped would be a lengthy absence, but he only visited the silver mines and turned up again, to his compatriot's annoyance, 'to stand it out' when the Queen's ambassador, Lord Halifax, arrived in May 1706 with Sophie's copies of the Regency and Naturalisation Acts. It was only when he proposed himself for a visit in the following year that he was asked by the Elector to stay away 'for meddling in politics', while Leibniz was always to regard the unfortunate letter as 'an eternal reproach to the Whigs' for not taking the decisive action that would have saved England much disquiet in the years to come.

Lord Halifax's visit was not particularly welcome to Sophie. 'My son would gladly pay out good money to anyone who stayed Milord Halifax in his design,' she wrote, displeased at being put to the trouble and expense inevitably connected with such visits. Surely, she said, Howe was quite capable of handing over whatever documents the Queen was wishing upon her. However, new Mathildas were put in hand, as was a new gold dinner service for Her Majesty's envoy, who in return presented her with a quantity of ornamental locks which, she complained, would oblige her to have all her doors changed.

Sir John Vanbrugh, who carried the Garter, accompanied Lord Halifax, but 'my son does not wish the Electoral Prince to grant audiences while he himself is alive,' wrote Sophie to Louise, surprised that this information, conveyed to her English visitors by an ordinary footman, should have put their noses out of joint. No actual slight, said Sophie, had been intended, but perhaps Benedicta had been right in observing that Hanoverian forthrightness was often taken for rudeness by strangers.

In the event the ceremony, in which George August was allowed after all to receive his new titles, brought him some disappointment. Queen Anne made a point of saying that she was creating her most dear cousin Baron of Tewkesbury, Viscount of Tallerton, Earl of Milford Haven and Marquis and Duke of Cambridge—Sophie had to jot them down; she said she could not possibly remember so many titles at once in her head— so that he might be 'in a manner present to our Parliament and Councils'. Physical presence, she stressed, would be out of the question, as the darling and ornament of Germany could hardly leave his native country 'while the neighbouring states were tossed with such violent tempests'. The darling fumed, unable to go to England or, because his father absolutely refused to have him tossed about, to the front in person.

During her own meeting with Lord Halifax Sophie, as always, played her part superbly. Once again she stood under her canopy flanked by her ladies, listened to speeches, received *étuis* and responded suitably, presumably living up to Burnet's description of her as 'the most knowing, most entertaining woman of her age'. Lord Halifax, however, never gained her affection, and his name among the fourteen nominations for the Regency Council, from which Sophie was to choose seven, was among those she deleted.

When George Louis succeeded to Celle—oaths of loyalty were being sworn during Halifax's visit—he ironed out the difficulties with the King in Prussia. Frederick's letters to Sophie grew warm again, and he took a lively interest in Caroline, now pregnant.

Against expectation, she did not miscarry when she escaped from a fire which swept from her wing of the Leine palace right down to the *Schlosskirche*. It melted the new organ which Sophie had donated, because 'something was needed to make the caterwauling of the congregation easier on the ear'. Frederick recommended new organ-makers, and told his own tale of woe regarding burning buildings: he was having Charlottenburg repaired because that rogue Schlüter—one of the few great German Baroque architects—had been so careless about chimneys. Herrenhausen, too, was to have its share of fires, but not as many as it would have had if Sophie had not trained herself to act quickly, and more than once pulled down the curtains of her bed when they began smouldering, set alight by the candle she used for reading before going to sleep. Numbers of her ladies were walking about with scarred and painful faces because they were less energetic than she in pulling their *fontanges*—notorious fire-catchers— off their heads; and when at the last Carnival the Electoral Princess and her suite had appeared dressed in paper pyramids, Sophie's youngest son had expected to see them all go up in flames at any moment. Fires were such a problem that Leibniz, taking time off from more considerable works, wrote a paper on improved pressurised fire hoses, which he published under the imprint of the Berlin Academy.

His painted coach still intermittently rumbled to Berlin, but now that there was no Figuelotte to promote his schemes he was increasingly ignored. The King did not even use his services when it came to arranging the marriage of his son, Frederick William, and Sophie's Hanoverian granddaughter, Sophie Dorothea.

From the moment her granddaughter had passed through the stage between child and human being which Sophie always found trying in girls, references to Sophie Dorothea had begun to appear in the Electress's letters to Prussia. Really, said Sophie, the child was becoming so agreeable that a visit of inspection seemed appropriate. The King and his Prince came for a visit, and saw that Sophie Dorothea, though neither witty nor particularly pretty, was modest and at the same time self-confident, which gave her a certain air.

They declared her perfection, and handed Sophie and the Elector written requests for her hand. Such had been the late Mme von Harling's skill that the Princess, who was sensitive to noise and almost jumped out of her skin at a slammed door, did not, as usual, excuse herself during the gala dinner when every royal health was accompanied by three thunder claps from no less than fifty cannons. Electoral healths were accompanied by booms from between twenty and thirty pieces. The Princess knew that on this occasion there could not be the slightest departure from ceremonial in the King in Prussia's presence, and sat wringing her napkin while the changing colour in her face was reflected in the table-settings. Gold only was the order of the day. The King could hardly be expected to eat off less, although, at his instructions, a single silver setting was laid for M von Wartenberg, who could not expect to eat off more precious metal.

From the moment the engagement was settled the Princess's trousseau became a matter of the first priority. Before his departure the King had personally discussed all plans for the nuptials with Hanoverian Court officials, but politely left the final arrangements to Sophie.

Once again she ordered bridal clothes from France. Liselotte was asked for help. Although the only instructions she ever gave to her own tailors were to keep her clothes light in weight and simple to manage, she took an unaccustomed interest in *manteaux* and furbelows for Sophie Dorothea and for George August, who was to be proxy-groom and would, the King feared, cut a poorish figure unless he too was dressed from head to foot in Paris clothes and covered with as many precious stones as the bride.

Jewels came pouring in from Prussia. The Princess spent hours each day in front of her looking-glass arranging them on her head, arms and fingers and around her throat, but feared that she would never learn to handle the train, twelve ells long, of her robe of state.

By the end of September Frederick became impatient. He had himself supervised the furnishing of his daughter-in-law's apartments, and approved and sent to Hanover the illustrated programme for three weeks of solid wedding celebrations in Berlin, and he was beginning to wish the clothes to the devil. Like his father before him, he feared that his usual winter ailments might interfere with his enjoyment of the treats he was providing. By the end of October the things were at last truly on their way to Berlin. Dresses, *manteaux* and accessories, *fontanges*, fans and gloves, shoes and slippers, *andriennes* and dressing-gowns would, hoped Sophie, meet with his approval. Louis XIV had said he wished all German princesses might have such extravagant trousseaux, it was so good for trade.

In case Frederick was not familiar with it, the strange-looking ivory object was a scraper for removing excess powder from the face—so useful in Prussia, where they still went in for kissing and where, Sophie complained, 'one's nose and eyes are filled with powder after each salute, so that one can neither breathe nor see'. Sophie Dorothea had after all become adept at walking about in her robes provided she had four young ladies to carry the train. The only worry was the crown, which, Sophie suspected, would be too modest. Did the Princess really need such an object? It was just as well that she included it in the bride's luggage—though without stones, as 'Your Majesty's are better than mine'—because Frederick wrote by return of post that of course a crown was vital, and that he would himself place it on her head 'since she cannot, after God, receive it from anyone else'. He sent the time-table for the day of the Princess's arrival: entrée, cannons, chapel and confirmation of proxy promises, cannons, banquet, cannons, *Fackeltanz*, bedding, and the prospect of twenty-one days of unrelieved joyousness.

After being given in proxy-marriage to her brother George August and enduring the Hanoverian celebrations—which, said Liselotte, tiresome though they were, distinguished royal weddings from those of chamber-maids—Sophie Dorothea travelled to Prussia. The King wished her horses to gallop all the way. However, 'it is a good thing that she is travelling slowly,' wrote Sophie to Louise, 'for if she arrived as red-eyed as she left, His Majesty would hardly be overcome by her beauty.'

She herself put away her wedding finery—black silk, embroidered with gold festoons and flowers so natural-looking that they might have grown there—and put up her feet. Dancing had become strangely tiring. She had marvelled at Eleonore d'Olbreuse's twinkle-toes that still seemed to remember every step of the ancient minuets which had long become unfashionable, and the energy with which she performed them at the wedding. On the whole, thought Sophie, she herself was ageing more gracefully. Mme de Celle, although younger, looked older through lack of teeth: as if age were not tiresome enough by itself, she complained of a thousand aches and pains, and gave details of every twinge and every one of her remedies. She seemed, moreover, to be sinking into an odd religious condition which caused her to cover her person with medals of saints. She was living in Celle, no longer in the palace but in a little house with a small suite of servants, whom she was later to dismiss regularly for very unlikely crimes, such as running her establishment as a bawdy-house. What else, thought Sophie, could one expect?

It was lucky that young Sophie Dorothea had turned out well, and more than one could say of her brother George August. Liselotte much pitied her aunt for being left in the company of her 'mad grandchildren, now that the pleasant ones have left'. Neither Sophie nor her niece could approve of the young couple's way of life. Caroline was unaware, owing to her inability to keep count, of when to expect her baby. Meanwhile she was keeping to her bed behind barricaded doors and shuttered windows, and no one was allowed to come near her. Sophie considered such behaviour not only unfriendly but unwise, in case her son Max, in his periodic bids for what he considered his rightful inheritance, 'might be of a mind to dispute the genuineness of the baby' if and when it appeared.

Prince Ernst August no longer believed that a baby was on the way. 'Wind, I expect,' he said when discussing Princess Caroline's condition—but it was generally agreed that he knew very little about women. When he joked about Sophie's *cour des anciennes* it was less for his own sake than for the sake of other gentlemen that he deplored the lack of beauties. Liselotte was convinced that, so far as love was concerned, 'something must have happened to put him off the idea'. She had never heard of a young man who was not attracted to at least one of the sexes. 'A virgin at eighteen!' she had exclaimed, and would shortly say, 'A virgin at thirty-six! Impossible!' Whether or not she knew of Ernst August's passionate friendship with a fellow-officer—'Have you given me a philtre to make me love you so much?', and 'I would rather embrace you than the most beautiful courtesans in Venice'—it was clearly no use hoping for a daughter-in-law from that direction, and Sophie made the most of her correspondence with her granddaughter in Berlin.

In letters that grew shorter as she grew more exhausted, Sophie Dorothea reported on fairy-tale decorations and on parties that followed one another so closely that she scarcely had time to catch her breath. The sky over Berlin seemed hung with fiddles. Her entrée had been somewhat spoiled by a tremendous downpour, but even the bridegroom had to admit that the procession of more than a hundred carriages, accompanied by hundreds of extra lackeys in colourful liveries and horses in brilliant trappings, made a brave sight. For himself, Frederick William would have preferred to see them march in military formation, dressed in plain clothes of the special shade of blue newly invented in Prussia, and before even a week had passed he wrote, tired of it all, 'It is to be hoped that everyone will be heartily sick of fêtes by the time the three weeks are finally over.' But huge crowds attended every event in spite of the inclement weather. The unusually high November winds prevented the main fireworks from being seen in their full splendour; a rocket, deflected off course, killed a man by hitting him on the head, and several people were squashed to death in the crush. Sophie Dorothea caught a cold. 'I retire to my fireside corner not to see the poor animals killed,' she wrote on the day when the entertainment consisted of bull-baiting. 'You know how bloodthirsty I am. But you would be amazed to see me stand up to the booming cannons.'

Frederick was delighted with his show. Shortly before Christmas—was invention running thin?—he gave a Feast of Spring, during which a hundred and twenty courtiers danced a sylvan ballet on a specially constructed gallery, large enough also to hold an orchestra of more than a hundred members. Sophie ran out of adjectives to praise the magnificence that was rapidly exhausting her granddaughter. She promised to send all the descriptions on to Liselotte so that they might exclaim over them at Versailles. 'No doubt they'll laugh at us,' Frederick wrote more modestly than sincerely, 'and say "*Voyez les sots Allemands!*". But we'll just carry on

H

in our good old German way, and shan't care a fig about being laughed at.'

Shortly after the final lottery, at which Sophie Dorothea drew the gala-prize—a charming set for coffee and tea—she was horrified to learn that her doting father-in-law had arranged to hold a small carnival in order to console her for missing it in Hanover. His kindness, Sophie feared, would kill her granddaughter in the end. Sophie Dorothea had the King's gracious permission to wear her *manteau* instead of the regulation Court *décolletage*, but her cold was truly dreadful by now, and she said that each day it took her longer to make herself beautiful. There were, however, increasing numbers of ornaments to pin and hang about her. She had begun by sending Sophie lists of the jewels that were raining upon her, but soon stopped because the list needed amendments on every post-day. 'If I wore everything at once, I should look like an actress,' she told her grandmother, and it was a relief when Lent came and only tortoise-shell jewellery was worn.

By February she had so far recovered her strength as to conceive. Sophie begged her to take care of her health. 'You need a son to make the King happy,' she wrote, imploring her to give up coffee. As an extra precaution she sent a golden *cafetière* 'for when you serve it to the Prince. He will be safer if you brew it in pure gold.' This pot had the honour of dispensing coffee to Frederick in person, who admired it almost as much as he had a statue of himself, finely gilded, which the Crown Prince had set up in his forecourt to welcome his father.

In 1707 Sophie became a great-grandmother twice over. In the summer Caroline gave birth to a son behind locked doors, with no Hanoverians and only a handful of people from Ansbach in attendance. Sophie, outraged at not being admitted to the birth-chamber, first met this baby at his quiet, private christening, where he was named Frederick. She said he was huge, beautiful and healthy. Although she was wrong about his robustness, he lived to become the object of his parents' loathing, and in time repeated history by excluding them from the birth of his own first child, having carried his wife out of their reach, wrapped in table-cloths, just before she produced 'a little she-mouse'.

Sophie's Prussian great-grandson, born in November in the full glare of Court publicity, did less well. The celebratory cannonade at his christening party threw him into a fit from which he never wholly recovered, and he died soon afterwards.

Since the Hanoverian baby was proving clever enough to survive the seizures that dogged his early days, George August, dynastic duty done for the time being, hopefully prepared to go to the wars. 'He's already picked his *cheval de bataille, celui de marche, celui de poursuite et celui de parade*' reported Ernst August, convinced that the Prince would be 'forced to drive about in comfort at home' for a long time yet. Indeed, it was not until the following year, 1708, that George August at last went into battle, making his debut at Oudenarde, where his *cheval de bataille* was promptly shot from under him. Marlborough praised his courage and said he was an inspiration to his troops, and Hanover rejoiced at the Prince's gallantry and the famous Allied victory.

The French defeat was so serious that only whispers of it were heard at the Court of Versailles, and the French nation was left as far as possible in ignorance. The Allies were able to enter France in consequence, and Lille surrendered in October. Secret peace talks, instigated by Louis XIV, began in Holland soon afterwards, and continued during the winter that was the worst in living memory. Ears and noses were freezing off all over Western Europe, and peasants were dying of the terrible cold. Sophie and Liselotte were obliged to thaw out their ink-wells before writing to each other, and Sophie shivered even in her bed, but bore up, 'because our brave soldiers in Lille must be colder still.'

Although France was at the end of her tether, the peace talks eventually foundered on an article in the Allied conditions which Sophie herself regarded as unchristian and inhuman. The French negotiators, who had been received by the Allies in a chamber 'lined with all the treaties their monarch had broken in the past', were informed that Louis XIV was required not only to renounce Spain to the Habsburgs but personally to drive his grandson from the throne. If fight he must, said the King, he preferred to fight his enemies rather than his own flesh and blood. He borrowed money, sent his golden tableware to the mint to be transformed into Louis d'Or with which to pay his troops, and fought on.

Since the Electoral Prince had proved to the world that 'he was not afraid of the smell of powder', Sophie hoped that he would not again be permitted to risk his life, but she heard with pleasure that the Prussian Crown Prince was at last allowed to go soldiering. The King in Prussia had, understandably, refused 'to risk the life of his single jewel' before the succession was secure, but since Sophie Dorothea had failed to provide living babies he had decided to make arrangements for producing heirs in person. In his hunting lodge, dressed in green even down to his stockings, he had proposed marriage to a plain Mecklenburg Princess—Ernst August said that from the point of view of looks the couple was ideally matched. In view of the bride's age—she was some thirty years younger than the groom—and her reputation, Sophie thought it a happy coincidence that her coat of arms featured a pair of horns, and felt that the ageing King must have taken leave of his senses in marrying for a third time. And what a perfectly ridiculous wedding breakfast! Frederick, in a coat embroidered with pierced hearts interspersed with Prussian eagles, faced his new Queen, while by each of their *couverts* cupids on silver platters spouted verse, aiming their darts at the centre-piece, which was enlivened by a fat lady representing Venus.

Frederick sent assurances of undiminished kindness to his children—'I know what it is to have a stepmother'—but Sophie firmly instructed Sophie Dorothea not to address the new Queen as Your Majesty, which the girl wisely disregarded. In spite of early reports that the newly-weds 'caressed each other furiously in public', Sophie was not sorry to hear that things seemed not to be so well in private. Only two good things came out of the match, so far as she could see: Mme von Wartenberg was sent away from the Berlin Court, and Frederick William could go campaigning, which made it possible for Sophie Dorothea to come to Hanover for a long visit. The girl seemed thin and lacking in *bonne mine*, but a few weeks of the air of her native land, together with a longish rest from her difficult husband, who was given to scenes of groundless jealousy, would, Sophie was sure, work wonders. Indeed, when Frederick William came to Hanover in the autumn of 1709, after the Battle of Malplaquet—another victory, though won at the cost of an enormous loss of Allied lives—he was transformed. 'All clocks,' observed Sophie, 'sometimes go wrong, but if they are made by a good master craftsman they soon come to rights again.' She noted with approval that Frederick William was polite even to his cousin George August, and that he treated his wife as a loving husband should and no longer like an uxorious drill sergeant.

She was delighted. Her opinion of love between the sexes was as high as ever. She counselled her granddaughter against coyness, and when the girl wondered about the propriety of sharing her husband's apartments advised her to dismiss such doubts and to disregard the prim Raugravine

Louise—'she talks like an old maid'. She especially warned Sophie Dorothea against Liselotte's well-known low opinion of marriage because, 'never having been in love in her life, she doesn't know what she's talking about'.

This time, the departure of the Prussian party did not leave Sophie high and dry, for Caroline had become a loving, attentive and very intelligent companion. Together the two ladies were able to discuss the ups and downs of the English succession, in which Caroline was taking a proper and personal interest, although she regretted that it was deepening the rift between her Prince, burning with enthusiasm, and the Elector, whose attitude was barely lukewarm.

Since the death of Anne's consort in 1708, and her announcement that she would not remarry, the issue should have become more clear-cut, as no hypothetical and improbable English royal babies any longer entered into the speculations. In fact, however, the Hanoverian cause had not appreciably advanced since the farcical incident of Sir Rowland Gwynne's letter three years ago. Sophie had grown increasingly disenchanted with her prospects.

When, in the previous year, the Union between England and Scotland had been established, she had refused to discuss its implications with Leibniz—'as I shall get nothing out of it, I'm not interested'. She had, fleetingly, remembered her Scottish blood, and had not been surprised that there were 'Scottish Milords' who did the same and therefore supported the Hanoverian succession. But she had also taken a genuine interest in James Edward Stuart's attempts to benefit from Scottish Jacobite elements: helped by Louis XIV, he had planned to go to Scotland in a French man-of-war on 1st April 1708, but the expedition had miscarried.

Sophie and her sister Louise Hollandine indignantly decided that 'the King of France made an April fool of him', and agreed that, far from publicising the venture, Louis should have kept it a dead secret, as Charles II and Montrose had done in former days. They marvelled that there was hardly anyone alive who remembered those stirring times, and when Louise Hollandine died at Maubuisson in 1709, aged eighty-six, Sophie became almost the sole survivor of her generation. Messieurs les Etats, she thought, could hardly have dreamt that their godchild would draw her pension for so long . . . 'people don't usually live to so great an age'. She sent them a polite note of thanks, and thought of all the Palatines, Oranges and Stuarts who had shared her youth—all long dead and gone, as were all too many of their children and even their grandchildren. Should she wish to relive her youth, she was now obliged to turn to books, notably Clarendon's *History of the Revolution*, which she enjoyed in spite of the author's frigid assessment of her brothers 'because I know all the people in it.'

There was, however, not much leisure for reading, and she could hardly do justice to the piles of books which Schütz, the Hanoverian envoy to London, sent her so as to keep her informed of English thinking. Thanking him for yet another parcel into which she had barely dipped, she observed that 'Solomon was right—there is nothing new under the sun: everything has been said before, and it is only the way in which it is said that's different'. As for a book on the English language, she didn't even bother to skim through it. 'I know as much English as the author. I've passed it straight on to the Electoral Princess—she has more need of it.'

Caroline was faithfully keeping up her English. She liked to excel at whatever she undertook, and had lately acquired an English lady-in-waiting for conversation and reading aloud. The other members of Sophie's Court appeared to have given up their linguistic studies. The Elector had never made any progress worth mentioning; and Ernst August, once highly praised by his mother for fluency and pronunciation, seemed to have forgotten all he had ever known. It was agony for him to be asked, as he occasionally was, to preside over meals with English visitors, and hardly more amusing for them. He didn't mind when they spoke English—on the contrary, it was a relief 'not to have to entertain them'—but when they laboriously tried to address him in bad French, 'it was a great embarrassment for a man like me, who understands nothing and does not know what to say in reply'. Not every meal was enlivened by the timely swooping of a bat across the table, which he despatched with a sword borrowed from the page behind his chair—'an act of heroism without any danger to myself', for which he was much applauded. Decidedly, he said, it was a grave mistake to expect him to do '*les honneurs de la maison . . . comme la reine de France*'.

Guests had more enjoyable parties when Sophie herself attended the meals. Whenever possible she personally entertained the English visitors, who still crowded into Hanover, still keenly supporting her succession—

and in her opinion 'likely to go on doing so as long as they think it will pay them'. Often she took her place at table—with a vacant *couvert* on either side as a mark of respect—when her physicians had begged her to remain in bed, since recurrent bouts of erysipelas had begun to trouble her. Her opinion of doctors was still low. She might go so far as to have herself carried in a chair down the draughty corridors, but she absolutely refused to 'give them the opportunity of hastening her departure into the next world.' Far better, she thought, to '*mourir de ma propre mort*', without 'doctors and clergymen murmuring over me without being able to do any good'.

From the moment Sophie reached her seventy-ninth birthday she made capital of being in her eightieth year, though never without profoundly thanking God for preserving her health and spirits. When, in inclement weather, she and her ageing ladies toured the gardens in her coach, she liked to add up the ages of her fellow-travellers, as she did those of her visitors: 'Anton Ulrich and Eleonore are expected today: two hundred and twenty-five years for dinner'—and she always took care to point out that she was the oldest and fittest of the lot.

Insuring against the day when she would 'no longer be agreeable company for people', she acquired an aviary of canaries, whose singing obliged her friend the Countess of Bückeburg to raise her voice as she read aloud, while Sophie, doing fine embroidery without spectacles—'my eyes seem to get sharper the more I use them'—sat in the Orangerie 'like a melon ripening in the sun'.

For the time being, however, there was no shortage of society. For Anton Ulrich, as for her other visitors, Sophie would order special performances at the opera house, where Handel, the Elector's new musical director, kept the standard high. 'He plays the clavichord more perfectly than anyone else,' said Sophie, 'and composes too. Such a good-looking man.'

The theatrical performances, on the other hand, no longer rose to the same heights as in the magic days when the ninth Electorate had first been celebrated. George Louis, when present, could be observed to yawn during comedy and laugh during tragedy, and when he was absent the actors did not play even as well as their waning powers allowed. The company was ageing. Its leader, Châteauneuf, trained by the great Molière himself, was still bearable, but his wife, once a beautiful actress, had grown so old and weak that her son and grandson, who followed in the family profession, unceasingly corrected and chivvied her even on stage. The Harlequin, by now almost useless for anything more exacting than shifting chairs, was not much good even at that. Prime Minister Grote, attending a production of *Adam and Eve*—notable mainly for the pink taffeta into which the players were sewn for realistic nakedness—found his reserved seats occupied, and Harlequin proved unable to provide others. There was a nasty scene, which so affected the poor devil that he walked through his part with hanging head. He was kept on only for the sake of his daughter, a useful actress with looks and talent but so peremptory a manner that she upset all the others: two leading ladies, one toothless and therefore unintelligible, the other old and fat; the actress whose health no longer permitted her to dress for the men's parts in which she had excelled, and who had taken to dragging out her speeches so much that the audience forgot the beginning before she reached the end; and the celebrated M Préfleury, who might still have starred in the roles of kings and fathers had he been capable of memorising lines, which, owing to drink, he was not.

It was as well, perhaps, that Anton Ulrich was growing too deaf to hear them—a fact that had not escaped his own opera company, who nowadays did little more than hum. But Sophie was able to produce an ideal entertainment for him—a new invention which by means of a mysterious machine conjured up fortified cities on her lake, together with a flotilla of men-of-war to bombard them. Rousing battle noises rang in the ears of all whose hearing was intact, and Sophie only hoped that her guest was not missing too much through deafness.

Most of her entertaining was done at Herrenhausen, where Quirini made constant improvements, though Ernst August said he was spoiling it all. There was now a lime avenue leading straight to Hanover, and a system of twice-daily public transport which was patronised by courtiers, laundry women with their bundles, chickens, geese, peasants and citizens.

Sophie's gardens had become grander since George Louis' accession. He had installed dozens of statues of Roman emperors and many pavilions, of which he was so fond that the grounds of 'La Fantaisie'—the villa that he had given to Mme von Kielmansegg—fairly bristled with *petites maisons* and resembled, said Ernst August, a military camp; and to make the fountains soar higher even than those at St Cloud, he authorised experiments with an embryonic model of a steam machine half a century or so before Watt's engine revolutionised the world.

But although the Elector took a proper interest, his heart was in his hunting lodge at Goehrde. The place was dull beyond description and the shooting poor, said Ernst August—'partridges invisible again, the Elector bagged an owl'. But here George Louis could cast off the melancholy humour that sometimes made him threaten to throw himself into the Leine, and Sophie naturally took an interest in his building plans. Palatial stables, she thought, were all very fine, but the Court had grown too large for the theatre there, and unless George Louis followed the lead of Berlin, where ladies were desired to leave the hoops off their skirts in order to take up less room, a new one was needed.

Under her auspices Tommaso and Quirini created a removable stage for the great hall, which was newly decorated with frescoes copied from the town hall at Lüneburg. The sight of the mediaeval Guelphs from Henry the Lion onwards, in Saxon attitudes with their broad swords dangling from the centre of their belts, amused Sophie, 'but no doubt future generations will find our fashions equally absurd'. The hall was inaugurated by a ball which guests were bidden to attend as characters from the mural—such a good grounding, commented Sophie Dorothea, in history.

Sophie Dorothea was constantly occupied with the production of babies. All died soon after arrival, except for pretty, precocious Wilhelmine, who looked, they said, like Figuelotte. Caroline's expected baby seemed once more so long in arriving that Ernst August, complaining of inordinate secrecy in *'cette petite famille'*, was unable to discover whether the Princess had miscarried, was about to miscarry or whether she was pregnant at all. But Caroline had only miscalculated again, and gave birth to a daughter, Anne, in 1709.

Sophie doted on all the babies. On the principle that *'les petits cadeaux entretiennent l'amitié'* she showered them and their elders with acceptable gifts. Often these were of her own making. Over the years she had manufactured chenille flowers, baskets, purses—'I wish I were making money instead'—altar-cloths and chair-covers to her own design, or from adaptations of whatever came to hand, including some antique mosaics that Carllutz had sent from Greece years ago. At other times she would give them objects bought at the great annual fairs, where the latest *à la mode* inventions were always on sale.

It was at the Brunswick fair that she solved the problem of a birthday present for the King in Prussia, who, she hoped, would be impressed by a gold-headed cane 'of a single piece of tortoise-shell, or at least so cleverly made that the joint is invisible'. Presents of suitable magnificence and originality for Frederick I were always a problem, but Sophie was able to come to the aid of Sophie Dorothea, in despair as to what to give her father-in-law. Liselotte, Sophie wrote, had sent her the description of the French King's *nef*—an object made in the shape of a ship which held the royal napkin. Surely even a King who had everything would consider this a novelty? Should Sophie send for a drawing? There was bound to be a clever French goldsmith in Berlin.

French artefacts, sent from Paris by Liselotte, always created great excitement in Hanover. When she despatched a pair of fat, jewelled Buddahs whose nodding heads contemplated their navels—Liselotte described herself as resembling them in shape, 'only with clothes on'—Sophie's whole Court had come to file past them in her cabinet. Her great-grandson had been delighted with them, although he had not dared to touch them for fear of causing damage. He had been equally entranced by a landscape painting populated with figures animated by clockwork, so that the gentry bowed and nodded, artisans plied their crafts, vehicles moved and the clock in the church-tower kept time. 'Moving pictures...' said the Prussian King, to whom Sophie sent an enthusiastic, detailed description. 'It'll be talking pictures next.'

The autumn of 1710 brought another ambassador from Queen Anne. This time it was Lord Rivers, a Tory peer, sent to acquaint Hanover with the ministerial changes that had taken place in England. The Whigs had fallen and Robert Harley, later Earl of Oxford, and Henry St John, later Viscount Bolingbroke, were engaged in forming a Tory government. Every letter that Lord Rivers received while staying in Hanover announced further new appointments. Much to Sophie's amazement loyal letters began to arrive from Tories who had not written to her for years. She had nothing against them, even though Marlborough was stressing that the future of *la maison* lay with the Whigs.

The new government did not share his commitment to 'no peace without Spain', and a scheme to unseat him as supreme commander, and to substitute George Louis as the Allies' figurehead, was at present being discussed. The Elector, on being approached, declined to have anything to do with this plan, which he recognised as a political manœuvre. But as he rarely informed his mother of such affairs, Sophie continued to hope for this attractive command for her son who had been wasting his talents at the Rhine, where there were no laurels for the gathering. Lord Rivers, with whom she discussed this in the following year, surprised her by declaring 'that he knew nothing about the war', when previously 'he had talked about nothing else'. England was growing weary of the long and expensive war, but Sophie still believed that the Queen would stand by her allies and that the Tories, like the Whigs before them, would countenance no peace without Spain. However, the Queen desired peace even at the cost of leaving Louis XIV's grandson on the Spanish throne, while assuring the Allies of the contrary.

In the spring of 1711 both the Emperor Joseph, brother of the Austrian claimant to Spain, and the Dauphin of France died. 'The face of Europe is changing,' wrote Sophie, since the Dauphin's son, the French 'King of Spain', had moved up in the line of succession to the throne of France (his previous renunciation was thought to be unreliable), while the late Emperor's brother, the Archduke Charles, was the only available candidate for the Imperial throne.

Hanover, at long last admitted to the Electoral College, sent representatives to the Archduke's subsequent election and coronation. Grote, unlucky as usual in the matter of seating, had bribed an attendant, hoping for a pew with a view, but was instead shown to the privy. By the time the misunderstanding was cleared up all the best seats had been taken, and Sophie got her description from her niece Louise. Remembering the past, she said, 'The play is the same. Only the actors are different.'

The present change in casting gave the English government even better reasons for pursuing its separate peace policy, while still assuring the Allies that the fight would continue with undiminished vigour until a treaty acceptable to them all had been hammered out. Sophie hoped that 'Whigs and Tories will share the glory of restoring liberty to Europe', but heard from London that they were 'such enemies that they sit at different sides even at the Opera', so this seemed unlikely.

And what would happen to the Hanoverian succession if Queen Anne's health, alarmingly poor, further deteriorated was anybody's guess. 'God knows in what mood the Whigs and Tories will be if the Queen should die,' wrote Sophie to Leibniz. 'What Parliament does one day it undoes the next. Even those who wanted to see me in England, and to give me a pension fitting for the heir to the crown, no longer mention the subject.' 'What a mad nation,' agreed Liselotte, who would have been as amazed as Sophie and George Louis to learn that even Marlborough was secretly promising support to the Pretender. But it caused Sophie no surprise that the Queen herself was showing every sign of desiring her brother to succeed her. 'Very natural,' she said, 'he's closer to her than I am.' But she thought it decidedly odd that, apart from sending regular compliments, the Queen treated all members of *la maison* as though they were perfect strangers. Anne had even ignored Caroline's last baby, her own godchild and namesake, until the child was two years old. Then, on being tactfully reminded, she sent, along with the usual letters assuring Hanover that everything possible was being done in the interests of the succession, 'a portrait . . . encircled by diamonds, the sort that one gives to ambassadors' for the little Princess.

None of the Queen's communications, *'fort gracieux'* though they invariably were, increased Sophie's belief in her sincerity. Like Leibniz she thought that only actions—specifically an invitation and a grant—would show that Anne meant what she said. Nevertheless, she refused to utter a word of criticism of the Queen except to her confidants, and even then tried to find excuses. When Anne harshly dismissed Marlborough on New Year's Eve 1711—'small thanks for the glory he has won for her arms'— Sophie thought that Milady Marlborough's behaviour was to blame. Leibniz shared her view and observed that personal animosities often, regrettably, influenced the course of history. Had the Duchess not over-reached herself, Marlborough, whose nature Sophie had thought 'subtle enough to maintain him in the Queen's favour' against all odds, might have remained in command and there would have been a chance of a good peace. Now that the Duke, one of the chief objectors to a separate peace agreement between England and France, had gone, the philosopher trembled for the European liberties. No matter what Louis XIV might sign, France would neither disarm, nor abandon hopes of installing the Pretender on the throne of England. Sophie agreed—'France's recognition of the Hanoverian succession is meaningless'—and when Lord Rivers began to lay claim to ever greater presents and special treatment it seemed to her 'as if the crown of England was up for sale', and she was in no doubt that

Sophie with her family by Jacques Vaillant, *ca* 1685. *L to R* (*probably*): Frederick August, Duke Ernst August, Charles Philip, Maximilian, George Louis. Sophie Dorothea with her son George August, Prince Ernst August, Sophie, Christian.

The Mathilda Medal by Lamballé.

Figuelotte and Frederick I by F. W. Weidemann.

'the King of France would be able to outbid us on behalf of the Pretender'.

While the future of Europe was being decided at the Peace Congress of Utrecht, which opened in January 1712, Leibniz was advising his patrons to look east. 'Peter the Great is someone who will make a great noise in the world. . . . He will be a sort of Grand Turk of the North. . . . He means to be Alexander the Great at the very least.' Anton Ulrich took his advice and shocked Europe by announcing the betrothal of one of his granddaughters to the Tsarevitch. Never, said the Prussian King, would he dream of sending a child into that barbaric country, but Sophie insisted that the groom, though evidently lacking in manners, was a *bon garçon* at heart; she did not like to hear her friend the Tsar criticised, even by implication.

She longed to go to the wedding in Dresden—planning, no doubt, said her youngest, 'to be *la reine du bal*.' Her embroidered French gala skirt was set to rights—'I save it for all Brunswick Princesses. I only wish I could dance in it at your pretty Princess's wedding,' she wrote to Sophie Dorothea, 'but alas, clothes last longer than people.' Sophie did not go to the wedding after all, but Leibniz was there. Ernst August was quite wrong in his prediction that Peter would take *Mlle Philosophe* for Anton Ulrich's fool. On the contrary, the Tsar thought him a *fort honnête homme*, and invited him to create an academy in Moscow on the lines of that in Berlin, a welcome offer, since his *au revoir* to Berlin had in effect turned out to be goodbye. None of his customary ploys—letters sent to Sophie to send on to Sophie Dorothea to hand to the King—had reinstated him in Frederick's favour, and George Louis had stopped paying his stipend because of his constant absences.* He more or less divided his time between Vienna and Brunswick, to the regret of Sophie, who would have preferred him closer at hand. While he was considering the Russian offer† Anton Ulrich sent her reports of the Russian marriage.

The bride, she learned, had at first been put off by her groom's shaggy mane and common expression, but things were looking up: he was having his hair curled and powdered, taking dancing lessons and studying the customs of the west. Although Ernst August had reported that the

---

* It was in this connection that Sophie wrote to her old friend, 'The likes of us do not seem to be among the lucky ones, fated to enjoy success'—an odd pronouncement for the twelfth child of poverty-stricken parents who against all odds became a reigning Duchess, an Electress and a royal heiress.

† In the event, he died before he could take it up.

Tsarevitch '*fait caca dans sa chambre*' and used the curtains for wiping, he seemed cleaner and politer than at first. As for apparent unfamiliarity with handkerchiefs, Sophie said that if the King of France took to blowing his nose in his fingers it would at once be considered the height of fashion by all Europe.

Although she was scathing about German princes who emulated the French King—'we seem to copy all their bad habits and none of the good' —she admired Anton Ulrich's château at Salzdahlum, which he liked to think of as a second Versailles. All the time he could spare from marrying off his granddaughters to Tsars and Emperors and from writing his novel —now in its tenth volume—was spent on this house and the garden, with its pagoda hung with bells that chimed in the wind. Sophie paid frequent visits, was impressed by his seven picture galleries, and exclaimed over 'vases painted by Raffael d'Urbino' and the portraits of old friends that lined the walls. Only Queen Christine looked less than lifelike—no wonder, for Anton Ulrich explained that she had been painted while she was lying in state. Sophie shuddered, as she often did at Salzdahlum, which was very grand but freezingly cold. To reawaken her numbed feet she took her lady-in-waiting by the hand and, humming a little air, proceeded to dance with her across the parquet floor. The Duke, not to be outdone— 'he wants to show that he is three years younger than I am'—followed suit, and the ageing threesome hopped and skipped along the glacial galleries, while an odious pug called Mops, from which Anton Ulrich was inseparable, skated behind them.

Sophie was not sorry to return to her own house, where, she said, her internal mechanism worked more smoothly, and where she could play with her great-grandchildren, to whom Caroline had added a second princess. Sophie gave a children's ball for Prince Frederick, his elder sister and their friends. She feared that she was 'growing so old as to embark on her second childhood', for she loved seeing the tots pace gravely round the room in miniature versions of grown-up party clothes. It was a pleasure, too, to see Frederick, who had been worryingly slow in walking and talk-ing, do both at last. She could tease him to the point of tears by saying that Wilhelmine of Prussia, whom he considered his fiancée and whose por-trait he cherished, was plain. Not that she was, Sophie assured her grand-daughter—on the contrary.

Another great-grandchild had arrived in Prussia, in January 1712:

Sophie Dorothea's third Frederick, the first one who looked like surviving —and did, to become the Great. Frequent couriers from Berlin brought news of his progress, and his doting grandfather personally announced each tooth.

The first half of 1712 also brought news of the deaths of almost the entire French succession. Frederick I was convinced that it was Louis XIV's punishment 'for so many Palatine Electors and Electresses dragged from their tombs—God's judgement for sure.' Only one infant prince—later to become Louis XV—was saved from the clutches of the Court doctors. These tragic events meant that there was now only a single life between the old King and his grandson, the King of Spain. This made the prospect of a separate peace between England and France—dependent, as it was likely to be, on English approval of Bourbon rule in Spain—even more menacing to the Allies. Queen Anne was annoyed that George Louis refused to dissociate himself from the Emperor, and remained deaf to the request of Prince Eugene, Castor to Marlborough's Pollux, who had rushed to London to persuade her not to abandon the Allies. Except for a handsome diamond sword, the Prince had nothing to show for his visit: the Queen, it was clear, wanted peace.

Leibniz tried to incorporate articles to secure the Hanoverian succession into the eventual peace treaty, but although Sophie heard that students had carried a banner 'on which were to be seen the devil, the Pope and the Pretender' around the Court on the Queen's birthday, she felt sure that nothing would come of her chances 'if France keeps the upper hand'.

In June Lord Oxford's cousin, Thomas Harley, arrived in Hanover with further documents, drawn up to ensure Sophie's precedence directly after the Queen. Sophie admired the *étui*—'painted with flowers all round, as though it's from Persia'—but the Act of Precedence itself left her cold. No one had ever dreamt of disputing *le pas* with any of her brothers, so what was the point of it now, especially as neither income nor invitation accompanied the scroll? Her recurrent discussions of the English grant were prompted not by cupidity, but by the wish for practical steps which would affirm the succession. 'Should the pension come,' she told Louise, now mistress of her household at last, 'I shall have to create a separate English court, and you would have plenty of English ladies under you.' On the whole, however, she thought it more likely that her niece would continue to live unencumbered and in '*santa pace*'.

In December she wrote to Sophie Dorothea that she was not unduly disturbed by the recurrent rumour that the Queen secretly favoured her Stuart brother, who was still expected to change his religion in order to qualify for the crown. 'Mine will come in the next world,' she said, 'although if I were twenty or thirty I might have more to say. But England looks on while France refers to the Pretender as the Duke of Gloucester, when in William's day war was made because Louis XIV called him the Prince of Wales. . . . Once upon a time Queen Anne herself believed that he was a changeling, and tried to make her sister* believe it too. That Princess wept, and confided in my daughter. Then, when the two sisters quarrelled, Anne declared publicly that she had no doubt the Pretender was her true brother. It's an old story, but you see how much store I can set by the great documents that I hold.'

Frederick I agreed. 'Since England now calls the Pretender the Duke of Gloucester, it means that he's assumed to be the rightful heir. But the English, as you know, are so unreliable that there's no trusting them. The Allies have been badly deceived, and in the future they'll have to take care not to make treaties with England without proper guarantees. I'm sorry for you, though, being fobbed off with empty phrases . . . but if you're clever you'll take my advice, not show that you mind, and treat them as politely as before. In this way you'll put them even more in the wrong.'

He congratulated her in October on hearing that her eighty-second birthday had been celebrated in London, but Sophie knew that there had been enthusiastic birthday celebrations for the Pretender in Scotland, so she was not unduly elated by the news. She danced at the great hunt ball on St Hubertus' Day, and thanked God that age was her only ailment. She commiserated with Queen Anne, suffering from gout which forced her to extend in greeting her left hand, swathed in nasty bandages like the right but less painful, and wrote to Prussia expressing her profound hope that Frederick's wife, that unworthy successor to Figuelotte, would shortly recover from her ominous bouts of madness. However, in February 1713 she learnt that, far from getting better, the Queen had as good as killed the King. Escaping from her keepers, she had wandered into his presence through a French window, closed at the time, in a white shift spattered with blood from the cuts. The shock of seeing the *Weisse Frau*, a ghost said

* Queen Mary, William III's co-ruler.

to presage Hohenzollern deaths, was too much for Frederick, and he took to his bed. 'The only pleasure the King ever had from the marriage was the wedding itself,' wrote Sophie. 'I expect he would be not sorry to be planning the Queen's funeral now.' However, it was the King himself who died, on 25th February.

'Weeping and wailing help no one and are a poor comfort, my dear Queen,' wrote Sophie to her granddaughter, 'so I shan't send you anything but congratulations and good wishes for the King's happy reign. We'll go into deep mourning as soon as the Tsar has departed. We didn't like to receive him in such gloom, and in any case the King has not yet officially informed us of our great loss. The Tsar wept hot tears, and we ourselves were too sad to cheer him up, though we tried.'

Frederick William was in his element at last. He himself drilled the troops that accompanied his father to his last resting-place, marched them out of the church, and personally gave the command for the last salvo. Although the poor chaps, said Ernst August, had been on the march for hours, he marched them out of the town again directly after the ceremony, because he was afraid that the girls who were leaning out of their windows would debauch them if they got the chance.

The new King's first royal act was to remove all the evidence of his father's extravagance. Out went the precious tapestries, the *objets d'art*, the porcelain for which Frederick I had personally scanned Dutch merchant ships as they returned from the east. Anton Ulrich offered to swap the porcelain for grenadiers, and Sophie was disgusted to hear that her grandson also planned to exchange the priceless Prussian art collection for eighty Saxon cannons. She hoped that he would not be so foolish, and reminded him that she 'would shortly be in a position to blacken his name in Paradise'. As always, she longed to see her dear grandchildren, but the new King could not spare the time. He was busy drilling a detachment of *Lange Kerle*—a friendly gift from the Tsar—and Sophie had to make do with a set of the new coins showing his profile, which she pronounced 'very like'.

It was likely that her martial grandson would soon be playing with his soldiers for pleasure only, for England and France were reaching agreement, and the general peace would inevitably follow. In the spring of 1713 the Anglo-French treaty was finally signed, to the disgust of the Empire, and the end of the war duly celebrated at St Paul's Cathedral. Handel, having moved to England, composed the Te Deum which lost him George Louis' favour for some time to come.

One of the peace stipulations had been that the Pretender should be removed from St Germain. He became a guest of Liselotte's daughter and her brick-coloured husband, the Duke of Lorraine, who in due course became one of a number of rulers to receive a round robin from Sophie's English supporters begging him to refuse the Prince asylum. A current joke concerning the Pretender amused Sophie: 'They say that if they banish him everywhere, there'll be nowhere to send him but Hanover'.

The Queen's speech before the general election in the autumn, when the Tories were again returned, failed to make any mention at all of the Hanoverian succession. Leibniz thought this significant, and told Caroline that 'in England they've been saying that the first Parliament would bring the Whigs to their knees, the second one make the peace, and the third work on changing the law of succession.' The Queen, however, wrote yet again that Hanover's interests were her own, and a further visit from Thomas Harley was announced. He was to discuss the question of the Pretender's domicile, and also the pension, wrote Sophie to Leibniz in Vienna, whence he did not stir in spite of her desire to have him by her bedside to discuss affairs of state. She was not actually ill, but sometimes stayed in bed 'in order to fade away as slowly as possible', having been told by her doctors that this might happen without warning at any moment. But 'our Princess of Wales is wonderfully well,' wrote Caroline to Leibniz early in 1714, adding 'the Electress' in brackets, for the Queen had vetoed the use of the former title, together with that of Royal Highness, and Sophie herself declined to be addressed by any of the royal-sounding forms of address which her well-intentioned friends occasionally invented for her. 'Royal Highnesses are becoming very common,' she had decided. 'Electress sounds much more distinguished.'

Health bulletins passed between her and Leibniz while she waited for Harley's arrival. Anton Ulrich, 'three years better than me, and intent on finishing his novel before his end', failed to do so, and preceded Sophie to the gates of Paradise, which she considered impolite to say the least. It was the loss of his overfed pug Mops that had been too much for the old man to bear. Youthful though he had seemed—'Wigs are so advantageous for old men,' said Sophie, who thought him *vif* and hearty—he died while Lutheran and Catholic clergymen fought over his soul across his bed. Always fanatical on points of detail, the Duke had left precise instructions down to the tying of his cravat for the lying-in-state, and as soon as the breath left his body a messenger sped to France with his apologies to Liselotte for leaving his book unfinished, and an outline of how it would have ended had he had time to write it.

It was to have been such a romantic ending, Sophie wrote to Leibniz, adding, 'My own would be *plus belle* if, as you desire, my bones were interred in Westminster Abbey.* But my spirit still governs my body and does not at present give me such gloomy thoughts. Discussions about the succession grieve me. So many books have been written for and against it that I no longer trouble to read them.'

Of Queen Anne, again reported to be at death's door, Sophie wrote in March, 'She'll have to hurry up with her dying if I'm to be Queen, as you desire'. But 'the Queen *se porte à merveille*' she wrote shortly afterwards, when young Baron Schütz, son of the former envoy, sent good reports of Anne's health from London. 'Creaking waggons go far'—there would be no chance, Sophie feared, of obliging her friends, 'who seem to be waiting to strew palms at my entry,' by outliving the Queen, who could, after all, almost have been her daughter.

April came, but there was still no sign of Harley. 'No doubt he is delaying in Holland in order to promote this outrageous peace,' wrote Leibniz. 'If his journey is taking so long because of the weight of caskets filled with gold which, as we read in the *Gazette*, he is carrying to enable *Votre Altesse Electorale* to hold Court in England, he must be pardoned his slowness. But if he is only coming to tell us that the Protestant succession is in no danger, he can keep his views for the coffee-houses of London.'

He also mentioned that he had made the acquaintance of a Scot, who preferred to remain anonymous (he was the Duke of Roxburgh), who felt strongly that Hanover needed to take some action to encourage Sophie's supporters in England. Since it would not do for the Electress to do so in person, 'I thought of the Raugravine Louise, who, as affairs approach the point of crisis, could regularly correspond with him and his friends. No one would be more suitable than the Raugravine, intelligent and zealous as she is. With a little ink and paper she might procure intelligence that

---

* It was this repetition of Leibniz's remark, says Onno Klopp, which gave rise to the frequently quoted myth that Sophie herself, untypically, longed to be buried in London under a stone inscribed 'Here lies Sophie, Queen of England'.

would otherwise cost us dearly. Of course I leave the decision to the superior wisdom of *Votre Altesse Electorale*, but I feel one should accept this offer to correspond, with due precautions which would be assured by the Raugravine's prudence.' He added that if Sophie would send the Scot a Mathilda, no medal would ever have been better employed.

Sophie read this letter with attention, as she did Leibniz's note to Louise. This stressed once again that Hanover's potential English supporters were doing less than they might because Hanover's enemies were insisting that the heirs cared nothing for the crown. The Hanoverian envoy had done what he could to alter this unfortunate impression, but it was up to Louise, provided Sophie agreed, to keep on with the good work.

When Harley finally turned up in May he brought letters from the Queen and his cousin, the Earl of Oxford, stating in the most explicit terms that both were in favour of the Protestant succession. But instead of an official parliamentary grant he brought only the offer of a private annuity from Anne, which Sophie politely refused—'just as the Queen herself had refused a similar offer from William III, as history tells us'.

'Meanwhile, the English people thought that he had come to invite me to England,' she wrote to Leibniz. 'There was not the least mention of this, but they nevertheless concluded that I don't want to come. So I commanded Schütz to ask the Chancellor if the Electoral Prince, as Duke of Cambridge, should not have a writ enabling him to take his seat in the House of Lords. The Chancellor replied that he had the writ ready, but that it was usual to apply for it in person, *sur le lieu*, and that he would speak to the Queen. It seems that this alarmed both her and the council. The Chancellor was finally told to act according to the law, and therefore sent Schütz the writ. Simultaneously the Queen forbade Schütz to show his face at Court, and he returned home by the post without knowing how he has offended. Then, suddenly, Harley took his leave from the Elector, and two days later from me, and departed with all his Englishmen, of whom he had great quantities.'

Leibniz wrote by return of post that he was amazed by Sophie's English news. Surely a writ was no more than the Prince's due, and to demand it showed that Hanover really cared about England. Presumably Schütz had acted on the Elector's order, but even if he hadn't he could in Leibniz's opinion 'be likened to a general who had won a battle without orders from the chief of staff'.

George August and Caroline by Godfrey Kneller.

Sophie Dorothea of Hanover after Hirschmann and her husband the Crown Prince Frederick William of Prussia by F. W. Weidemann.

'The Golden Age under George I' by James Thornhill.

The great question was—now that the writ had been issued, would the Prince actually go? Leibniz told Caroline that he must: not to do so would look like repugnance. Caroline replied that she and the Prince were vainly moving heaven and earth to gain the Elector's consent. Then in the middle of the crisis, at noon on 6th June, Sophie, George Louis and George August all received angry letters from Queen Anne, whose reaction to the demand for the writ had been so violent as to astonish and worry all who were with her, accustomed though they were to her bad temper on the subject of Hanover.

The three letters were identical in substance. The succession, said the Queen, had long been declared to belong to Hanover, but would be endangered 'unless the Prince wearing the crown maintained her prerogative and authority'. There were, unfortunately, too many seditious persons in England, only too eager to use the establishment of what would be a rival Court for their own purposes. To Sophie she said that she had always been under the impression that 'Madam, cousin and aunt' understood this as well as she did, and begged for other suggestions to secure the Hanoverians in her country, short of having her grandson reside in England. To George Louis she wrote accurately that she was sure no Prince possessed of such knowledge and penetration as he could ever have been party to the writ affair. With George August she was bluntest of all. She said that, first, the matter should have been raised with herself personally, and, secondly, that nothing could be more dangerous to the tranquillity of her estates and the right of the succession in his line, and consequently more disagreeable to her, than his coming into England at this juncture. This letter, of a violence that Caroline thought worthy of Bolingbroke, well known for his Jacobite sympathies, so upset George August that Caroline 'feared for his health and even his life'.

Sophie, too, was agitated by these harsh communications. 'This affair will surely make me ill,' she told the Countess of Bückeburg. '*J'y succomberai*, but I'll have that gracious letter printed to show the world that it is not my fault if my children lose the three crowns.' Eventually she would have come to share Leibniz's view that she should console herself about this *petit contretemps*, and that in the long run it was all for the best as it would force the Elector to take a decisive stand, but Sophie's time was running out.

That evening her head ached as she took her customary tour round the garden. 'The miserable affair weighed on her heart,' wrote Bückeburg. 'Our good Electress has never minded anything so much as the Queen's refusal.' Sophie took supper as usual, and went to bed to spend a disturbed, miserable night. Against all advice she rose in the morning at her accustomed hour, but felt sick during dinner and returned to her apartments, from where she ordered that copies of the letters should be sent to her friends in London. At 6 pm the Countess of Bückeburg was successful in persuading her to take two successive *lavements*, which eased her, and she rose to sup with her son. On the following day she had so far recovered that she not only dined in public but set off for her habitual promenade in the late afternoon. Although it was overcast and looked like rain she refused to hear of sedan chairs, sent the porters away, and marched briskly as usual, discussing the English affair with Caroline.

Bückeburg, out of respect, kept a few paces behind with the rest of the suite, but soon, 'in that gracious and obliging manner of which she alone was capable', Sophie turned and took her arm, continuing her walk between the Princess and the Countess. She talked of all manner of things with her normal vivacity, including the beauty of Mme von der Bussche, who was walking with her sister at the other end of the avenue.

In the centre of the garden, by the little painted pavilion near the first fountain, Sophie swayed and faltered as though she were very tired. Caroline asked if she was feeling unwell and Sophie, clasping her diaphragm with her hands, said with a great sigh, 'It's here, it's here'. Bückeburg suggested opening her stays to ease the feeling of tightness, but Sophie demonstrated that her bodice was quite loose. She agreed to rest in the pavilion before returning to her apartments, but after ten paces or so, in the rain that was now falling hard, it became clear that she could walk no further. 'I feel very ill,' she said, 'give me your hand.'

Bückeburg, alarmed, sent Sophie's ladies for doctors, gold-powder, sedan chairs and bearers. In that avenue, now quite deserted because of the rain, Caroline, Bückeburg and an attendant gentleman ministered to her in her last moments, as Sophie sank into their supporting arms. They placed her gently on the ground, the courtier's arm still around her shoulders, Bückeburg's lap cushioning her head; while they prayed for her Bückeburg removed the kerchief from her throat, and with her knife cut open her stays to allow her to breathe. They noticed that her colour was changing, and that a deathly pallor appeared on her face. Sophie gave one anguished sigh and half-opened her eyes, 'only to show us that their lustre was extinct and that the spirit that had so wonderfully animated them had left its illustrious abode'.

The tears and cries of that little huddle on the path by the pavilion gradually attracted the whole Court. 'They brought what we had sent for, but too late,' the Countess of Bückeburg told Louise, 'although they did all they could to revive our dear Electress'. An hour later they were still torturing her in their attempts to bring her back to life. They bled her arms and feet and flattered themselves that her colour was changing, but the looking-glass they held up to her lips remained unclouded. Sophie had escaped the ministrations of both sorts of charlatans—the priests and the doctors—who never help the dying but only torment them. She had long been at peace with her Maker, 'and quite prepared to meet him, as late as possible'. There had been no death-bed, no terror, and never, said Bückeburg, had a death been *plus douce et plus heureuse*.

It was not for Sophie that he was sad, wrote Leibniz to Caroline. It was not she who had lost, but Hanover, England and himself. He wrote another poem on her death and she was, according to her wish, buried with a minimum of pomp in a plain pine-coffin in the family tomb.

George Louis wrote to Queen Anne that understandable grief had prevented him from replying to her letter, and when he did so a week later it was to express surprise and sorrow at its contents. Six weeks after that the Queen herself was dead, and Sophie's son was proclaimed George I of England.

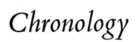

Chronology

	Personal	General
1630	Sophie b. 14 October.	
1632	Winter King d.	Gustav Adolph of Sweden d. his daughter Christine succeeds. Ferdinand III Emperor.
1635		Peace of Prague between Emperor and most Protestant States.
1641/2	Sophie moves to The Hague.	Richelieu d. Mazarin becomes first minister. Civil war in England.
1643	Sophie's first official engagement. Edward, Prince Palatine, m. Anna Gonzaga.	Louis XIII of France d. Louis XIV succeeds.
1645		Wedding of Mary Stuart and William II of Orange.
1647		William II of Orange succeeds his father as Stadholder.
1648	Charles Louis restored as Elector Palatine.	Peace of Westphalia. Second civil war in England.
1649	Charles Stuart, Prince of Wales, courts Sophie.	Charles I beheaded. England republic under Cromwell.
1650	Charles Louis marries Charlotte of Hesse-Cassel, and Sophie moves to Heidelberg. Philip, Prince Palatine, d.	William II d. William III born.
1651	Electoral Prince Charles b. in Heidelberg.	Charles II crowned in Scotland.
1652	Electoral Princess Liselotte b. in Heidelberg. Maurice, Prince Palatine, lost at sea.	
1652/3	Prince Rupert arrives in Heidelberg.	Diet of Ratisbon.

Personal	General
1654 Proposal of marriage from Prince of Zweibrücken, followed by proposal from George William of Brunswick-Lüneburg.	Queen Christine abdicates. Charles X succeeds.
1658 Sophie marries Ernst August, youngest Duke of Brunswick-Lüneburg.	Leopold I becomes Emperor. Death of Oliver Cromwell.
1659 Liselotte comes to Hanover and accompanies Sophie on visit to the Winter Queen.	
1660 George Louis, Sophie's first son, b.	Charles II restored. 'Princess Royal', Mary of Orange, d.
1661 Ernst August becomes Bishop of Osnabrück. Frederick August b.	Death of Mazarin. Louis XIV begins his personal rule.
1662 Winter Queen d. in England. Sophie moves to Iburg.	
1664/5 Sophie in Italy.	
1665 Christian Louis d. John Frederick's *coup d'état*. George William's *mariage de conscience* to Eleonore d'Olbreuse.	Charles II of Spain succeeds his father.
1666 Maximilian b. Sophie Dorothea of Celle b.	Quadruple alliance between Netherlands, Brandenburg, Brunswick and Denmark.
1667	French War of Devolution against Spain. Louis XIV claims Spanish Netherlands.
1668 Sophie Charlotte b. John Frederick m. Benedicta.	Peace of Aix. France obtains Flemish border fortresses. Anna Gonzaga's brother-in-law, John Casimir, abdicates Polish throne.
1669 Charles Philip b.	
1671 Christian b. in Heidelberg. Electoral Prince Charles m.	

	Personal	General
	Wilhelmine Ernestine of Denmark. Liselotte m. Monsieur.	
1672	Move from Iburg to fort-fied Osnabrück.	William III becomes Stadholder. —1678 England and France at war with Netherlands.
1673		Alliance of Empire, Holland, Spain and Pope against France.
1674	Prince Ernst August, Sophie's last child, b.	
1675		Battle of Conz-Saarbrücken.
1676	George William's official marriage to Eleonore d'Olbreuse.	
1678		Peace of Nijmegen.
1679	Sophie visits France.	Installation of French Chambers of Reunion.
1680	John Frederick d. and Ernst August becomes Duke of Hanover. Charles Louis d. Sophie begins Memoirs.	
1681		France occupies Strasbourg in peace-time. Elector of Brandenburg forms defensive alliance with Louis XIV.
1682	Rupert d. George Louis m. Sophie Dorothea.	—1689 Turkish War. Emperor allied to Venice and Poland.
1683	Primogeniture in Brunswick-Lüneburg. George Augustus, the future George II, b.	Siege of Vienna.
1684	Sophie Charlotte m. wid-owed, Electoral Prince of Brandenburg.	
1685	Sophie's nephew the Elector Charles d.	France claims Palatinate for Liselotte. Charles II of England d. James II succeeds.

Personal	General
	Louis XIV revokes Edict of Nantes. Persecution of Protestants in France.
1686 Sophie in Berlin for birth of Sophie Charlotte's first, short-lived baby. Sophie Dorothea II born in Hanover.	League of Augsburg formed against France.
1687	Ernst August in short-lived alliance with France.
1688 Great Elector d. succeeded by Frederick III. Frederick William, the future Soldier King of Prussia, b.	–1697 War of League of Augsburg against France. William III of Orange called to rule England. James II flees to France.
1689 Enrico Leone performed in new Hanover Opera House.	William III and Mary II King and Queen of England. Melac devastates Palatinate. Bill of Rights excludes Catholics from English succession. Peter the Great proclaims himself sole ruler of Russia. James II defeated by William III at the Boyne.
1690 Charles Philip and Frederick August d.	
1691 Maximilian's plot against primogeniture.	
1692 Ninth Electorate created for Ernst August.	
1694 Königsmarck scandal; George Louis divorce.	Queen Mary II of England d.
1697 Peter the Great at Coppenbruck.	Peace of Ryswick. Louis XIV recognises William III as King of England, and Anne as Heir Presumptive.
1698 Ernst August d.	First Spanish partition treaty.
1700 Sophie meets William III at Het Loo.	Second Spanish partition treaty. Charles II of Spain d. Louis' grandson nominated as sole heir. Emperor claims Spanish inheritance for his son, the Archduke Charles.

	Personal	*General*
1701	Act of Succession nominates Sophie and issue as heirs to throne of England. Elector Frederick III of Brandenburg crowns himself King Frederick I in Prussia.	–1714 War of the Spanish Succession.
1702	Christian d.	William III of England d. Queen Anne succeeds. Imperial Diet decides to join war against France.
1704		Marlborough and Prince Eugene victorious at Blenheim.
1705	Sophie Charlotte d. Caroline of Ausbach m. George August.	Archduke Charles recognised as King of Spain in some Spanish provinces.
1706	Sophie Dorothea II m. Frederick William, Crown Prince of Prussia.	
1707		Act of Union between England and Scotland.
1708		Battle of Oudenarde Pretender's bid for Scotland fails.
1709	Louise Hollandine d. at Maubuisson.	Battle of Malplaquet.
1710		Godolphin's Whig ministry replaced by Tory Cabinet.
1711		Archduke Charles succeeds his brother Joseph I as Emperor Charles VI. Marlborough dismissed. Preliminary peace between England and France.
1713/4		Peace of Utrecht.
1714	Sophie d. at Herrenhausen, June.	Queen Anne d. August. George I succeeds.

Bibliography

BIBLIOGRAPHY

Sources

Briefe der Elisabeth Stuart, Königin von Böhmen, an ihren Sohn den Kurfürsten Karl Ludwig von der Pfalz, ed. Anna Wendland, Literarischer Verein Stuttgart, 1902.

The Letters of Elizabeth Queen of Bohemia, ed. L. M. Baker, The Bodley Head, 1953.

Leibniz, Briefwechsel mit der Kurfürstin Sophie, Briefwechsel mit der Königin Sophie Charlotte, 1873 ff, ed. Onno Klopp, *Die Werke von G. W. Leibniz*, Vols. VII–X, Hanover, 1873.

Neuentdeckte Briefe der Herzogin Sophie von Braunschweig-Lüneburg, ed. J. G. Weiss, Niedersächsisches Jahrbuch, 1934.

Die Memoiren der Herzogin Sophie, nachmals Kurfürstin von Hannover, ed. A. Köcher, Leipzig, 1879.

Die Mutter der Könige von Preussen und England. Memoiren und Briefe der Kurfürstin Sophie von Hannover, ed. Robert Geerds, Ebenhausen, Munich and Leipzig, 1913.

Briefwechsel der Kurfürstin Sophie mit dem Preussischen Königshaus, ed. G. Schnath, K. F. Koehler, 1927.

Briefe der Kurfürstin Sophie von Hannover an die Raugräfinnen und Raugrafen, ed. E. Bodemann, Publikationen aus den Königlichen Staatsarchiven, 1888.

Briefe der Herzogin, später Kurfürstin Sophie von Hannover an ihre Oberhofmeisterin A. K. von Harling, ed. E. Bodemann, Hanover/Leipzig, 1895.

Briefwechsel der Herzogin Sophie von Hannover mit ihrem Bruder, dem Kurfürsten Karl Ludwig von der Pfalz, ed. E. Bodemann, Publikationen aus den Königlichen Preussischen Staatsarchiven, 1885.

Briefe des Kurfürsten Ernst August an seine Gemahlin die Kurfürstin Sophie, ed. Anna Wendland, Niedersächsisches Jahrbuch, 1930.

Die Briefe der Kinder des Winter-Königs, ed. Karl Hauck, Neue Heidelberger Jahrbücher, Heidelberg, 1908.

Schreiben des Kurfürsten Karl Ludwig und den Seinen, ed. W. L. Holland, Literarischer Verein Stuttgart, 1884.

A Collection of Original Royal Letters, Sir G. Bromley, London, 1837.

Briefe des Herzogs Ernst August von Braunschweig-Lüneburg an Johannes Franz Diedrich von Wendt, ed. Graf von Kielmansegg, Hahnsche Buchhandlung, 1902.

Der Königsmarck Briefwechsel, G. Schnath, Quellen und Darstellungen zur Geschichte Niedersachsens, 1952.

Prinzenbriefe 1685–1701, ed. Anna Wendland, Hildesheim, 1937.

Briefe der Königin Sophie Charlotte von Preussen und der Kurfürstin Sophie von Hannover an hannoversche Diplomaten, ed. R. Doebner, Publikationen aus den Preussischen Staatsarchiven, S. Hirzel, 1905.
Letters from Liselotte, ed. Maria Kroll, Gollancz, 1970.
Aus den Briefen der Herzogin Elisabeth Charlotte von Orléans an die Kurfürstin Sophie von Hannover, ed. E. Bodemann, Hahnsche Buchhandlung, 1891.
The Letters and Diplomatic Instructions of Queen Anne, ed. Beatrice Curtis Brown, Cassell, 1968.

Books Used

ARKELL, R. L., *Caroline of Ansbach*, Oxford University Press, 1939.
BAILY, F. E., *Sophia of Hanover and her Times*, Hutchinson, 1936.
VON BOEHN, MAX, *Modes and Manners*, Harrap, 1935.
——*Der Tanz*, Berlin, 1925.
Cambridge Modern History, Vols V. & VI.
CHAPMAN, HESTER, *Privileged Persons*, Jonathan Cape, 1966.
——*The Tragedy of Charles II*, Jonathan Cape, 1964.
CHURCHILL, WINSTON, *Marlborough, his Life and Times*, Harrap, 1933.
DOVE, ALFRED, *Die Kinder des Winter-Königs*, Ausgewählte Schriften vornehmlich historischen Inhalts, Leipzig, 1898.
ERLANGER, PHILIPPE, *Louis XIV*, Weidenfeld & Nicolson, 1970.
——*Monsieur, Frère de Louis XIV*, Hachette, 1970.
EVELYN, JOHN, *Diary*, ed. William Bray, Everyman, 1951.
GREEN, DAVID, *Sarah Duchess of Marlborough*, Collins, 1967.
——*Queen Anne*, Collins, 1970.
HAMILTON, ANTHONY, trans. Peter Quennell, *Memoirs of the Comte de Gramont*, Routledge, 1930.
HAMILTON, ELIZABETH, *William's Mary*, Hamish Hamilton, 1972.
HAUCK, KARL, *Karl Ludwig von der Pfalz*, Leipzig, 1903.
HAUPT, A., *Die bildende Kunst in Hannover zur Zeit der Kurfürstin Sophie*, Hannoversche Geschichtsblätter, 1903.
HÄUSSER, LUDWIG, *Geschichte der rheinischen Pfalz*, Heidelberg, 1924.
HAVEMANN, W., *Geschichte der Lande Braunschweig und Lüneburg*, Göttingen, 1853–57.
HUEHNS, G., ed. Selections from *Clarendon*, Oxford University Press, 1956.
KNOOP, MATHILDE, *Kurfürstin Sophie*, August Lax, 1964.
KÖCHER, ADOLF, *Geschichte von Hannover und Braunschweig 1648–1674, Vols. I & II*, S. Hirzel, Leipzig, 1884/5.
——*Denkwürdigkeiten der Cellischen Herzogin Eleonore*, Z. H. V. Nds., 1878.
MALORTIE, C. E. VON, *Beiträge zur Geschichte des Braunschweig-Lüneburgischen Hauses und Hofes*, 4 vols., 1847–1860.
MELVILLE, LEWIS, *The First George in Hanover and England*, Pitman & Sons, 1908.
——*In the days of Queen Anne*, Hutchinson, no date.

NÖLDEKE, W., *Sophie, Kurfürstin von Hannover*, Hanover, 1864.

OMAN, CAROLA, *Elizabeth of Bohemia*, Hodder & Stoughton, 1938.

——*Henrietta Maria*, Hodder & Stoughton, 1936.

PEPYS, SAMUEL, *Diary*, ed. John Warrington, Everyman, 1966.

ROBB, NESCA A., *William III*, vols. I & II, Heinemann, 1962–66.

SACKVILLE-WEST, V., *Daughter of France*, Michael Joseph, 1959.

SCOTT, EVA, *Rupert, Prince Palatine*, Constable, 1899.

SCHNATH, GEORG, *Die Kurfürstin Sophie und ihr Kreis*, Hanover, 1930.

——*Festschrift*, 1931.

——*Der Königsmarck Briefwechsel—eine Fälschung*, 1930.

——*Ernst August, der erste Kurfürst von Hannover*, Han. Magazin, 1929.

——*Geschichte Hannovers im Zeitalter der neunten Kur und der englischen Suk-zession 1674–1714, Vol. 3, 1674–1692*, Lax, 1938.

SCHNATH, HILLEBRECHT PLATH, *Das Leineschloss*, Hahnsche Buchhandlung, Hanover, 1962.

SCHUTH, LUDWIG, *Italienreisen im 17 und 18. Jahrhundert*, Vienna, 1959.

STOLPE, SVEN, *Christina of Sweden*, Burns Oates, 1966.

THACKERAY, W. M., *The Four Georges*, Falcon Press, 1948.

VARNHAGEN VAN ENSE, K. A., *Biographische Denkmäle*, Brockhaus, Leipzig, 1872.

VEHSE, EDUARD, *Geschichte der Deutschen Höfe seit der Reformation*, Hoffman & Campe, 1851.

VOLTAIRE, *The Age of Louis XIV* (sel. & ed. W. Hadley), Dent, 1961.

WARD, ADOLPHUS W., *The Electress Sophia and the Hanoverian Succession*, Goupil & Co., 1903, Longmans, Green, 1909.

WEDGWOOD, C. V., *The Thirty Years War*, Jonathan Cape, 1938.

WENDLAND, ANNA, *Beiträge zur Geschichte der Kurfürstin Sophie*, Zeitschriften des Historischen Vereins für Niedersachsen, 1910.

——*Hannover-Herrenhausen im Leben der Kurfürstin Sophie*, Hanover, 1914.

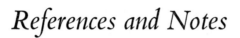

References and Notes

REFERENCES AND NOTES

Although every work cited in the bibliography informed some aspect of this book, the references below list only those from which specific statements or quotations were drawn.

Relevant passages are identified by page numbers and key-phrases. Titles of recurring sources are abbreviated as shown below; all others, though shortened, are self-explanatory. Unless otherwise stated, Sophie is the writer of the quoted phrases.

BEB	Baker: Elizabeth of Bohemia's letters
BSCL	Bodemann: Sophie to Charles Louis
BSR	Sophie to Raugravines
BSvH	Sophie to Mme von Harling
DSFD	Doebner: Sophie and Figuelotte to diplomatists
GSL	Geerds: Sophie's memoirs and letters
HWL	Hauck: Winter children's letters
HCL	Biography of Charles Louis
HCLF	Holland: Charles Louis' family letters
KEA	Kielmansegg: Prince Ernst August's letters
KL	Klopp: Leibniz papers.
Mems	Sophie's memoirs, Koecher.
SSP	Schnath: Sophie's correspondence with Prussia
SK	Königsmarck correspondence.
WEB	Wendland: Elizabeth of Bohemia's letters
WPL	Princes' letters
WEA	Ernst August's letters

page   *Prologue and Chapter One*

22   Stuart Palatine wedding . . . Oman, *Elizabeth*

23   Rupert's rescue . . . Scott, *Rupert*

23   Duke of Saxony and Queen's monkey . . . 1655 Weiss

24   'les viandes ordinaires' . . . Christoph v Dohna 21 January 1627 (HCL)

24   Wine-cellar and family portraits . . . Frederick V 20 June 1622 (HCL)

24   Frederick's dislike of idleness . . . Frederick V 9 November 1925 (HCL)

27ff Sophie's birth and childhood . . . Mems

27   Queen Victoria's restrained disapproval . . . her letter 16 July 1870, cit. in *Your Dear Letter*, Roger Fulford, Evans, 1971

29   Mme de Maintenon, fellow-sufferer . . . Charlotte Haldane's biography, Constable, 1970

30　Sophie's boredom . . . Knoop cites delighted report of diversions from a tutor visiting Leiden with young charges

30　'the *canaille* of Holland' . . . Frederick V quoted in *Memoires de la Princesse Palatine*, Blaze de Bury (HCL)

31　'. . . but exchanged a father' . . . Charles I 26 December 1632 (HWL)

32　The Queen's grief . . . her letter of 24 December 1632 (BEB)

32　'. . . as a Christian and a woman' . . . Queen 27 July 1636 (BEB)

32　'the sweet Elector' . . . John Dineley 29 October 1633 (HWL)

33　'. . . much embracings' . . . Sir Thomas Roe 1 May 1636 (HCL)

33　'that tunne of beer' . . . Queen 1 November 1638 (BEB)

37　Orange/Stuart wedding . . . Pieter Geyl, *Orange and Stuart*, Weidenfeld 1969

37　'. . . the honour you doe him' . . . Charles Louis 12 December 1640 (HWL)

38　'. . . sometimes contrary to my own sense' . . . Charles Louis 20 August 1642 (HWL)

39　'. . . his honour engaged' . . . Queen 20 April 1643 (BEB)

39　'. . . to remove all impression' . . . Queen 13 April 1643 (BEB)

42　'foul damps of sensuality' . . . Charles Louis 1645 (HWL)

46　'. . . cares no more for those cursed people' . . . 13 April 1649, cit. in Scott, *Rupert*

47　'Mistress Barlo' . . . 8 July 1685 (BSvH)

50　'absolutely displeased therewith' . . . Charles Louis 16 August 1650 (WEB)

51　'if Carray says' . . . Queen 18 May 1654 (BEB)

51　'I will never keep any' . . . Queen 29 August 1650 (WEB)

page　　　　　　　　　　　*Chapter Two*

55ff Sophie's journey and arrival . . . Mems

52　'. . . only someone whom the Electress neither envies nor despises' . . . Princess Elizabeth 21 October 1652 (HWL)

56　Visit to Württemberg . . . Mems

56　'the movables have nothing to do with you' . . . Queen 24 August 1650 (WEB)

57　Henriette's wish to please . . . 18 September 1650 (HWL)

57　'. . . affliction enough' . . . Princess Elizabeth no date 1650 (HWL)

59　'a *gros crime*' . . . 24 September 1652 (BSCL)

60　'I could not stoop so low' . . . Mems

60　'the discontent and grief' . . . Queen 27 February 1651 (BEB)

60　'. . . to see the place so spoiled' . . . Queen 6 June 1656 (WEB)

61　Butcher's wife . . . Queen 6 June 1656 (WEB)

61f Report from Heidelberg . . . 24 September 1652 (BSCL)

62　'. . . would not have gone a-gossiping' . . . Princess Elizabeth 21 October 1652 (HWL)

63   '. . . whether the realities' . . . Queen 4 November 1652 (BEB)
64   'we danced our feet off'. . . Princess Elizabeth 27 February 1653 (HWL)
64   'incredible as it may sound' . . . Mems
65   'no great enquirie for Maurice' . . . Charles Louis 13 July 1654 (WEB)
66   Inefficient hunt servants . . . Rupert 22 October 1655 (HWL)
67   Montecelso and Rosalinda . . .(HCLF)
67   *La coquetterie* . . . Charles Louis August 1655 (HWL)
68ff Scenes in Heidelberg . . . Mems. Louise von Degenfeld, no date, Charlotte
        11 March 1657 (both HCLF). A further lurid description is given in
        Bilder Deutscher Vergangenheit by Gustav Freytag, Leipzig 1859. This,
        however, is based on one of the numerous *Histoires Secrètes* by the Baron
        von Poellnitz—a kinsman of Figuelotte's favourite—a hopelessly
        unreliable reporter even of events that did not, as did these, take place
        long before he was born.
69   Dismissal of rumours regarding Sophie . . . Queen 12 June 1656 (WEB)
69ff Proposals of marriage . . . Mems
72   Charles II's consent . . . 'bounde by contract to acquaint the King of her
        marriage . . . hear you have forgott' . . . Queen 6 October 1654 (WEB)
73   'Simmern . . . ever an elder brother's portion' . . . Queen 1 April 1652
        (BEB)
74   'hatching some very curious plans' . . . Rupert 26 January 1658 (HWL)
74   Charlotte's ill-temper with her children . . . Charles Louis 16 August 1658
        (HCLF)
74   Divorce document . . . (HCLF)
75   'my servants are naked' . . . Queen 10 April 1656 (WEB)
75   Louise's budget . . . (HCLF)
75   'happy Easter-eggs', green hangings . . . Charles Louis 13 April 1658
        (HCLF)
76   'a patient Gricill' . . . Queen 12 June 1658 (WEB)
76   'all persons in misfortune, . . . Queen 14 July 1659 (WEB)
77   'the very youngest Duke' . . . Queen 23 May 1658 (WEB)
77   Living hot water bottle . . . Charles Louis 1 May 1658 (HCLF)
77   'Indian ambassadors' . . . Charles Louis May to June 1658 (HCLF)
78   Inkwell incident . . . Charles Louis 1 May 1658, Edward May 1658 (both
        HCLF); Queen 13 May 1658 (WEB)
78   'in coelibatu' . . . Mems
79   'the change in Sophie's marriage' . . . Queen 24 June 1658 (WEB)
79   'Adorable Princesse' and Louis von Rothenschild's quandary . . . Knoop,
        Sophie

page   *Chapter Three*
                (Source: BSCL unless otherwise stated)
80ff Sophie's wedding . . . Mems

80   Charlotte watches from upstairs . . . Charles Louis October 1658
          (HCLF)

81   Liselotte in tears at sight of groom . . . Charles Louis 17 October 1658
          (HCLF)

81   Electoral menus and economies . . . (HCL)

81   'Pantagruel' . . . Charles Louis 18 October 1658 (HCLF)

82   'much as he had come' . . . Mems

82   'brother Ned too full of *raillerie*' . . . Charles Louis to Louise, 26 August
          1658 (HCLF)

82ff Wedding journey . . . Mems

83   'the land of Pumpernickel' is a phrase that recurs throughout Sophie's
          correspondence with her brother, and was later borrowed by Thackeray
          in *Vanity Fair* to describe a fictional German principality

83   John Frederick's and Christian Louis' description by their mother . . . 12
          June 1645 and 23 October 1652, cit. in Koecher, *History*

84   'as from Paradise' . . . 26 December 1658

86   'the miracle of the century' . . . 6 February 1659)

86ff Hummlingen . . . 18 April 1659

87   Requests for ointments . . . no date 1659 (BSvH)

87   'where do we find bread in the desert?' . . . 19 January 1659

87   ' . . . drawn from my own body' . . . 29 May 1659

88   'you don't want her to become a Schurmann' . . . 18 April 1660

89   'it looks as though you'll be an uncle' . . . Queen 17 November 1659
          (WEB)

89   '*quel crève-cœur*' and the Queen's opinion that Liselotte 'is not leik the
          House of Hesse, schi is leik ours' . . . 17 November 1659

91   Sophie's new coach . . . 24 November 1659

91   Fire in Cloppenburg . . . 24 March 1660; Queen April 1660 (WEB)

92   'the *affamées* of The Hague . . . 17 November 1659

92   '*me voici*' . . . 29 May 1660

93   Trios by Sophie's bedside . . . 24 June 1660

94   Distribution of leeks in Heidelberg . . . Mems

96   Queen's last will and testament . . . (WEB)

96   Birth of Frederick August . . . 26 October 1661

96   '*en caquant des paternosters*' . . . 6 May 1660

97   'we play at nine-pins' . . . 6 June 1663

97   Spanheim's congratuations . . . Knoop, *Sophie*

97   '*de la merde au bout de baton*' . . . 26 March 1662

98   'miles of pure silver' . . . January 1663

99ff Italy . . . Mems; correspondence 1664–65 (BSCL and BSvH)

107   'it will be like the Palatinate' . . . 15 April 1665

108   'might have given his *fille*' . . . 11 November 1665

108   'a more exciting *passe-temps*'. . . Mems

page *Chapter Four*
(Source: BSCL unless otherwise stated)

109ff Eleonore d'Olbreuse's background . . . Koecher, *Duchesse Eleonore*

110 Clorinde . . . Koecher, *Duchesse Eleonore*

110 Sophie's description . . . Mems

110 *'mariage de conscience'* . . . 15 November 1665

111 'who but George William' . . . 8 April 1666

112 Eleonore's household . . . 17 March 1666

112 'all skin and bone' . . . 18 March 1667

112 'as large as the round tower' . . . 9 December 1666

113 Anna Gonzaga's bulky pillow . . . Cardinal de Retz, *Memoirs*, Strasbourg 1913

114 Informal meeting between Charles and Wilhelmine Ernestine . . . 5 June 1669

114ff Mlle de la Mansilière . . . Mems

116 The Meisenbugs . . . Schnath, *History*

116 *'beaucoup de pouvoir'* . . . D'Arcy cit. in Schnath, *History*

116 'well-beaten to such usage', Cresset's day-book, BM add MSS.

117 *'il faut commencer avec la mariage'* . . . Anna Gonzaga 10 September 1667, Koecher, *History*

117 'daughters of gallant mothers' . . . 11 April 1669

117 'like a woman about to give birth' . . . 21 January 1668

118ff Eleonore's inelegant pining for fricassées and journey to Heidelberg with Princess of Denmark . . . Mems

119 John Frederick repacks fireworks . . . 26 February 1670

119 'in matters which he did not understand' . . . Mems

120 'such a bagatelle' . . . Anna Gonzaga 7 August 1671

121 Liselotte 'hopes that the Elector will forgive her' . . . no date 1671

121 'a daughter brought up to love truth' . . . Charles Louis no date 1671

121 'how am I supposed to sleep with that?' . . . reported by la Grande Mademoiselle, quoted in V. Sackville-West's biography, Michael Joseph 1959

121 'did the bride please her husband?' . . . Ernst August 8 December 1671 (WEA)

122 Workmen at Osnabrück . . . 20 April 1673 (BSvH)

123 'our Duke wants to become a farmer' . . . 18 April 1673 (BSvH)

123 The Aesculapius of Clèves . . . 24 November 1677

123 'finest heritage' . . . 5 January 1678

124 'dust raised by Turenne' . . . Charles Louis August 1674

124 'no difference whether country gobbled up by friend or foe' . . . Charles Louis 23 November 1674

124 ' . . . allowed to do exactly as they like' . . . Charles Louis 16 August 1674

145 'all beginnings are *incommode*' . . . February 1680 (BSCL)
146 Smoke-filled rooms . . . 15 March 1680 (BSCL)
147 Dinner for the five mitres . . . 2 May 1680 (BSCL)
147 Prince Charles' hypochondria . . . Häusser, *Palatinate*
148 Vipers and adders . . . Häusser, *Palatinate*
149 Louis XIV ignorant of Elector's troubles . . . 5 July 1680 (BSCL)
150 'no heavier cuirass' . . . Charles Louis 10 August 1680 (BSCL)
151ff Elector's last illness, death and lying in state . . . Doctor's reports (BSCL)
152 'in this world he had nothing but *fâcheries*' . . . 27 September 1680 (BSR)
153 'like Rupert *tout craché*' . . . 19 September 1675 (BSCL)
153 Ceremonial at the town hall . . . Nöldeke
155 Overtures from Whitehall . . . Rupert 9 January 1680 (HWL)
156 'now thou art chosen' . . . Rupert 21 September 1682 (HWL)
159 '*il en vaudrait plus la peine*' . . . cit. in Varnhagen
159 'we'll soon have company . . .' . . . 15 June 1684 (DSFD)
160 State-bed and coach . . . 1 September 1684 (DSFD)
161 *Mme la poupée* . . . 27 October 1684 (DSFD)
161 Frederick's ring . . . Varnhagen
162 'taste not as *fin* as elsewhere' . . . 29 September 1684 (DSFD)
163 Frederick's pillow . . . Varnhagen
163 'Does the egg . . .' Duke Ernst August no date 1685 (WPL)
164 'your father's intentions' . . . no date 1685 (WPL)
164 '. . . for a king's daughter' . . . 13 January 1685 (WPL)
165 'I smile by day and cry all night' . . . 10 November 1685 (GSL)
165 'I am not so fortunate' . . . 23 February 1685 (BSR)
166 Charles' reign in the Palatinate . . . Häusser, *Palatinate*
166 'the succession goes to the Duke of Neuburg' . . . 3 June 1683 (BSvH)
168 Sophie Dorothea changes her tune . . . 8 July 1685 (BSvH)
169 Christening of the Moslem boy . . . 19 January 1686 (GSL) (This was possibly one of the gentlemen of the backstairs whom George Louis imported to England after his accession)
170 '. . . *poudre de la succession*' . . . 6 July 1687 (BSR)
170 '. . . we felt as if we had been caned' . . . 16 August 1687 (BSR)
171 'things will go badly' . . . no date 1688 (GSL)
172 'Your Majesty would think me insincere' . . . no date (GSL)
173 '. . . the benefit of second sight' . . . no date (KL)
173 '. . . put into the world to inherit England' . . . 17 June 1689 (KL)
174 '. . . the least we can do' . . . 15 May 1688 (BSR)
174 Research journey to Modena . . . Leibniz January 1689 (KL)
174 '. . . a worthy chapter to our story' . . . 27 January 1689 (KL)
175 Enrico Leone . . . Malortie
176 Economy edicts . . . Malortie
176 The dogs' petition . . . Malortie

199 Sophie's Jacobite letter . . . (KL)
200 ' . . . others of whom they might like to take their choice' . . . 22 February 1701 (BSR)
200 The Electresses admire Het Loo . . . 21 September 1700 (BSvH)
201 'Player-Queen' . . . Varnhagen
201 'all the bother without hope for the benefit' . . . 14 April 1701
202 'is Louis XIV buying English support?' . . . 13 June 1701 (DSFD)
202 'so that the son's efforts to make me Queen' . . . 25 May 1701 (DSFD)
202 'to give *en reine*' . . . 13 June 1701 (DSFD)
203 Reception of embassy in Hanover . . . John Toland cit. in Malortie
204ff Feast of Trimalchion . . . Leibniz 25 February 1702 (KL)
205 Young Lord Monthermen . . . 5 May 1702 (DSFD)
206 'with the Queen we've got' . . . 31 March 1702 (DSFD)
206 'to curb the exorbitant power of France' . . . Queen Anne 1702 Curtis Brown, *Letters*
206 'Milady Marlborough herself . . .' . . . 5 August 1702 (BSR)
207 ' . . . a paradise without the apples' . . . 6 June 1702 (BSR)
207 ' . . . so much pleasure and my health as well' . . . July 1702 (BSR)
208 'Like cupido, especially when his hair is done' . . . 5 September 1700 (BSR)
208 'no one would have known it was Max' . . . 31 January 1712 (BSR)
209 'the German nation appears to have a death-wish' . . . Leibniz 6 March 1703 (KL)
210 Marlborough's present, 'I send you the universe' wrote Sophie when she sent a set of tapestries showing the Creation, cit. in Churchill, *Marlborough*
211 Figuelotte's death . . . Varnhagen
211 'that death had taken her instead' . . . 2 February 1705

page   *Chapter Seven*
                 (SSP unless otherwise quoted)
212 'the jealous heavens' . . . Caroline no date 1705 (KL)
213 At a single stroke transforming . . . Leibniz 18 March 1705 (KL)
214 'I who never bought a single jewel' . . . 28 March 1705
214 Frederick William's views of funerals . . . his letter 30 May 1705
214 'truly one must regard it as predestination' . . . 27 July 1705
214 ' . . . grateful not to be taken for a fool' . . . Frederick I 7 August 1705
215 ' . . . *dépit amoureux*?' . . . 12 August 1705
216 '*un meuble plus précieux que moi*' . . . Leibniz 18 March 1705 (KL) (He was to use the identical expression in writing to Caroline after Sophie's death)
216 'our faces were wreathed in smiles' . . . 5 September 1705
217 ' . . . prevented him from showing his tender love' . . . 4 December 1706

217   'I live in quiet and contentment' . . . 3 November 1705 (KL)
218   'I shall depend on your kindness' . . . Queen Anne 13 November 1705,
          Curtis Brown *Letters*
219   Leibniz and Sir Rowland Gwynne's letter . . . (KL)
220   'my son would gladly pay good money' . . . 23 March 1706 (KL)
221   'while the neighbouring states are tossed' . . . cit. in Melville, *Queen Anne*
221   Deletion of Halifax's name . . . Ward, *Sophie*
221   ' . . . to make the caterwauling easier on the ear' . . . 1 October 1704 (BSR)
221   Sophie's fire drill . . . 30 August 1712 (BSR)
221   Leibniz' improved hoses . . . (KL)
222   ' . . . between child and human being' 26 September 1696 (GSL)
222   Arrangements for Sophie Dorothea's engagement dinner . . . Malortie
223   'one's nose and eyes are filled with powder' . . . 7 October 1711 (BSR)
223   'your Majesty's stones are better than mine' . . . 6 November 1706
225   'have you given me a *philtre*' . . . Prince Ernst August 11 August 1707
          (KEA)
225   '*les sots Allemands*' . . . Frederick I 28 December 1706
226   Tortoise-shell jewellery during Lent . . . 4 December 1706
226   Sophie's great grandson repeats history . . . Arkell, *Caroline*
227   'he has already picked his *cheval de bataille* . . .' . . . Prince Ernst August
          15 July 1707 (KEA)
227   'our brave soldiers in Lille' . . . 13 October 1708 (BSR)
227   'not afraid of the smell of powder' . . . 5 June 1708 (BSR)
228   Frederick's green courting suit . . . Prince Ernst August 27 August 1708
          (KEA)
228   'lucky her coat of arms features horns' . . . 7 October 1708 (BSR)
228   Wedding breakfast . . . Prince Ernst August 9 December 1708 (KEA)
228   'all clocks' . . . 15 May 1709
229   'she talks like an old maid' . . . 20 April 1709
229   'the King of France has made an April fool of him' . . . 19 April 1708
          (BSR)
230   'because I knew all the people in it' . . . 12 April 1704 (KL)
230   'I know as much English as the author' . . . no date 1712 (DSFD)
230   '*les honneurs de la maison* . . .' . . . Prince Ernst August 17 June 1706
          (KEA)
231   Sedan chair to negotiate corridors . . . 14 February 1711
231   '*mourir de ma propre mort*' . . . 7 January 1712 (BSR)
231   Two hundred and twenty-five years for dinner . . . no date 1713
231   'my eyes seem to get sharper' . . . 20 September 1711 (BSR)
231   'like a melon' . . . 21 March 1714
231   'Handel plays the clavichord' . . . 14 June 1710
231   Assessment of theatrical troupe . . . Platen cit. in Malortie
232   Sea-battle on Herrenhausen lake . . . 8 January 1710

232 Improvements at Herrenhausen . . . 4 June 1710
233 Early steam-machine (Sophie reported that the inventor, Wellin, submitted it in January 1705) (KL)
233 Mediaeval frescoes at Goerhde . . . 30 September 1711
233 'so secretive in that *petite famille*' . . . Prince Ernst August 9 March 1708 (KEA)
233 Sophie's embroidery after Carllutz's mosaics . . . Knoop, *Sophie*
234 Tortoiseshell cane . . . 26 March 1707
234 Louis XIV's *nef* . . . 7 March 1708
234 Jewelled Buddhas . . . 28 February 1711
235 ' . . . knew nothing about the war. . . . 11 November 1711 (KL)
235 ' . . . only the actors are different' . . . 20 October 1711
235 'sit at different sides at the Opera' . . . 4 April 1711 (BSR)
236 'what Parliament does one day' . . . 5 May 1711 (KL)
236 'small thanks for the glory' . . . 4 December 1712 (BSR)
236 'Milady Marlborough deserves the blame' . . . 5 November 1711
236 ' . . . the crown of England for sale' . . . 22 December 1711 (KL)
237 ' . . . a sort of grand Turk of the North' . . . Leibniz 21 March 1711 (KL)
237 'clothes last longer than people' . . . 26 August 1711
237 Tsarevitch and his bride . . . 11 February 1711 (BSR)
238 '*fait caca dans sa chambre*' . . . Prince Ernst August 13 July 1712 (KEA)
238 'we seem to copy all their bad habits' . . . 15 November 1711
239 ' . . . so many Electors Palatine dragged from their graves' . . . Frederick I 7 March 1712
239 'the devil, the Pope and the Pretender' . . . 5 March 1712
239 'as though it came from Persia' . . . 6 July 1712
239 'no one had ever disputed *le pas*' . . . 9 June 1712 (KL) & 6 June 1714 (GSL)
240 'Queen Anne herself believed he was a changeling' . . . cit. 21 September 1712
240 'since England now calls him the Duke of Gloucester' . . . Frederick I 4 October 1712
240 'old age the only ailment' . . . 6 March 1713
241 'weeping and wailing help no one' . . . 3 March 1713
241 Frederick I's funeral . . . Prince Ernst August 17 March 1713 (KEA)
241 ' . . . in a position to blacken his name in paradise' . . . 22 July 1713
242 ' . . . there'll be nowhere to send him but Hanover' . . . 8 December 1713 (KL)
242 'in England they're saying the first Parliament' . . . Leibniz no date 1713 (KL)
242 'our Princess of Wales is wonderfully well' . . . Caroline no date 1713 (KL)
243 'my own would be *plus belle*' . . . 29 February 1714 (KL)
243 ' . . . waiting to strew palms' . . . 2 April 1714 (KL)

243 'for the coffee-houses of London' . . . Leibniz no date 1714 (KL)
243 'with a little ink and paper' . . . Leibniz May 1714 (KL)
244 'just as the Queen herself' . . . 20 May 1714 (KL)
245 Queen Anne's letters . . . Curtis Brown and Melville, *George I*
246f Sophie's death . . . report by the Countess of Bückeburg (KL)

INDEX

by H. E. Crowe

Brunswick-Lüneburg, Anna Eleonore (1601–1659), Duchess of, mother of Ernst August 83, 88

Brunswick-Wolfenbüttel, Duke of, *see* Anton Ulrich

Brussels 89

Bückeburg, Countess of (1673–1743) 231, 245, 246, 247

Burnet, Gilbert (1643–1715), Bishop of Salisbury 47, 155

Bussche, Albrecht Philip von der (1639–1698), governor to Sophie's sons 123, 178

Ca'Foscari, palazzo, Sophie at 100

Calenberg-Göttingen 70

Cambridge, Marquis and Duke of, title of George August 220

Carnival of first Electoral (1693) 180

Caroline of Ansbach (1683–1737), wife of Prince George August; ward of Frederick King of Prussia 208; refuses Archduke Charles 209; and Figuelotte's death 213, 214; marries George August 216, 255; birth of Frederick 226; and Sophie 229; learns English language 230; daughter Anne born 233; Queen Anne ignores baby 236; Leibniz writes 247. Mentions 214, 215, 221, 238, 242, 246, *facing page 24*

Carray, The Misses, Sophie's maids 29, 40, 51

Casa di Brunswick 99

Cassel 98

Catherine of Braganza marries Charles II 95

Catholic League, army of 23

Celle 130

Celle, Duke of, *see* George William of Brunswick-Lüneburg

Celle, Mme de, *see* Eleonore d'Olbreuse

Charbonnier and son design gardens 122, 155

Charles Edward (1668–1690), Raugrave son of Charles Louis, killed in battle 176

Charles, Electoral Prince (1650–1685), son of Charles Louis, Liselotte's brother; marries Wilhelmine Ernestine 112–13; swears to care for sisters 132, 151–2; religious mania of 133; hypochondriac 147; learns father's death 151–2; breaks promise 165; plays soldiers 166; death of 253. Mentions 56, 94, 119

Charles Louis, Elector Palatine (1617–1680), son of Frederick V and Elizabeth Stuart, Sophie's brother; married (1) Charlotte of Hesse Cassel (2 morganatically) Louise von Degenfeld, Raugravine; visits England 32–3, 38; prisoner 34; returns and loses battle 34; writes to Charles I 37; Charles dislikes 38; political embarrass-

ment over Edward's change of religion 42, 45; and Charles I 46; enters Heidelberg 47; marries Charlotte of Hesse Cassel 48; and illegitimate son 48; restores estate 48–50; love of wife 53; and Henriette's marriage 57–8; and Elizabeth 58; love of theatre 58; at Electors' Diet in Prague 61; meets Emperor 62, 63; Imperial Arch-Treasurer 63; and Louise von Degenfeld 66 ff., 74, 75; quarrels with Rupert 73; desires to rid himself of Charlotte 74; finds precedents for living with Louise 74–5; joy at Louise's pregnancy 75; and Imperial crown 77; assaults Bavarian Ambassador 78; and Sophie's marriage 79, 80; son by Louise 81; publishes divorce documents 82; and Liselotte's habits 87; and Ernst August's absence 91–2; and Queen's will 96; relations with Rupert 96; asks Sophie for return to Liselotte 97; ailments of 124; and George Louis 131; children by Louise 131–2; mourns death of Louise 132, and Wilhelmine Ernestine 132; and France's strength 134; illness of 140, 147, and death of Princess Elizabeth 141–3; and Benedicta 147; protests to France 149; sends son to England for support against France 150; death of 150–1; inheritance 166. Mentions 17, 28, 32, 41, 60, 63, 69, 72, 80, 83, 86, 94, 97, 100, 108, 114, 119, 120, 125, 126, 139, 166, 251, 253, *facing pages 32, 97*

Charles Louis (Carllutz) (1658–1688), Raugrave son of Charles Louis by Louise; Captain at Trèves 125; sent to France 150; dies at Negroponte 171. Mentions 81, 169, 233

Charles Maurice (1670–1702), Raugrave son of Charles Louis 204, 205

Charles Phillip (1669–1690), Sophie's son 153, 154; death of 176, 252, 254, *facing page 236*

Charles I of England (1600–1649), marries Henrietta of France 24; and Frederick V's death 31; has Charles Louis released 34; and the Princess Royal's marriage 36–7; and Charles Louis' request 38; angry with Charles Louis 38–9; suggests that Charles Louis becomes a Catholic 39; prisoner on Isle of Wight 44; executed 45, 46, 251; furore created by 46

Charles II of England (1630–1685) writes to Sophie 79; marries Catherine of Braganza 95; receives George Louis 155; and Louis XIV 171; and Sophie 202; crowned in Scotland 251; restored